From Queenston to Kingston

From Queenston to Kingston

The Hidden Heritage of Lake Ontario's Shoreline

RON BROWN

NATURAL HERITAGE BOOKS
A MEMBER OF THE DUNDURN GROUP
TORONTO

Edited by Jane Gibson
Copy-edited by Allison Hirst
Designed by Courtney Horner
Printed and bound in Canada by Webcom

Library and Archives Canada Cataloguing in Publication

Brown, Ron, 1945-
        From Queenston to Kingston : the hidden heritage
of Lake Ontario's shoreline / by Ron Brown.

Includes bibliographical references and index.
ISBN 978-1-55488-716-3

        1. Ontario, Lake, Region (N.Y. and
Ont.)--History. I. Title.

FC3061.B756 2010   971.3'5   C2009-907472-9

1   2   3   4   5   14   13   12   11   10

We acknowledge the support of **The Canada Council for the Arts** and the **Ontario Arts Council** for our publishing program. We also acknowledge the financial support of the **Government of Canada** through the **Canada Book Fund** and **The Association for the Export of Canadian Books**, and the **Government of Ontario** through the **Ontario Book Publishers Tax Credit** program, and the **Ontario Media Development Corporation**.

Care has been taken to trace the ownership of copyright material used in this book. The author and the publisher welcome any information enabling them to rectify any references or credits in subsequent editions.

J. Kirk Howard, President

www.dundurn.com
Published by Natural Heritage Books
A Member of The Dundurn Group

Front cover photos: (top) Fishing colony at the tip of Point Traverse; (bottom left) Former blacksmith shop in the village of Stella; (bottom right) Lighthouse in Presqu'ile Point Provincial Park. Photos by Ron Brown.
Back cover photos: (top) The Guild Inn's "garden of ruins"; (bottom) One of Kingston's Martello towers at Fort Henry. Unless otherwise indicated, all images are credited to the author.

Dundurn Press	Gazelle Book Services Limited	Dundurn Press
3 Church Street, Suite 500	White Cross Mills	2250 Military Road
Toronto, Ontario, Canada	High Town, Lancaster, England	Tonawanda, NY
M5E 1M2	LA1 4XS	U.S.A. 14150

Mixed Sources
Product group from well-managed forests, and other controlled sources
www.fsc.org Cert no. SW-COC-002358
© 1996 Forest Stewardship Council

Contents

Chapter 9: The Old Stones of Kingston

Acknowledgements

The author wishes to acknowledge the helpful staff at Ontario's many fine archives and museums. Archivists and curators at the facilities in Napanee, Archives Ontario, the City of Toronto Archives, and the Toronto Reference Library provided excellent service. I would, however, like to single out the staff at the Oshawa Community Archives and Museum and at the County of Prince Edward Archives for their generous assistance in this project. The staff at the Ministry of Natural Resources at Glenora and the Presqu'ile Point Provincial Park were also generous with their time and resources. Thanks to them as well. Many fine archival images are available on a series of excellent websites. The Niagara Public Library, the Queen's University Archives, and in particular the website for the tiny community of Deseronto, which, despite its small size, has one of the finer archival websites online. To my family, my wife June, thanks for your patience with my various absences while prowling the shores of this unusual and historic lake. Finally, I am most grateful to my editor, Jane Gibson of Natural Heritage Books, and copy editor, Allison Hirst of the Dundurn Group, for unearthing and rectifying my various grammatical slip-ups. Any errors in content are strictly mine.

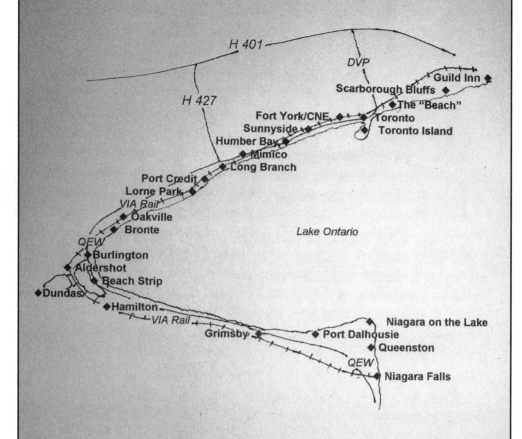

MAP ONE

H 401

DVP

H 427

Scarborough Bluffs ◆ ◆ Guild Inn

The "Beach"

Fort York/CNE
Sunnyside
Humber Bay
Mimico
Long Branch
Port Credit
Lorne Park
VIA Rail
Oakville
Bronte
QEW
Burlington
Aldershot
Beach Strip
◆Dundas
Hamilton
VIA Rail

Toronto
Toronto Island

Lake Ontario

Niagara on the Lake
Grimsby   Port Dalhousie
Queenston
QEW
Niagara Falls

WESTERN LAKE ONTARIO

N

Maps are not to scale

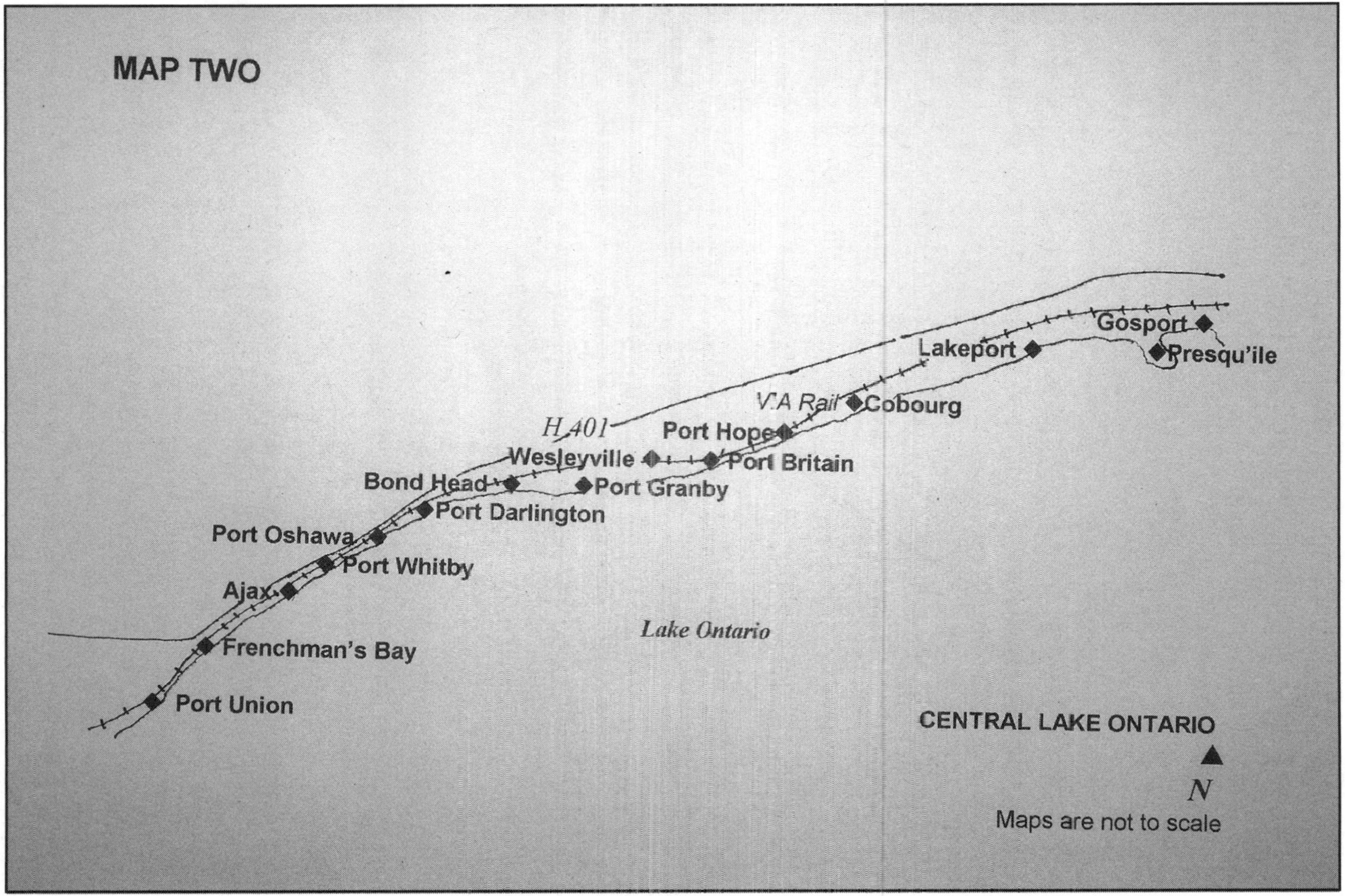

MAP TWO

Port Union

Frenchman's Bay

Ajax

Port Oshawa

Port Whitby

Bond Head

Port Darlington

Wesleyville

Port Granby

H401

Port Hope

Port Britain

VA Rail

Cobourg

Lakeport

Gosport

Presqu'ile

Lake Ontario

CENTRAL LAKE ONTARIO

N

Maps are not to scale

MAP THREE

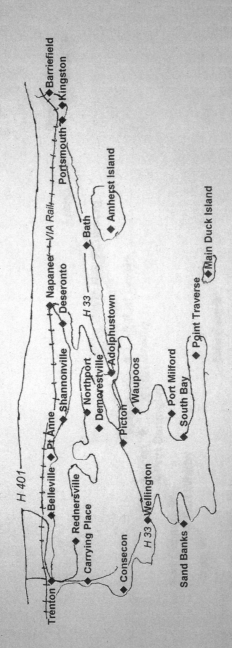

EASTERN LAKE ONTARIO

N

Maps are not to scale

Introduction

The Shaping of the Lake

L ake Ontario's shoreline is not old. In geological time it is but a newcomer. Exactly what the land looked like before the last ice age is anyone's guess, but it was after the last great ice sheet finally trickled away that today's lake began to take shape.

For about two hundred thousand years, massive glaciers moved back and forth over the land that is now Ontario, gouging gullies and depositing mounds of sand and gravel. As the ice began to melt, around twenty thousand years ago, the waters pooled behind the ice, creating lakes of varying shapes and levels. The earliest postglacial lakes formed to the western end of what is now Ontario, draining in a southwesterly direction. Later, as the ice continued to retreat northeast, the lakes found another outlet, and drained southerly through the Mohawk Valley of New York. At this time, the body of water that would one day become Lake Ontario, what geologists call Lake Iroquois, began to form. Due to the ice dam to the east, its level was much higher than Lake Ontario is today.

While at that level, the lake washed into glacial deposits, leaving behind a series of shore bluffs that today stand high and dry. As the ice sheet shifted from the east end of the lake, the water found a new outlet — down the St. Lawrence River — resulting in the lowering of the lake level. The land, suppressed from the weight of the ice sheet, remained low, and ocean waters moved into the area of today's Brockville, bringing with them marine life. (The discovery of whale bones in these oceanic deposits gave rise to a myth of whales in Lake Ontario.)

When the ice left for good, the east end of the lake, now freed from that weight, rebounded, raising the levels at the western end of the lake and flooding existing river mouths. This inflow created lagoons along the shoreline that provided shelter for aboriginal villages, and later for the schooners and small boats of the early settlers. By then, Lake Ontario had assumed the configuration that it retains today — 311 kilometres long and eighty-five kilometres at its widest point. Of its nineteen thousand square kilometre surface area, more than ten thousand lie within Ontario, as does most of its 1,146 kilometres of shoreline.

When the ice melted, arctic flora and fauna flourished, creating a tundra-like landscape and paving the way for early aboriginal populations. Archaeologists have labelled these peoples as "fluted point" for the shape of their spearheads. These artifacts and a few burial mounds such as the Serpent Mounds on Rice Lake and the Taber Hill Mound

Lagoons that formed the lake's early harbours were a result of rising lake levels caused by the melting of the glaciers more than ten thousand years ago.

in Scarborough constitute the scanty physical evidence that remains of those early populations.

Human migration continued, and by the time the first Europeans arrived, the land north of Lake Ontario was inhabited primarily by the Huron people. The first Europeans had come looking for China, the land of silk and gold. In fact, Samuel de Champlain, when he first portaged his way up the rapids of the St. Lawrence in 1608, called them the "Lachine" Rapids, French for "China." Guided by members of the Algonquian First Nation, he followed the traditional aboriginal route into the Great Lakes, up the Ottawa, across Lake Nipissing, and down the French River into Georgian Bay. Convinced he had at last arrived at the Pacific Ocean, he called it a *mer* or "sea." But the absence of salt meant it was not the ocean he was seeking.

Again, guided by his Algonquian friends, Champlain's group made their way into Lake Simcoe, which he called Lac Taronto, and then followed the Kawartha and Trent River System into the Bay of Quinte. From here he crossed the lake to help his allies attack a Seneca village on the south shore of Lake Ontario, only to suffer a defeat that exacerbated the animosity between the Iroquois and the Algonquian.

When the French finally realized they were a long way from the riches of the Orient, they settled for fur, as well as trying to convert the indigenous inhabitants to Catholicism. Missions were established, such as the one on Georgian Bay, known today as Sainte-Marie among the Hurons, and Kente, on the Bay of Quinte. It was at Saint-Marie that the culmination of Iroquois incursions into Ontario in 1648 resulted in the deaths of Fathers Brébeuf and Lalemant and the near eradication of the Huron and the Neutrals.[1]

By 1670, six Native villages were in place along the lake's north shore, including Ganestiquiagon, a Seneca village at the mouth of the Rouge River; Ganaraske, a Seneca site at the mouth of the Ganaraska River; and Quintio, at the neck of the Prince Edward Peninsula. Near Napanee stood the Oneida village of Ganneious.[2] With the bulk of the Iroquois still south of the lake, these villages were small, and after 1701, when the French and Iroquois concluded a peace treaty, were abandoned. Once the Iroquois had left, an Algonquian group known as the Mississauga moved in along the lake from their lands north of Georgian Bay. Although their home territory remained farther north, they used the lakeshore primarily as seasonal hunting and fishing camps.

For the next half century, the French maintained a series of forts along the lake, largely as fur-trading outposts, though they were garrisoned to guard against the British, whose territory lay along the lake's south shore. By 1758 the French had abandoned their outposts, and in 1763 the Lake Ontario shore became British.[3]

Twenty years would pass before full-scale migration swamped the lake. In 1783, Britain's American colonies had won their independence and did not take kindly to those who had chosen to remain loyal to the British. These Loyalists were beaten, killed, or at the very least lost their property. To help resettle those who survived, by then officially called United Empire Loyalists, the British government laid out a series of townships, primarily at the east end of Lake Ontario and in the Niagara area, in which to disseminate free land as well as grain seed and farm utensils. During 1783–84, the government concluded agreements that would allow Loyalist settlements between Montreal and Trenton.

The ruins of the early French fort, Fort Frontenac, have been unearthed in downtown Kingston.

After the first influx tapered off, more followed, taking up the shoreline between Trenton and Toronto. Upper Canada's first lieutenant governor, John Graves Simcoe, arrived in 1792 and relocated the legislative capital from Newark (now Niagara-on-the-Lake) to what is now Toronto Harbour and named the site York. Further treaties with the Mississauga between 1787 and 1805 freed up more land for settlement between Trenton and Toronto. Meanwhile, the Mohawk followers of Joseph Brant took up territory along the Grand River and on the north shore of the Bay of Quinte, between today's Shannonville and Deseronto, today the Tyendinaga First Nation Territory. Although the Missisauga retained some small areas along Lake Ontario for fishing, the bulk of their population wound up on reserves in the Rice Lake and Kawartha Lakes areas, as well as on a parcel near Brant's Six Nations settlement on the Grand River.

To provide the new arrivals with a steady supply of building materials, the government ordered sawmills to be built at Kingston and on the Humber and Don rivers at York. Industry gradually took hold as gristmills appeared, as well. Wharves were built into the lake to ship grain and lumber, as often as not by the individuals who just happened to own that shoreline. Fishing at the time was very much an individual occupation, and usually consisted of lakeshore farmers setting nets close to shore to provide for their needs and those of their neighbours. As more migrants arrived, more industry developed. Distilleries were constructed in conjunction with the gristmills. Ontario's first steamboat, the *Frontenac*, was launched at Finkle's Tavern in Ernestown (now Bath) as was its first brewery. Steamboats appeared and gradually replaced the wind-powered schooners, giving the larger harbours an advantage over the little coves and lagoons. Towns selected as district and later county administrative seats grew larger.

Still, transportation remained difficult. Lake travel was seasonal, while roads were usually muddy quagmires. Simcoe opened roads to Lake Simcoe and the Thames River in the 1790s while Asa Danforth gamely carved out a winding road from York to the Bay of Quinte. His trail proved to be poorly located and unpopular with settlers, and was replaced with a straighter Kingston Road in 1817. Still, stage travel between Kingston and York could take anywhere from three to five days.

Much changed with the arrival of the railways. While such projects had been proposed as early as the 1830s for Hamilton and Cobourg, the first steam-powered rail operation did not commence until the early 1850s. The Grand Trunk Railway (GTR) and Great Western Railway (GWR) followed the shore of the lake, while resource lines like the Cobourg and Peterborough, the Central Ontario, the Kingston and Pembroke, the Bay of Quinte, and the Midland railways tapped into the hinterland. Communities that acquired a rail link added foundries and factories to their roster of industries. By this time the lumber industry was losing its supply of logs, but farming and fishing became more specialized.

Canals also altered the industrial landscape: the Desjardins Canal linking the lake with Dundas opened in 1837; the Welland Canal linking Port Dalhousie with Lake Erie opened in 1828; the Rideau Canal opened between Bytown and Kingston in 1832; and the Murray Canal connected the Bay of Quinte with Wellers Bay in 1889. Locks were improved along the St. Lawrence, permitting ever larger vessels to enter the lake, and forcing many small ports to close. During the Prohibition era of the 1920s, many of these hidden coves returned to life, as fishermen made their late-night runs, carrying boatloads of whisky and beer to the thirsty Americans.

As cities and towns grew, so did the workforce. Seeking respite from their smoky urban environs, city dwellers sought out bucolic lakeside retreats, even if just for the day, and the tourist boom was underway. Beaches and waterfronts soon became the haunt of amusement parks, pleasure grounds, and "casinos" or dance halls. Places like Port Dalhousie and Hamilton Beach, along with Sunnyside, Hanlan's Point, and The Beach in Toronto, all hosted major amusement parks, while smaller grounds were common nearly everywhere.

By this time, the many sturdy forts that protected Ontario against possible American attacks had either been downgraded or had fallen into outright ruin. Some were rebuilt or restored as Depression-era make-work projects, while Fort Henry and Fort York housed prisoners of war during the Second World War. The end of that conflict ushered in the auto age, one that would once more transform the towns and cities along the shore. In addition to the shoreline railways, there were now high-speed highways, with the Queen Elizabeth Way becoming North America's first limited-access freeway in 1939. By 1955, the Toronto Bypass was on its way to becoming the 401, and piece by piece connected Toronto with Kingston and beyond.

As railways changed from coal to diesel, the coal boats no longer called, and tracks were lifted from most of the lake's port lands. Kingston, Deseronto, Belleville, Trenton, Cobourg, Port Hope, and Whitby all lost their rail links to the lake. New industries preferred truck-friendly locations by the highway and away from the antiquated harbour sites. The fishing industry all but vanished, with only a handful of fishing boats still operating in the Prince Edward County area. Many municipalities were pondering the fate of their waterfronts, and several undertook major overhauls, ripping up old wharves and replacing them with marinas. Warehouses and grain elevators made way for hotels and condominiums — Kingston and Toronto being the main culprits here. In many locations, public access was restored and rebuilt, allowing for a renewed era of waterside recreation. Cobourg, Hamilton, Toronto (despite its wall of condos), and Burlington are prime examples of such concerted efforts. Others, such as Port Darlington and Deseronto, await their turn.

Despite the waves of sweeping change that have altered the Lake Ontario shore, its heritage lingers today; some well-known and heavily promoted, some known to only a few. In these pages, I hope to open a modern-day window on the evidence of Lake Ontario's hidden heritage, all the way from Queenston to Kingston.

Chapter 1
The Niagara Frontier

Niagara: it's a word that brings to mind different images. To movie buffs it's a classic 1953 Marilyn Monroe film of the same name; to history buffs it's the many battles that raged across the torrential river; to tourists it's the foaming falls that leap from a limestone precipice; to wine lovers it's the home of the latest VQA; and to comedians it's the age old joke about the falls being the second biggest disappointment on a new bride's honeymoon.

But beyond the tour buses and the neon cacophony of Clifton Hill, Niagara hides a treasure trove of Ontario's lesser-known heritage features — the vestiges of a strange buried gorge, the ruins of an ancient fort, a forgotten ghost road, some of Ontario's oldest surviving homes and churches, as well as a tale of heroism, and a long forgotten camp movement. For this Lake Ontario adventure, only that portion of Niagara that links to the lake is explored, mainly the area north of Queenston.

To get the whole picture, it is necessary to return to the ice age. As noted earlier, for an estimated two hundred thousand years, mighty glaciers came and went across the landscape that today is Ontario, the latest finally beginning to release its icy grip around twenty thousand years ago. Even as the ground of central Ontario began to emerge from the ice, a mighty lobe remained lodged stubbornly against the stone ramparts of the Niagara Escarpment. Before doing so, it had disgorged a massive deposit of sand and gravel that completely submerged a preglacial gorge that had served as an outlet for what had been an earlier version of the Niagara River.

When the ice lobe finally receded from the escarpment, Lake Erie once more began to empty northward. With its old outlet now sealed, the waters sought another path, and began to carve a new defile, creating today's Niagara Gorge. Flowing northward, the waters entered a lake that was much higher than the Lake Ontario we know today (Lake Iroquois). As the waters lapped against the escarpment's cliffs, they left behind a series of gravely beach ridges and sandy lacustrine deposits, both of which would define the history of Niagara.

With the glaciers finally gone, early animals and humans began to filter onto the landscape. In Niagara, however, there were two major impediments blocking their easy movement. One was the craggy cliff-lined ridge of the escarpment, which in the Niagara area is at its steepest. This left only one feasible route, that which followed the buried gorge wherein once flowed the pre-glacial river. The second impediment was that posed by the raging new river itself. Thus, movement both north–south and east–west was severely restricted.

Once the first aboriginal populations were gone, either by annihilation or assimilation, the tribe known as the Neutral moved in to occupy much of the western side of the river. The various nations of the mighty Iroquois Confederacy roamed the forests to the east, and eventually the Neutrals succumbed to Iroquois supremacy and disappeared from history.

Next came a parade of Europeans, beginning with the French: La Salle, Father Hennepin,[1] and Champlain all trouped through Niagara, each awestruck by the mighty falls, but also by the strategic importance of the river and the high cliffs. The British were next. In 1763, having gained much of North America from the French during the French and Indian War, they constructed important military outposts on both sides of the Niagara River at its Lake Ontario outlet — Fort Niagara on the east, and Fort George on the west.

More war was to follow. In 1776, England's thirteen American colonies decided they had had enough of England's domination and declared their independence. Seven years later they achieved it. The east side of the river became American, the west side stayed British. While the falls remained the focus above the Niagara Escarpment, two key towns began to take shape below — Queenston and Butlersburg, which later went on to become Newark and then Niagara (and now Niagara-on-the-Lake).

Queenston

In 1807, the deputy postmaster-general of British North America, George Heriot, toured the Niagara area and noted that

> Queenstown is a neat and flourishing place, distinguished by the beauty and grandeur of its situation. Here all the merchandise and stores for the upper part of the province are landed from vessels in which they have been conveyed from Kingston.... Between Niagara and Queenstown the river affords in every part a noble harbour for vessels, the water being very deep, the stream not too powerful, the anchorage good, and the banks on either side of considerable altitude.[2]

At first Queenston was the more important of the two. Situated at the immediate base of the escarpment, it became the terminus of a key portage around the falls and the gorge. Beginning at the end of navigation on the Niagara River above the falls, at Chippewa, the portage struck inland and followed a winding route, descending through the buried gorge to the head of navigation of the lower Niagara River, namely Queenston. To this day, Portage Road in Niagara Falls follows much of that early trail.

Named by Upper Canada's first lieutenant governor, John Graves Simcoe (who introduced Anglo-centric nomenclature to most of his domain), Queenston quickly attracted the shipping business of local industrialist Robert Hamilton.[3] Here, in the dying years of the eighteenth century, he built wharves and storehouses from which he shipped flour, guns, and other necessities, offloading them from schooners and placing them onto wagons for the tiring trek up the escarpment.

But the Americans were never far away, and neither was their ambition to bring England's remaining North American colonies into their rightful fold, namely as part of the now-named United States of America. To their surprise, most of the Loyalist inhabitants of Upper Canada didn't share that goal. Thus began the War of 1812. Battles raged back and forth. York was burned in 1813; in retaliation, Washington was put to the torch, although private businesses and homes were spared. It is said that the White House was so named following a whitewashing to remove the smoke stains on the building. After the British took Fort Detroit, the Americans launched a series of raids throughout southwestern Ontario. One of the more decisive battles took place early in the war at Queenston Heights.

Because of Queenston's strategic importance as the terminus of the vital Niagara portage route, it was defended by General Isaac Brock and a force of British troops. Its significant location was also the reason that the Americans wanted it. On October 13, 1812, American troops slipped across the river and surprised the British, killing Brock early in the battle. At first seeming victorious, the Americans then had to face a Native force. Although small in number, the warriors, led by Major John Norton,[4] bottled up the Americans until General Roger Sheaffe arrived from Fort George with reinforcements. Fearing the chilling battle cries of the Iroquois, the remaining American forces refused to cross the river, and the invaders were put to flight.

As commander of the British forces in Upper Canada, and being provisional lieutenant governor, as well, Brock in death warranted a special monument. After having been completed to a height of 14.5 metres, construction on the first Brock Monument was halted in 1824 when a cornerstone was found to contain a rendering of William Lyon Mackenzie's rebellious *Colonial Advocate* newspaper. A second monument on the same site was completed in 1828, but was destroyed in 1838 by a suspicious explosion attributed to rebels sympathetic to Mackenzie. Finally, the monument that stands on the site today was completed in 1853. It soars fifty-six metres into the sky, and the cut-stone structure is inlaid with carvings of lions and the four figures of Victory. From its apex, Brock's sword points north down the Niagara River, and can be seen on those rare clear days from the shore of the lake.

The little-known building to which Brock's body supposedly was carried still stands in Queenston as the Stone Barn at the rear of 17 Queenston Road. So does the only Anglican church in the world dedicated to a layman, the Brock Memorial of St. Saviour, located at 12 Princess Street. It was completed in 1879.

Another hero was Queenston resident Laura Secord, who, after overhearing American soldiers billeted in her home talking of a pending assault on the British, undertook a gruelling hike, guided in part by aboriginal allies, to the headquarters of Lieutenant Fitzgibbon where she

Over the years, there has been remarkably little change to the built heritage of the main street of Queenston.

delivered her warning. Her actions on that muggy night in 1813 helped the British to repel the American assault. While her home has been restored, the headquarters used by Fitzgibbon is but a ruin.

William Lyon Mackenzie, too, has a link with Queenston, for it was here that he initially published his anti-establishment *Colonial Advocate* newspaper. After moving to York (now Toronto) in 1824, he went on to become the very first mayor of that city in 1834. Mackenzie pushed for a more representative form of government, the upshot of his actions culminating in the ill-fated rebellion of 1837 for which he was exiled. But villains can just as easily become heroes and, following his return to Canada, Mackenzie once more became involved in politics.

His Queenston printing office deteriorated until, by 1935, only the walls remained. Although restored between 1936 and 1938, it served as little more than a municipal office until 1958. Finally, in 1991, shortly after the 200th anniversary of the Niagara Portage Road, thanks to the Niagara Parks Commission and the Mackenzie Printery Committee, old-style printing presses were installed, and today the building houses the hands-on Mackenzie Newspaper and Printery Museum and the lithography studio of Canadian artist Frederick Hagan. Meanwhile, in Toronto, Mackenzie's Bond Street home (once thought to be haunted) contains his original presses and is also open as a museum of his exploits.

Following the war, Queenston resumed its importance as a transportation route around the Niagara Falls. An important road followed an early glacial beach ridge at the base of the escarpment, west to the village of Ancaster — another key pioneer settlement at the head of the lake. In 1839, Queenston became the terminus of Ontario's first railway operation. Known as the Erie and Ontario Railway, it was a simple horse-drawn tram that rocked along on wooden rails covered with only a strip of iron. This new mode of travel linking Queenston with Chippewa effectively eliminated the old portage trail. From Queenston, passengers would be shuttled from the rail station to the wharf, where they could board a steamer to Toronto, while from Chippewa, travellers could sail to Buffalo.

Soon after the line was opened, William H. Smith, compiler of the *Canada West Gazetteer*, visited Queenston. "Before the opening of the Welland Canal," he wrote in 1846, "Queenston was a place of considerable business, being one of the principal depots for merchandise intended for the west ... which now finds its way by the Welland Canal."[7] The railway, he noted, was "commenced in 1835 and completed in 1841 ... which passes close to and above the falls of Niagara, and during the summer the cars run daily and steamboats from Buffalo meet the cars at Chippewa."[8] At Queenston "during the season, boats ply here regularly from Toronto, and stages run from Hamilton to meet the boats.[9]" In 1846, he also noted that "a horse ferry-boat plies across the river from Queenston to Lewiston."[10]

Six years later he would add in *Canada: Past Present and Future* that "a suspension bridge is now nearly completed across the river.... It is supported by wire cables, ten in number carried over stone towers ... the total length is twelve hundred and forty five feet (and) is supposed to carry a weight of eight hundred and thirty-five tons without breaking."[11]

By 1886 the *Illustrated Historical Atlas of the Counties of Lincoln and Welland* was noting that "the bridge which gave way to the more convenient one at Clifton (now Niagara Falls) had its cable wire stays broken by the ice gorges in the river it spanned and today all that is left of the bridge, which excited the wonder of all when finished, are several large twisted wire cables that span the river, still securely fastened to massive stone towers on either side."[12] In 1854, the Erie and Ontario railway line changed its name to the Erie and Niagara Railway, and was extended to Niagara (the name changed from Newark to Niagara in 1798) and then on to Fort Erie. Steam locomotives had by then replaced the horses. Today, those Queenston wharves are the site of a busy jet-boat tour of the rapids, while the rail line is now a walking and cycling trail.

In 1893 another railway arrived in Queenston, the Niagara Park and River Railway. The eighteen-kilometre route began at Niagara Falls, Ontario, and followed the brink of the Niagara River Gorge, providing tourists with vertigo-inducing views deep into the tumultuous abyss. In 1899 a new suspension bridge was built across the river, linking Queenston with Lewiston, New York, and the tourist line was then able to cross to the American side and follow a circle route. After seeing the river from above on the Canadian side, travellers would cross at Queenston and follow the bottom of the gorge to Niagara Falls, New York. However, following a series of rock falls, the route was abandoned, and the bridge removed. Today, the stone-block abutments, now overgrown, and the weed-filled pavement of the road that once led to it are the only "ghosts" of this once vital link across the border. The high level Queenston–Lewiston Bridge now connects the Queen Elizabeth Way with Interstate 190 in the United States, completely bypassing Queenston.

Although its transportation role is now history and its traditional businesses replaced by B & Bs, Queenston offers many vestiges of those grander days. Several of Ontario's earliest and grandest homes can be found on the quiet backstreets of this riverside village. One of the more prominent landmarks of the former main street is the South Landing Inn (21 Front Street). Built in 1827, it retains its two-storey porch, while modern additions provide accommodation for today's travellers. It was here that one-time owner James Wadsworth earned a Prohibition-era reputation as a rum-runner to the United States shore, at the same time allegedly returning with illegal immigrants.

Two homes that date from the 1820s sit at 48 Queenston Street and 25 Princess Street, and a red-brick house at 93 Queenston may well be the oldest in Queenston and one of the oldest in Ontario. It was built in 1807 by Robert Hamilton, who had earlier helped launch Queenston into its role as a transportation node.

Unfortunately, the elegant mansion, known as "Glencairn Manor," is not visible from the road, but its southern pillars and twenty rooms overlook the riverside site where John Hamilton, Robert's son, built steamers for the Queenston to Toronto run.

The River Road

One of Ontario's most scenic drives, although short, is along the Niagara Parkway. Administered by the Niagara Parks Commission, it links Queenston with its sister riverside town, Niagara-on-the-Lake. The route itself is not new. An earlier and more twisting dirt version was the one that met George Heriot, who followed it in 1807. He recounted that journey, enthusing that "the scenery from Niagara to Queenstown is highly pleasing, the road leading along the summit of the banks of one of the most magnificent rivers in the universe."[13]

Due to the scenic appeal of the river, and its access to a navigable section of the Niagara River, wealthy Loyalists and army officers chose its banks on which to build their grand homes. And, being farther from the American bombardments during the War of 1812, a few of those early mansions remain standing.

What is arguably one of the grandest homes visible from the Niagara Parkway is the southern-style "Willowbank." Built in 1834, it is considered a classic Greek revival-style house, with grand pillars lining the east façade. Its history is linked to that of Queenston, as its builder was one of Robert Hamilton's sons, Alexander. The eighteen-room limestone structure sits on a bank overlooking the river, on a seven-hectare property. Though not open to the public, the house has processional steps, hand-carved capitals, and classical mouldings. A grand spiral staircase graces the inside of the rear entrance.

The Parks Commission has been careful to balance the privacy of property owners with the public appeal of the river road. Newer homes generally are accessed by service roads that parallel the main road, while scenic pull-offs allow travellers to follow the pathways to the riverside. Historic plaques describe the many heritage highlights of the route, such as Vrooman's Battery, from which cannon fire harassed American troops attempting to cross the river during the War of 1812, or Brown's Point, where Adam Brown opened a tavern and operated a wharf from which local settlers could ship their produce. Two of the river road's grander homes are also highlighted. Built in 1800, a plaque describes the "Field House" as being one of Ontario's oldest brick homes. Located at 15276 Niagara Parkway, the house remains in private hands (after briefly being used by the Ontario Heritage Foundation) and is protected by covenant.

Another grand home of similar age is the "McFarland House." Built by His Majesty's boat-builder James McFarland in 1800, the house served as a hospital for both British and American troops during the 1812 conflict. King George III had granted McFarland 240 hectares of land, and he and his sons fired bricks in their own kiln to build the impressive structure. Now owned by the Parks Commission, the house, since 1959, has operated as a museum, complete with a nineteenth-century style yard and garden. The McFarland House is located at 15927 Niagara Parkway. Despite its proximity to Niagara-on-the-Lake, it was one of the few buildings from that community to survive the torching of the town by the Americans.

Niagara-on-the-Lake

Today's Niagara-on-the-Lake has evolved into one of Ontario's major tourist attractions. While the annual Shaw Festival draws tens of thousands of visitors, the city's situation as a jump-off point for Niagara-area wine tours draws even more. Its heritage homes and historic main street are lures for tourists year-round.

Originally, the location, due to its proximity to water transportation, its bountiful supply of fish, and its defensive advantages, attracted the Neutral Nation. The British, too, saw its military strengths, and established a fort here in 1781, calling the community Butlersburg. In 1792, lieutenant governor John Graves Simcoe, who was fond of naming anything he could after locales in his cherished England, renamed it Newark and established Upper Canada's first parliament here. But he soon realized that it was too vulnerable to the Americans, who had built Fort Niagara just across the river, and moved that function to a safer location across the lake, to a place he called York. Shortly after Simcoe returned to England in 1796, the town restored its original name, or at least one close to it: Niagara.

In 1807, Heriot wrote that Niagara may not have been particularly healthy: "a swamp [between the fort and the town] becomes, at particular seasons, from the vapours exhaled from it, prejudicial to the health of those whose residence is by the river, and sometimes to that of the troops in the garrison."[14] This was an observation in stark contrast to the healthful properties being promoted less than a century later. But of the town itself he wrote, "The houses are in general composed of wood and have a neat and clean appearance, their present number may amount to two hundred," [houses which would lie in a smouldering ruin a mere six years later]. "The streets are spacious ... so that the town when completed will be healthful and airy."[15]

While Queenston thrived as the terminus of the Niagara portage road, the town of Niagara grew into a key port of entry for goods destined for the area's settlers. Its location on the Niagara River made it a focus for many of the battles that raged during the failed attempt by the United States to annex their wayward cousins in Upper Canada. In 1812 the Americans slipped across the river and burned the town to the ground.

"Nothing but heaps of coals and the streets full of furniture that the inhabitants were fortunate enough to get out of their houses met the eyes in all directions," one visitor was quoted as saying in the *Atlas of Lincoln and Welland Counties*. "We were very apprehensive that a mine was left for our destruction."[16]

The ruins of Ontario's best "ghost fort," Fort Mississauga, are now surrounded by a golf course in Niagara-on-the-Lake.

But once the occupying forces had retreated across the river, Niagara began to rebuild, many of the owners building on the original foundations despite orders to move their homes farther away from the river. The British Army quickly rebuilt Fort George, also adding Butler's Barracks and the more strategically located Fort Mississauga. Although Fort George was too far from the river mouth to be useful, Fort Mississauga lay directly across the river from Fort Niagara on the American side. At this time, the land around the new fort was owned by James Crooks, a merchant and land speculator. In order to keep Crooks from developing the land around the fort, and thus possibly endangering prospective occupants, the government exchanged his property for a parcel of land farther from danger. (Crooks's former property is now the golf course.)

The fort was built on the site of the Mississauga Point Lighthouse. Dating from 1804, it was the first brick lighthouse built in Canada. Although it somehow survived the otherwise total destruction of the town, a new fort was more vital, and the stones from the lighthouse were incorporated into the new fort, as were many of the ruins of the town. But a light was still needed, and a new beacon was placed on the fort, where it remained in operation until the 1840s. For several years afterward, only the light on the American shore guided ships into the river. A number of shipwrecks convinced the government that new lights were needed on the Canadian side, as well, and in 1904 a pair of range lights flickered on. These lights continue to guide pleasure craft to the new yachting harbour.

Following the War of 1812, Niagara quickly re-established its role as shipping centre for the northern part of the Niagara Peninsula. Soon steamers began carrying tourists to Niagara, where they would board stages to see the wonder that was Niagara Falls. It also regained its role as the seat for the counties of Lincoln and Welland (a role it later lost to St. Catharines). To accommodate this new function, English architect William Thomas designed a simple, classic stone courthouse, built in 1847, that served as the district seat for fourteen years.

To house the growing number of tourists, hotels began to spring up, among them the Whale Inn and the Moffat Inn. In 1832, the Niagara Harbour and Dock Company built new wharves and shipbuilding facilities. Eight years later, Ontario's first railway, the Erie and Ontario Railroad, was completed between Chippewa and Queenston. It was extended to Niagara in 1854. But the bubble would soon burst.

Courtesy of the Toronto Reference Library, T 13472.

An early view of Niagara's courthouse, originally built as the county seat in 1849.

Back in 1851, the second Welland Canal had opened, replacing the limited capacity of the first, much smaller, canal. In 1853, the Great Western Railway extended its route well to the south of Niagara, allowing through east–west rail traffic to bypass the northern peninsula completely. In 1859, another new railway, the Welland Railway, with its north–south link, was built from Port Colborne to Port Dalhousie, its builders ignoring intense lobbying by Niagara for a link of its own to St. Catharines.

Writing in 1851, W.H. Smith noted the decline, observing that Niagara "was once a place of considerable business, but since the formation of the Welland Canal, St. Catharine's being the more critically situated, has absorbed its trade and thrown it completely in the shade…. The Niagara Harbour and Dock Company formerly did a large business and many first class vessels have been built here … however from some cause of other affairs did not prosper with them and the whole concern was sold by the sheriff."[17]

Smith did appreciate the tourist potential of the site: "[Niagara] is airily situated and is a pleasant summer residence frequented during the summer season by families having spare time and spare money by health seekers and hypochondriacs."[18] But most of Niagara's tourist prosperity was to materialize in the future.

Then, as if the stagnating village needed another blow, in 1862, ratepayers of the newly created Lincoln County chose St. Catharines over Niagara as the site of the new county seat, and the court house was downgraded to town hall. In the years that followed, Niagara's population plunged from more than three thousand to nearly one third of that.

But with its idyllic location at the mouth of the Niagara River, and its distance from the more prosperous but smokier growing cities, Niagara began to grow its tourist sector. Using money it received in compensation for losing the county seat, the town helped finance the building of the elegant Queen's Royal Hotel, as well as a golf course on the vacant grounds around the now abandoned Fort Mississauga. The majestic Prince of Wales Hotel made its appearance in 1882 on the main street close to the Michigan Central train station. Originally it was known by the less regal name Long's Hotel, and later The Arcade. Its princely re-appellation did not come until 1901, when the Duke of York, who very shortly would become the Prince of Wales, bestowed upon it its new name. The hotel's three-storey corner mansard dormer is one of the town's iconic images today.

In 1878 the Niagara Navigation Company launched steamships like the *Chippewa*, the *Corona*, and the *Cibola* to carry tourists between Toronto and Niagara. A new invasion from the United States began, but this time to see the sites. The Michigan Central Railway, which by this time was running the old Erie and Ontario line, had created a station stop overlooking Niagara Falls, and it, too, was drawing tourists into Niagara. Around this time, the town published a brochure promoting itself as a peaceful summer getaway, with somewhat more relaxed bylaws. By 1894, the St. Catharines and Niagara Central Railway was operating a daily interurban electrical train service into the town. Because its rails ran along the streets, no evidence survives of that long abandoned line.

In the 1880s there arrived yet another invasion of tourists: the Chautauquans. The Chautauqua movement was started in upper New York State, on the shores of Chautauqua Lake, in 1874 (although, as a later chapter will reveal, its real roots lay in Ontario). In an era before cinema and radio, Chautauqua provided a form of cultural entertainment. A community grew on the shores of the lake, with theatres, hotels, and several streets of elegant homes. In 1887, the Chautauquans established a Niagara assembly on the shores of Lake Ontario, just north of the town of Niagara. Here they built the three-storey Chautauqua Hotel, a four-thousand-seat amphitheatre, and a circular road lined with cottages. Although many tourists travelled from Toronto to the Chautauqua dock by steamer, the railway added its own spur line to the grounds. Activities at Chautauqua were many and varied. Far from being a religious camp, Chautauqua treated visitors to poetry, lectures, music, and theatre. But the Niagara assembly never really gained a sound financial footing. In 1909 the hotel burned, and by the 1920s the land was being subdivided for housing.

Following the end of the First World War, the auto age slowly began to arrive, and Niagara's distinctiveness as a summer resort began to lose ground to the lakes and woods of today's cottage country. Little remains of Niagara's Chautauqua. Its distinctive street pattern radiates out from its circular configuration, while street names recall many of the writers and philosophers who attracted the early crowds — Wilberforce, Wycliffe, and Wesley, to name a few. Chautauqua Amphitheatre Circle defines the location of the theatre, the focus for their riveting lectures. Few of the original cottages have survived, most replaced or radically altered. One which has retained its Chautauqua ambience is the Lakeview Bed and Breakfast, built in 1879 and located at 490 Niagara Boulevard. And, partly in deference to its theatrical origins and partly due to its popularity with Shaw Festival actors, the community has now earned the nickname "Camp Shaw."

Despite its many makeovers and economic ups and downs, the streets of Niagara-on-the-Lake (finally named as such in 1880 in order to distinguish it from the postal address of Niagara Falls) reveal its varied heritage. Many grand homes still survive from the post-1812 years. This is thanks in large part to a concerted effort by restoration architect Peter John Stokes, who authored the book *Old Niagara on the Lake*, published in 1971. He was spurred on by the heritage passions of such locals as Kathleen Drope and Carl Banke.

A few years earlier, in 1962, a local lawyer named Brian Doherty had launched the Shaw Festival using the spare space in the old town hall as its first theatre. Built to house the county offices, its role was reduced to that of town hall when the county seat went to the hated rival, St. Catharines, instead. Today it is the popular Court House Theatre and the main street's most prominent structure.

At the corner of King and Queen stands Ontario's oldest apothecary. Built in 1820, it is now maintained as a 1860s-era drug store museum by the Ontario Pharmacists Association. Kitty-corner to it, the elegant Prince of Wales Hotel, an iconic landmark, has been much extended. A few blocks away, the Pillar and Post Hotel occupies the shell of a one-time canning factory. The Oban Inn, near Front and Simcoe, was originally built as a private home by the town's first ship-owner. Moffat's Inn on Front Street was owned by Richard Moffat, and was one of twenty-eight taverns operating in the town during the bustling 1830s. One of Ontario's oldest Anglican churches, St. Marks, although refurbished after the 1812 war, was originally built in 1791 and stands on Byron Street. The Olde Angel Inn was established in 1789 and rebuilt in 1816 after it was burnt by the Americans during the War of 1812. Located at 224 Regent Street, it is considered Ontario's oldest operating inn.

Many black settlers who had escaped servitude south of the border, or had arrived as slaves before Britain abolished the slave trade, took up residence in Niagara. A typical example of one of their early dwellings, with its simple two-room layout, still stands at Gate and Johnson streets. In stark contrast, the rambling Victorian-style mansion at 177 King Street was built in 1886 by merchant Sam Rowley for his black wife, Fanny Rose.

Of all the historic streets in Niagara, perhaps one of the most significant is Prideaux. Several houses here were among the first to have been rebuilt after the destruction of the town by the Americans — some as early as 1815.

In contrast, the historic wharf area is much changed, with little to remind the visitor that the Michigan Central's tracks once ran beside a wharf-side station. Amid the new condos and wharf-side development, the King George III Inn is a reminder of the location's key role as a transportation hub. The downtown station on King Street also still stands, though altered somewhat by the addition of a small faux tower.

The most prominent of the military structures in the area is the much touted Fort George. Although a key outpost during the War of 1812, it was never completely rebuilt after its destruction by the Americans. Today's recreation came about as a Depression-era make-work project. Another military site, Navy Hall, originally consisted of five separate buildings built by the British as early as 1765. Destroyed by the Americans during their rampage through the town, Navy Hall was reconstructed after the war. Today, only one of those buildings still stands, and is now used for private functions. It lies on Ricardo Street, at the east end of the town, opposite Fort George.

Faring somewhat better is the complex known as Butler's Barracks, located at the corner of King and John streets. These five structures stand on what is known as the Commons, and today house the museum of the Lincoln and Welland Regiment, which was descended from the renowned Butler's Rangers.

The most haunting and original of the town's military buildings is the ghostly ruin of Fort Mississauga. Following its reconstruction by the British after 1812, it saw military service off and on until 1872, when it was finally abandoned. Today the ruins have been stabilized by Parks Canada. A trail leads through the golf course, marked by historic interpretive plaques. Its rival across the river, Fort Niagara, can be clearly seen from the parapets, though the only missiles hurled at it today are those of the golfers.

Twelve Mile Creek: Port Dalhousie

Before rail lines breached the peninsula, two main routes led from Niagara to Ancaster and the head of the lake. The more popular followed the old raised beaches at the foot of the Niagara Escarpment, left behind by the receding waters of Lake Iroquois. This alignment was higher and drier, allowing easier travel by stage or foot. Another route followed the shore of the lake itself. Although shorter, it was more difficult, as the many river and creek mouths to be crossed proved time-consuming. But this crude trail led to the naming of those same waterways. Quite simply, the rivers were named based on the distance they were from the mouth of the Niagara River. A short distance from Niagara, Four Mile Creek was the site of an early mill operation.

The first of the Loyalists to arrive at the mouth of Twelve Mile Creek were Peter Broeck and Lieutenant Benjamin Pawling. In 1821, Pawling founded a town site he called Dalhousie, for then governor general, the Earl of Dalhousie. The site also attracted William Hamilton Merritt, who saw the potential for an all-Canadian canal to link Lake Ontario with the upper lakes. The completion of the Erie Canal linking New York with Lake Erie led Canadians to see the need for an all-Canadian route from the Atlantic seaboard to their ports on Lakes Erie and Huron, as well as those on the upper lakes.

But the high cliffs of the Niagara Escarpment posed an engineering nightmare. The first thought was to dig a canal along Twelve Mile Creek to the base of the huge cliff, and from there drag the boats up by means of an incline railway. But Merritt convinced the government that the best route lay in a canal that mounted the escarpment by a series of locks, and then connected with the Welland River, thence to the Niagara River at Chippewa.

In 1824, the canal's president, George Keefer, turned the sod at Allanburg, and on November 30, 1829, the first two schooners sailed through the canal and into the Niagara River. Because there was insufficient water in the watershed to operate the canal effectively, more was needed, and a feeder canal was opened to Port Maitland to draw the water from the Grand River. However, because of the strong currents on the Niagara River and the shallow draft of the feeder canal, a third channel had to be dug, this one directly from Port Robinson to Port Colborne, right on Lake Erie.

But with forty locks, and ships increasing in size, the first Welland Canal was soon obsolete. A second was started. Completed in 1851, it followed the same route as the first, but the number of locks was reduced to twenty-seven, they were lengthened and deepened, and most wooden locks were replaced with stone ones. The success of the canal brought a boom to St. Catharines, but a decline for places like Niagara and Queenston. New towns sprang into existence along the route, such as Port Robinson at the old junction of the first canal and the Welland River, and Port Colborne and Port Dalhousie as the Lake Erie and Lake Ontario termini respectively.

The Thorold and Port Dalhousie Railway rolled into town in 1853, building its facilities on the east side of the harbour. This line later became part of the Welland Railway and then the Grand Trunk. The east side of the harbour was nicknamed the "Michigan Side" due to the annual winter migration of the tow boys — men who guided the horses that towed the sailboats through the canal to the lumber camps of that state. Even today the beach is known as Michigan Beach.

By 1866, the Muir brothers were operating a permanent dry dock at the north end of Martindale Pond, a business which survived for nearly a century. But many of the new locks remained inadequate, and so between 1873 and 1887 they were doubled in size, while a more direct route between Port Dalhousie and Allanburg was excavated. By 1907, it was evident that this one, too, was outdated, and yet a fourth canal was begun. Interrupted by the war, the new waterway opened in 1932. Now constructed of concrete, the locks were reduced to a mere seven, with a new Lake Ontario entrance at Port Weller. It is this canal (with another bypass at Welland opened in 1972) that today accommodates some of the world's largest lake and ocean freighters.

The success of the canal meant both boom and bust for Port Dalhousie. With the opening of the first canal, the mouth of Twelve Mile Creek became an overnight bonanza town, with a string of bars and taverns lining the lock side. Sailors, longshoremen, and tow boys all crowded into the smoky nighteries, often tumbling out onto the streets and filling the night air with the sounds of drunken brawling. It was little wonder then that in 1845 a small stone jail was built close by. Guests were invited to share two cramped cells and, if they became cold, would be allowed to stoke the fire in the single wood-burning stove.

When the swamp at the mouth of Twelve Mile Creek was filled in, a recreational park was opened, attracting tourists from Hamilton and Toronto. As early as 1884, the paddlewheel steamer *Empress of India* began carrying visitors to the park. In 1902, the Niagara, St. Catharines and Toronto Railway took over operations, with the ships *Northumberland* and *Dalhousie City* plying between the park and Toronto.

In 1903, Martindale Pond, originally a part of the first two canals, became the site of the Royal Canadian Henley Regatta. A branch of the Welland Railway ended at a station on the east side of the canal, while streetcars from the Niagara, St. Catharines and Toronto Railway also brought fun-seekers to the beach. Prohibition did not put a serious damper on the port's nightlife. Despite the restrictions of the Ontario Temperance Act, beer managed to make its way to the town on boats from Quebec. The park continued to expand, with rides, a water slide, a dance pavilion, and, in 1921, the arrival of a merry-go-round from Hanlan's Point in Toronto. The pavilion featured dance bands such as the Andy Spinosa Band. By the 1930s, nearly three hundred thousand visitors were arriving by boat each year, and radio station CKTB was regularly broadcasting lacrosse games from the park.

The relocation of the canal entrance to Port Weller had brought a slump in the economy of the port, and the years following the Second World War hurt the park, which, along with the boats, was being operated by the Canada Steamship Company (CSC). Steamers continued to call until a deadly fire on the *Noronic* in Toronto Harbour in 1949 tightened safety standards for the

Port Dalhousie's historic carousel is the sole survivor of the site's days as an amusement park.

lake-passenger ships. The cross-lake traffic died out, and Canadian National (CN), then owner of the CSC, decided to get out of the amusement park business altogether. In 1969 the park was closed and the rides sold; only the carousel and dance hall remained (the dance hall burned in 1974).

With considerable foresight, the St. Catharines council bought the property and, in 1978, declared the carousel a heritage site. By then the Queen Elizabeth Highway between Toronto and Fort Erie was bringing a new wave of tourists. St. Catharines' urban growth soon engulfed the port, and it gained new life as both a popular summer playground and an historic lakeside attraction. Today, sleek yachts crowd into the harbour and beery laughter fills the bars and patios on the warm summer nights.

Despite the urban growth around it, Port Dalhousie remains a heritage treasure trove. For starters, two historic locks remain. Lock number one from the second canal is part of a park on Lakeport Road, the main street along the canal, while lock number one from the third canal lies farther east on Lakeport Road where a lock master's shanty has also been preserved.

Several of the early hotels still stand on the portside streets, including the Port Mansion at 12 Lakeport Road, built in 1860, and the Non-Such Hotel, built in 1862, located at 26 Lakeport Road. Near the corner of Lock and Main streets are the Lakeside Hotel, built in the 1890s as the Austin House, and the Lion Tavern, dating from 1877 and originally known as the Wellington House.

The little stone jail also survives, just around the corner from the drinking establishments — but today it belongs to one of them. The lockup is considered to be the second smallest establishment of its kind in North America. Measuring just 4.6 by 5.8 metres, it is just a few centimetres larger than the jail at Rodney, in southwestern Ontario, which measures 4.5 by 5.4 metres.[19]

Martindale Pond was once the site of the Muir Brothers Dry Docks and Shipyard. The solitary reminder of that operation is the Dalhousie House, built in 1850, and now a community hall and seniors centre. A pair of small historic lighthouses still blink on and off, guiding ships in the hours of darkness. The outer light was constructed in 1879, the inner light in 1898. But of all the historic structures to see in Port Dalhousie, the most sought-after is the old-time carousel. Built in 1898 by the I.D. Loof Company of Rhode Island, it was restored in the 1970s and still offers rides for just a nickel.

Port Weller

Despite being Port Dalhousie's successor, Port Weller offers a minimal amount of heritage. A residential road along the east side of the canal leads to a small beach where the large ships can be seen entering the canal. A solid lift bridge carries the traffic across the canal, except during those lengthy intervals when it is raised to allow the massive freighters to inch through. (The best viewing spot for ship-watching is at the Lock Three Museum and viewing platform in St. Catharines.) The Port Weller Dry Dock on the south side of the bridge remains a busy operation, and at any time a massive vessel may lie high and dry while undergoing repairs or maintenance.

In 1931, a lighthouse and keeper's dwelling were built to guide ships into the new canal. Here, on the west side of the entrance, the Department of the Marine constructed a simple, unadorned concrete building, sturdy enough to withstand the fiercest of gales, with a twenty-nine-metre-tall steel frame light. Despite a seven-kilometre road connection, the location was sufficiently remote that the lighthouse keeper's wife began operating a ham radio connection. In 1953, a more commodious and modern-looking house was added for the keeper. Finally, in 1970, the newer house was removed and the old light tower torn down, keepers no longer needed to tend the new automated beacon. The site is no longer accessible to the public, but the older house is now being put to good use by the Canadian Coast Guard as a search-and-rescue station.

Twenty Mile Creek: Jordan Harbour

The village of Jordan began as a mill town adjacent to a steep gully on Twenty Mile Creek. The creek flowed into Lake Ontario through a wide lagoon, which, although shallow, could accommodate small vessels. In was here, in 1833, that the Louth Harbour Company (Louth was the name of the township in which Jordan developed) built 160 metres of piers. Shipments of lumber, flour, and clothing originated at the mills of Glen Elgin, a village located upstream where the creek tumbled over the brink of the escarpment. Shipments from Jordan Harbour also included ships' masts and tan bark, and the port enjoyed a short-lived shipbuilding industry. In 1853, the Great Western Railway extended a long trestle across the creek, effectively blocking the shipments from Glen Elgin.

The railway did, however, bring a new era to the little community. The Jordan Harbour Company added a large wharf on the east side of the bay in 1897, while the government dredged the sand spit covering the mouth. The area's tender fruit crops were loaded onto freight cars, destined for grocery stores in Hamilton and Toronto. A few fishing vessels sailed from the protected lagoon. A small street network was laid out around the station, and a new community grew — Jordan Station. By 1898 the sand beach along the spit had attracted a community of cottagers. A drawbridge allowed traffic to cross the harbour until 1939, when the four lanes of the QEW ended the shipping era for Jordan Harbour. As the highway was widened, the cottages were removed. Two motels and a small mall now line the lakeshore. Jordan Station remains a residential community, and although trains no longer call, the attractive wooden station was rescued from the CNR's wrecking crews and is now a private home close to its original site.

The original mill village of Jordan has become a popular stop on the Niagara wine route and boasts a main street of new boutiques. Glen Elgin, later renamed Balls Falls, fell silent and is now a ghost town within the Balls Falls Conservation Area. But a ghostly sight of a different kind greets motorists racing along the QEW. It is the gaunt remains of a listing and rusting "tall ship."

The strange tale begins on the St. Lawrence in 1914, when *Le Progress* was launched as a ferry. In 1991 it was rebuilt to resemble *La Grande Hermine*, the sailing ship used in 1553 by explorer Jacques Cartier to make his way across the Atlantic and up the St. Lawrence River. To avoid allegedly unpaid dockage fees on the St. Lawrence, the ship was towed to Jordan Harbour in 1997 and, six years later, became a victim of arson. Its owner now deceased, it remains a mystery at this writing as to just how long this landmark will remain in its current location.[20]

Forty Mile Creek: Grimsby Beach

While the world-renowned and historic Chautauqua Movement is associated with the lake of the same name in upper New York State, its roots lie firmly in Canadian soil with a Methodist camp on the shores of Lake Ontario.

In 1846, John Bowslaugh, a devout Methodist, dedicated a lakeside parcel from his extensive property east of Grimsby as a Temperance meeting ground. For the next thirteen years, the annual meetings occurred in different sites, but by 1859 Bowslaugh's land had become a permanent Methodist camp. For several years, followers sat and listened to lectures held in tents, and swam in the inviting waters of the nearby beach. Finally, in 1874, the Ontario Methodist Campground Company was formed, and the site became known as Grimsby Park. The company divided the land into fifty lots, and a community of decorative cottages grew up on them. These otherwise simple buildings became known for their elaborate fretwork façades.

In 1876 a dock was built and the Great Western Railway added a stop at the park entrance. Two hotels, The Lake View House and The Park House, provided accommodation for those coming on short visits. Camp rules prohibited alcohol and foul language, and lights were to be out by 10:30. Any scofflaws might be detained by the camp constable and incarcerated in a lockup below The Park House Hotel.

In 1888 an elaborate temple replaced the outdoor speaker's stand in Grimsby Park, a building thirty-seven metres in diameter with a dome that soared thirty metres high above. Unfortunately, the resonance within such a shape made the speakers' words nearly unintelligible. By the 1890s the rules were relaxed, and campers were entertained by fireworks, concerts, recitals, and a new device known as the stereopticon.

By 1912, the Grimsby Company was bankrupt and had been purchased by Henry Wylie. He had a decidedly non-Methodist vision for the property and effectively turned it into an amusement park. Eliminating most of the constraining rules of the Methodist days, he installed two carousels, a miniature railway, and a shooting gallery, as well as a "Figure 8" roller coaster. Following Wylie's death in 1916, the park was bought by Canada Steamship Lines, which also operated other parks such as Wabasso in Burlington and Lakeside in Port Dalhousie.

But as the buildings aged, fires began to take their toll. In 1914, thirty-four of the tiny wooden cottages were destroyed, along with the roller coaster and The Park House. Just four years later, the Lake View House Hotel was also consumed. In 1922 the rotting temple hall was demolished, and in 1927 another thirty cottages went up in flames. But despite the dwindling attendance and the disappearance of most of the park's attractions, the band played on, and the dance hall stayed open through the Depression.

The last grand addition to the park was in 1939 when a new stone-and-wood entrance to the grounds was erected in honour of King George VI and Queen Elizabeth's visit to Ontario. Ironically, that was the same year that the monarch opened the QEW, a route that took over much of the park property. Soon after, the lots were sold off to the cottage occupants, and the community became a year-round suburb of Grimsby.

Despite the overwhelmingly suburban nature of today's Grimsby Park, a visit to the site is like a visit to another era. The tiny streets are lined with many of the elaborately fretted little cottages, the stone section of the

The bell from the Grimsby Beach meeting ground is preserved in a park surrounded by camp cottages.

entrance still stands, a cairn sits in "Auditorium Circle," and the bell that once called worshippers rests in a parkette on Fair Avenue. By the water's edge, Grimsby Park offers a shady respite from summer's heat, as it did many years before, while down on the lake, traces of the pier remain, buried now under more recent fill.

The village of Grimsby was once quite separate from the Methodist Camp at Grimsby Beach. It began to grow as a mill town on the banks of Forty Mile Creek. The first settler on the Forty was said to be a Captain Hendrick Nelles, whose son Robert built the area's first mills on the creek. The sites lay along the St. Catharines Road, inland from the lake. In 1846, William H. Smith would describe Grimsby as "beautifully situated on the St. Catharines Road … in the midst of some very fine scenery…. During the summer it is a favourite destination of pleasure seekers from Hamilton."[21]

A harbour was developed where the creek flowed into the lake and where schooners called at the wharves to carry off such products as lumber and wheat. When the Great Western Railway built its line closer to the main road, business at the harbour decreased. Grimsby still boasts a powerhouse from this era, located on the lake along with the remains of the wharf. A busy marina now occupies most of the one-time harbour. Although the picturesque station built by the Grand Trunk in the 1890s burned a decade ago, the original Great Western station still stands close to the track, now a private business operation.

But it was the Nelles family who dominated much of Grimsby's early history, and much remains of their legacy. At 126 Main Street West the grand home built by Robert Nelles between 1788 and 1798 still survives. Other Nelles family homes are also still standing — the one at 139 Lake Road, known as the "Hermitage" was built by Robert's brother William in 1800, while William's son Adolphus built "Lake Lawn" in 1846, found today at 376 Nelles Road North.

Chapter 2
The Head of the Lake

Geographically, the head of Lake Ontario is somewhat complex. Two sections of the mighty Niagara Escarpment form a wide steep-sided valley where the walls converge to the west, creating the spectacular Dundas Valley. Here the waters of Lake Ontario reach their western extremity. But before they do, they encounter two hurdles.

One is a sand strip or beach bar separating the main body of the lake to the east from a bay known variously as Lake Geneva or Burlington Bay to the west. At the western end of Burlington Bay lies yet another, higher barrier, Burlington Heights — the remains of an ancient beach deposited by the waters of Lake Iroquois. Beyond this ridge lies the lake's westernmost body of water, Cootes Paradise, which breaches the Burlington Heights through a small stream known as Morden Creek. Burlington Bay flows into the lake through an occasional breach in the sandbar at the north end of the strip. At least that was how the first Europeans encountered it.

When John Graves Simcoe was obliged to relocate the province's capital from Newark, he chose a site a safe distance away, in fact so distant that he was told to abandon it. That site was to have been at the forks of the distant Thames River, the location of today's busy metropolitan centre of London. To access that location, he ordered that a road be laid out from the head of Cootes Paradise to the Thames. Simcoe named that starting point King's Landing, a landing which, along with the community of Dundas Mills, developed into the town of Dundas.

But Lord Dorchester refused to consider the manning of two garrisons, and ordered Simcoe to forget the Thames and instead locate the new capital near the ruins of an old French fort named Fort Toronto. But as was his custom, Simcoe eschewed the aboriginal name and selected the name York. The location had the advantage over the forks of the Thames in that, while the harbour offered a military advantage, it also lay on Lake Ontario, then the only means of moving troops and supplies. Thus, the head of the lake was no longer the jumping-off point to a new territorial seat of government.

Hamilton

Hamilton developed later than Dundas. The parcel of land that forms the old section of the city today was originally bought by James Durand, the local member of the British Legislative Assembly, who in 1815 sold it, along with his palatial house, to George Hamilton, a local early settler and son of Robert Hamilton, the Queenston entrepreneur. Hamilton, along with another local property owner, Nathaniel Hughson, went on to acquire and subdivide more parcels in 1813, naming early streets James, John, Hunter, and Catherine, after family members. In 1816 he convinced the government to designate the town site as the administrative centre for the District of Gore.

Hamilton was elected as the MLA for the Gore District and lobbied for improvements to Burlington Bay. Up until that time, any exported goods had be hauled across the sand spit, or poled through the occasional breach at the north end, into waiting schooners. Between 1823 and 1832, a canal was cut through the sand strip, allowing vessels to come and go from the harbour with greater ease.

As Smith described it in 1851: "The town of Hamilton was laid out in 1813, but for many years its progress was very slow.... The completion of the Burlington Bay Canal however gave it access to the lake and formed the commencement of a new era in its history."[1] Soon a bustling and doubtless rowdy little community grew at Port Hamilton, well to the north of Hamilton's original town site.

Railway days were soon to arrive. As early as 1837, lawyer Allan Napier McNab, who had moved to Port Hamilton from York in 1826, had earned

Grand Trunk Railway Station, Hamilton, Canada

Courtesy of Ron Brown Collection.

This early view from the mid-1870s shows Hamilton's Great Western rail yards and docks.

much of his fortune through land speculation, and was promoting the building of the London and Gore Railroad, which in the end failed to gain sufficient financing. He did manage, however, to start the Great Western Railway, and by 1850 it had been surveyed from the Niagara River to the Detroit River, with Hamilton as its headquarters. Smith saw potential there, too: "Hamilton is admirably situated for carrying on a large wholesale trade with the West — being at the head of navigation of Lake Ontario and in the heart of the settled portion of the province."[2]

Before the rails were laid, Port Hamilton consisted of several small streams that cut their channels into the soft silt of the lake bottom. Pilings more than ten metres deep were required to anchor the many private piers that stabbed out into the bay. McNab's first wharf originally stood near the foot of Bay Street and is known today as Pier 4. Nearby was the first location of the prestigious Royal Hamilton Yacht Club (RHYC). It lasted here until 1891, when encroaching industry began to reduce the ambience of the location, and an elaborate new clubhouse was built beside the Burlington Canal. Upon its completion, Queen Victoria consented to the use of the word *royal* — one of only ten yacht clubs in Canada to have earned that distinction. After the new clubhouse burned in 1915, the RHYC returned to its original Bay Street site, and erected a newer clubhouse in 1938 at the foot of nearby McNab, where it remains today.

Other early operations on Hamilton's bayfront were the Leander Rowing Club and H.L. Bastien's boathouse. During its heyday as the main passenger line on the Great Lakes, and while also operating several amusement parks, Canada Steamship Lines maintained an office at the foot of Wentworth Street. Following an investigation into the tragic fire on the *Noronic* in Toronto on September 14, 1949, which killed upwards of 140 people, the company was faulted for its lack of fire alarms, escape plans, and extinguishers. Partly as a result of those findings, Canada Steamships decided to focus instead on freight. McKay's Wharf, at the foot of James Street, was built to handle larger ships, which began to enter Hamilton Harbour as soon as the Burlington Canal was opened, and ferries such as SS *Lady Hamilton* puffed out from their slips near James Street.

McNab had by this time purchased a property on Burlington Heights, where he constructed the magnificent Dundurn Castle. From his new perch he could look down upon his railway empire, as the Great Western yards, docks, and station lay along the harbour, literally at McNab's feet.

Smith's foresight was prescient. By the late 1800s, Hamilton was indeed in Ontario's industrial forefront as two more rail lines converged on the growing city. In 1873, the Hamilton and Lake Erie began service between Hamilton and Jarvis, and five years later to Port Dover on Lake Erie. In 1879 the line was extended to Collingwood on Georgian Bay as the Hamilton and Northwestern Railway. This new route gave Hamilton rail access to both American coal from the south shore of Lake Erie and to western grain shipped down the Great Lakes.

In 1896 the Toronto Hamilton and Buffalo Railway (TH&B) laid tracks through the city, providing both Hamilton and Toronto (via running rights over the Grand Trunk) with their shortest rail link to Buffalo. Within a few years, the TH&B had extended a branch line to Port Maitland on Lake Erie, giving Hamilton yet another link to coal from the United States. By the time the TH&B established their headquarters and main yards here, those of the Great Western had largely gone. Following its merger with the GT, the new owner relocated most of the facilities to Stratford and London.

Because of the easy access to coal from West Virginia and Pennsylvania, iron from the Lakehead, and the presence of steel industries building locomotives for the Great Western, Hamilton was well on its way to becoming "Steel Town." In 1895, the Hamilton Blast Furnace Company began producing iron right in the city, and in 1899 it joined Ontario Rolling Mills to form the Hamilton Iron and Steel Company, which in 1910 became The Steel Company of Canada (Stelco, now US Steel Canada). The other iconic name in steel production, Dofasco, began more modestly as a small foundry, later merging with the Hamilton Malleable Iron Company to become Dominion Foundries and Steel Company, or Dofasco.

As more heavy industry arrived, attracted by the ready availability of steel, the old port of Hamilton became unrecognizable as landfill pushed the docks farther into the harbour. In this emerging industrial landscape, workers' suburbs also began to take shape. With minimal public transport available, living close to the factories was essential. Union Park was one example of a workers' subdivision created by land speculators in the east end of the city. Others were laid out by the local factory owners themselves. Most such homes were simple wooden structures of one or one and a half storeys, and often built by the owners themselves, who would enlarge them as money became available.

For many years, Hamilton was scorned for its endless industrial landscape and its yellow, rank air that spewed across the entire peninsula. In recent years the industries and the government authorities have drastically reduced the air pollution, and many of the aging factories have modernized and earned a place in the industrial heritage of Hamilton.

While most of the original industrial buildings have long since been replaced with brighter and safer working environments, a few early survivors remain. In a building set back from Biggar Avenue, Royal Recycling occupies a structure built by the Hoepfner Refining Company in 1899. A stone building fronting on Barton Street at Wellington, once closer to the water, dates from 1876 and began life as a malt house.

The oldest of the industrial buildings is the Hamilton Waterworks. Finished in 1859, it claims to be the only mid-nineteenth-century intact waterworks in North America. When in operation, two steam-powered pumps extracted water from the lake. This water then flowed three kilometres to a reservoir, and from there into the city's water system. As the city grew, a second pump was added, but by 1938 they could not keep pace with the growing demand, and the plant was closed. Today the buildings

Hamilton's historic waterworks, located on Woodward Avenue, were designated a National Historic Site in 1983.

complete with original boiler house, pump house, chimney, and fuel shed — have been preserved and deemed a national historic site. Inside are two original water pumps, fourteen metres high, one of which remains operational and is used for demonstrations. Visible from the busy QEW, the waterworks is situated at Woodward Avenue and Burlington Street.

Hamilton Harbour sports two faces. The industrial landscape lies largely east of the HMCS *Haida*, which was towed to Hamilton in 2002 and is now a popular national historic site.[3] West of the *Haida*, the harbour becomes recreational. The Hamilton City Yacht Club and the Royal Hamilton Yacht Club show off dock after dock of sailboats and yachts. Farther west are the Parks Canada Discovery Centre and Harbourfront Park, once the site of the Great Western Railway's dock facilities. Now a landscaped landfill, the park offers boat launches, cycling trails, a swimming beach, and fishing docks. Pier 4 Park nearby offers lookouts over the bay and play areas for children.

Though most evidence of old Port Hamilton has long gone, one link remains. The red-brick building at number 469 Bay Street once housed

William W. Grant's sail-making operation. Built in 1869, the exterior still looks much like it did when the nine-by-twenty-eight-metre interior was workspace. But the age of steam rendered the tall ships a thing of the past, and in 1907 the building became Reid's Gasoline Engine Company. Over the years it was put to a variety of uses, until 1985, when it fell into disrepair and was condemned. The new owner, recognizing the heritage value of this rare building, has begun to restore it — an unusual success story in demolition-happy Hamilton. Nearby streets also reflect the heritage of the harbour, and rows of early workers' homes are now undergoing gentrification.

Burlington Heights

One of the first Europeans to arrive at the head of the lake was Richard Beasley. Among the first of the Loyalists to flee the newly independent American colonies, he constructed a small house on the summit of Burlington Heights, overlooking Burlington Bay. This location would prove strategic during the War of 1812, for it was from these heights that on June 5, 1813, seven hundred British and Canadian troops, under Lieutenant Colonel John Harvey, set out for Stoney Creek. Here they surprised 3,750 American troops, putting them to flight and marking a key turning point in the war. A section of the British earthworks remains visible in the Hamilton Cemetery, across from Dundurn Castle, and is marked with a commemorative cairn.

Mention the word *castle* in Ontario, and two spring to most minds: Casa Loma in Toronto, and Hamilton's Dundurn Castle. While nearly eight decades separate the ages of the two massive structures, both were the accomplishments of men with vision and dreams. Casa Loma was built by Sir Henry Pellatt in 1912, a home that high taxes, combined with his dwindling fortune, forced him to vacate. Completed in 1835, Dundurn Castle was the dream home of parliamentarian and railway promoter Allan Napier McNab (later knighted by Queen Victoria in 1837 for his role in helping to repress William Lyon Mackenzie's rebellion).

The sprawling forty-room Regency-style villa, one of Ontario's grandest then and now, earned the nickname "castle," although architecturally it was not castle-like in its appearance. From its vast grounds, McNab enjoyed a wide view across Hamilton Harbour (then known as Lake Geneva) and within a few years would add to it the sprawling yards and shops of his pet project, the Great Western Railway.

Today the castle is a national historic site and Hamilton's most visited museum. Costumed guides lead visitors through the many rooms, refurbished to reflect the 1855 time period. In the basement is the brick and stone foundation of a much older building, the home built by Richard Beasley in 1799. The grounds also contain such unusual features as a one-hundred-hole birdhouse and the controversial Cockpit Theatre. In the late nineteenth century a small amusement park operated on the grounds. The stone Coach House was added in 1873 to shelter the family's horses and carriages. Now a restaurant, The Coach House is available for rental only. Curators have also recreated a Victorian kitchen garden similar to that which McNab would have harvested.

Although the McNabs resisted overtures from the city to buy the property, thirteen hectares were opened to the public in 1878. As the popularity of the park increased, sports fields and a small roller coaster were added. In 1899 the city finally purchased the park for fifty thousand dollars and closed the amusement facilities, although they opened a small zoo that remained until 1928. Opened as a museum in 1935, then renovated in the mid-60s, Dundurn Castle and its grounds now offer visitors access to the gardener's cottage and the Battery Lodge, currently housing the Hamilton Military Museum.

In 1839, Dundurn "Castle" was built atop Hamilton's Burlington Heights by railway entrepreneur Allan Napier McNab. Since the 1930s it has been a museum run by the City of Hamilton.

Another of the Heights' more prominent features is the striking Thomas B. McQuesten High Level Bridge. Son of Calvin McQuesten,[4] Thomas chaired the Hamilton Parks Management Board for twenty-five years, from 1922 until 1947, during which time, as provincial minister of highways, he helped launch the construction of the QEW. But to McQuesten, the highways of his day should be aesthetic as well as functional. The high level bridge, which at the time marked the York Street entrance into Hamilton, was built in 1931–32 to replace an earlier structure over the Desjardins Canal. The new bridge is noted for its four art-deco pylons, each of them twelve metres high and bearing the coat of arms for the city. In 1986 it was declared a historic landmark under the Ontario Heritage Act, and renamed for McQuesten.

The McQuesten legacy for which Burlington Heights is most noted is the Royal Botanical Gardens. Thomas McQuesten was an avid student of garden design and, as Hamilton's parks commissioner, promoted the beautification of Hamilton's northwest entrance by adding a botanical garden. Canada at the time had only two botanical gardens — those on the grounds of the University of British Columbia, and the Central Experimental Farm in Ottawa. At that time, both the highway and the shoreline leading into Hamilton presented an eyesore of billboards, shacks, and boathouses. In this age of urban beautification, McQuesten reasoned that Hamilton could do better.

In 1929 the parks commission acquired an abandoned gravel pit and converted it into a rock garden. In 1930, local farmer

The Royal Botanical Gardens in Burlington started out as a rock garden in an abandoned quarry. Work began in 1929, and it was opened to the public in 1932. Seven themed gardens cover an area of more than 1,100 hectares.

George Hendrie gifted forty-nine hectares of his Hendrie Valley farm, giving the new gardens a total of 162 hectares. That same year McQuesten received royal assent to bestow the designation *royal* on the gardens, after which the concept was altered from that of a more formal garden to one that reflected the various vegetative components of the world at large.

The garden was severed from the parks commission in 1941 and became its own entity. By that time it was spread over 486 hectares, and within a few years would approach one thousand hectares. Landscape architect Carl Borgstrom greatly altered the layout of the gardens and, now encompassing 1,100 hectares, they include an arboretum, various flower gardens — including the immaculate Rose Garden and an indoor garden — and a modernized visitor centre, as well as the original historic rock garden. The Cootes Paradise Sanctuary added another 250 hectares and comprises the largest freshwater marsh restoration project in Canada. Today, visitors can hike, drive, or board a shuttle bus to see the seven garden areas that make up the Royal Botanical Gardens.

Dundas

Geographically and historically, Dundas is the true head of the lake. To John Graves Simcoe, the site was critical. As noted earlier, anxious to relocate the colony's capital away from the vulnerable Newark, he ordered the surveying and clearing of a road to lead from the head of the bay, or Coote's Paradise, to the forks of the Thames River, where he would locate the new town.

Landing at the head of Coote's Paradise, the site of an earlier aboriginal landing, Simcoe named it the King's Landing. From this point he instructed his surveyor, Augustus Jones, to lay a road west to the forks of the Thames River. The road became known as the Governor's Road. However, when Lord Dorchester rejected Simcoe's site, he chose instead a protected bay on the north shore of Lake Ontario, and laid out the town of York. The road, never fully cleared, grew over, and would remain so for another twenty years. But the Dundas location still had its attractions. Water, potential power for mills, tumbled along the creek, and roads led not just to the Thames, but also to Guelph and Waterloo, and eventually to York.

Dundas was named for Sir Harry Dundas, secretary of war, though he never set eyes on the place. One who did was a Captain Coote, an avid hunter and member of the King's Eighth Regiment. The new settlement retained the name Coote's Paradise (the apostrophe has since been dropped) until 1814, when the post office opted for "Dundas."

One of the settlement's earliest colonists was Richard Hatt, an industrialist who had emigrated from England and originally settled in the Niagara region. In 1800 he moved to Dundas and built the area's first mill. Even as early as 1804 he realized the need for better access between Dundas and Lake Ontario, and financed the deepening of Morden Creek through Burlington Heights to Burlington Bay. Hatt dredged the winding channel just wide enough and deep enough to allow for the passage of the shallow Durham boats. He died soon after.

Hatt's business manager was another dreamer, a man named Pierre Desjardins. His vision was considerably more ambitious than that of Hatt, for Desjardins wished to build a canal that would link Dundas, not just with Lake Ontario, but with Lake Huron as well. But in 1833 he also died, and his nephew Alexis Begue assumed the grand project. Although the link to Huron was never realized, Begue succeeded in cutting through the looming Burlington Heights, and in 1837 the new Desjardins Canal was opened. By this time a canal had also been chopped through the sand spit separating Burlington Bay from Lake Ontario, and Dundas became the leading town at the lakehead. During his visit to Dundas in 1851, William Smith noted that the town "has a valuable supply of water power which is made use of to a considerable extent.... For some time the trade of the town had considerable difficulties to contend with having to be conveyed to Burlington Bay by land. The construction of the Desjardins Canal which is five miles in length enables the manufacturers and merchants to ship from their own doors."[5]

Smith recorded that the town had three flour mills, a large foundry, a paper mill, plus the usual range of early Ontario industries. Early hotels included the Boggs Swan Inn, Cain's Hotel, the Elgin Hotel, and the Collins Hotel. First opened in 1841, the latter survives today as Collins Brewhouse, its exterior largely unchanged since the late 1800s. It can be found at 33 King Street West. It was one of the few buildings to survive the extensive conflagration that consumed much of downtown Dundas in

The site of the Desjardins Canal is now in a peaceful setting.

1861, its owner distributing free beer afterward to those who helped save it from the flames.

During the 1830s and 40s Dundas glowed in its prosperity. Nearly five thousand dockings took place at the wharves during that period, bringing in coal, iron, and a wide assortment of dry goods while exporting more than five million board feet of lumber, as well as flour and farm produce. Three times each week steamers carried passengers from Toronto, taking two days to do so. But then another construction crew showed up in Cootes Paradise. These were the navvies of the Great Western Railway. In 1852 they hammered into place a high level bridge above the canal, and the following year trains started rolling with regular passenger service between Hamilton and Toronto.

It was along this route, and over the Desjardins Canal, that Canada's first, and one of its worst, railway tragedies occurred. On March 12, 1857, a Hamilton-bound train, a small Oxford steam engine pulling a pair of passenger coaches, derailed as it approached the wooden bridge, twenty metres above the canal. As the heavy steel wheels bounced along the ties and onto the bridge, the wooden structure crumbled, hurtling the engine and its coaches into the ice-covered canal. The *Illustrated Historical Atlas of the County of Wentworth* described the accident:

> The immense weight of the engine breaking through the bridge, the whole structure gave way and with one frightful crash, the engine tender, baggage car and two

first-class passenger coaches leaped headlong into the
yawning abyss below. The engine and tender crashed at
once through the ice, carrying the engineer and fireman
with them; the baggage car was thrown ten yards from
the engine; the first passenger car came after and fell
on its roof, breaking partly through the ice and being
crushed to atoms, and the last car fell endways on the ice,
and strange to say remained in that position.[6]

Fifty-nine people perished that day, either killed instantly or drowning
in the ice-filled canal. Although an inquest blamed a broken axel for the
derailment, speculation swirled around whether or not it was the cheaper
and softer pine used in the bridge that caused the structure to crumble
so easily. Sturdier oak was normally used for bridges. Today a steel bridge
carries the freights and the VIA passenger trains over the canal. A few steps
away, near the entrance to the Hamilton Cemetery, a stone monument
commemorates the members of the train crew who died in the wreckage.

With the arrival of the railway age, the canal fell into disuse: "[T]he
canal is now seldom used, except by raftsmen for the purpose of floating
timber into Burlington Bay."[7] By 1890, railways were bypassing Dundas
— to the north and east the Grand Trunk, and to the south the Toronto,
Hamilton and Buffalo Railway. Subsequently, the community went into
an economic decline.

Today the town is well within the Greater Hamilton Area, and malls,
suburbs, and condos line the old Governor's Road, stretching out from
the ancient town centre. The core has managed to retain a reasonable
collection of early heritage buildings, much of which remains near the
historic heart of the town, the junction of the roads to York, Waterloo,
Hamilton, and London.

The town hall, built in 1849, is considered to be Ontario's oldest
municipal building. It was begun immediately after the town received its
municipal status. Designed by a local contractor named Francis Hawkins,
the classic revival hall contained an opera hall on the second floor and
the council chamber on the ground level, while the basement of this all-
purpose structure contained Alfie Bennett's Crystal Palace Saloon, across
the hall from which, conveniently, stood the lockup.

Across the road stands the Merchants' Exchange Hotel, dating from 1847, while to the east, at 30 York Street, a stone building with a date stone of 1833 has been described by some historians as having been a customs house. An even earlier building is that which housed a blacksmith shop. Built of stone, but with newer windows, it stands at the corner of Main and the Governor's Road.

But one of most beguiling of Dundas's historic structures is the "doctor's house." Originally located on Main Street, it was moved in 1974, and is now a private residence on Albert Street. Constructed of board and batten, this tiny office was built in 1848 for Dr. James Mitchell, but was more popularly known as the "Bates' Office," named for its last practitioner, Dr. Clarence Bates, who practised in the building from 1935 until 1974.

In the oldest section of town, that bounded by York, Dundas, and King, handsome old homes line the shady streets. Number 32 Cross Street is one of the more interesting. Built by lawyer William Notman, the house for many years contained the famous Notman cannon. This six-pounder, a gift from Lord Selkirk, was used during the 1837 rebellion. Notman faithfully fired the cannon each May 24, up until his death in 1865. Today the famous cannon has found a home in front of the town hall, and grand homes still dominate Cross and Victoria streets, marking an historic part of town that is now a designated heritage district.

The famous canal today is little more than a weedy ditch, its turning basin now filled in. Its route through the Burlington Heights beach ridge remains, though its entrance to Cootes Paradise is now barred to boats. A paved cycling and walking trail leads from beneath the bridges to the Pier 4 Park at Hamilton's west end. Historic plaques recount the many historic chapters in the life of this early, yet often ignored, waterway. High overhead loom the bridges of CN Rail's tracks, the McQuesten High Level Bridge, and the later Highway 403 bridge. Stairs lead from the ends of the McQuesten Bridge on busy York Street to the water, where, about halfway down, tucked into the overgrown hillside, lie the stone abutments that witnessed the horrific train wreck of 1857.

The Beach Strip

Marking the far west end of Lake Ontario is a wave-washed sandbar. This long spit of land separating the lake from Burlington Bay (Lake Geneva) evolved over thousands of years. As the creeks that flowed down the Niagara Escarpment emptied into the lake, they met with easterly currents that slowed the flow, depositing the silt and sand carried by the waters. The sandbar was long an aboriginal trail that Simcoe incorporated into his network of military roads. To establish his presence, he ordered the construction of the King's Head Inn, the first permanent building on the strip. In 1813 the invading Americans burned the building (although its sign survived and is displayed in the Brant Museum in Burlington). At this time, the Beach Strip was a wilderness, its dunes covered with beach grasses and shrubs. At the north end, waves would occasionally cut through the sand, enabling small vessels to pole their way through and proceed on to Cootes Paradise and the village of Dundas at its head.

In 1826, at the urging of a local industrialist, James Crooks, who operated mills at the now ghost town of Crooks Hollow, a more permanent canal was cut through the sandbar, a change that would alter the destinies of the new town of Hamilton and of the older Dundas. Up until then, any goods being exported from Dundas had to be lifted over the sandbar to ships waiting on the other side, or poled through whenever the gap opened. On July 1, 1826, Ontario's lieutenant governor, Sir Peregrine Maitland, presided over the opening of the new channel. But it proved to be an inauspicious start. No sooner had the first vessel, the *General Brock*, navigated the new waterway, than it ran aground.

Vicious winter storms in 1829 and 1830 wrecked the piers and the first lighthouse. Finally, in 1832, the finishing touches were added, and the new canal, now properly constructed, opened. Two mast lights replaced the older light, but these proved inadequate, and in 1837 an octagonal wooden light tower was built on a sturdy stone foundation. A wooden ferry ushered any road traffic across the narrow channel.

But more devastation was to come. In 1856, the sparks from a passing steamer set fire to the new pier and lighthouse. Both were destroyed, and a new light tower had to be built the following year. Designed in the circular "imperial" style common on Lake Huron and Georgian Bay, the new

This historic lighthouse tower and keeper's house still survive beside the Burlington Canal. The light was replaced by a new structure in 1969.

tower could boast stone walls 2.2 metres thick. The keeper's brick house was also rebuilt beside it. This time the lighthouse was constructed to withstand storms and ships, which it did, until a new light was placed in a more prominent position atop the canal lift bridge in 1961. Though now abandoned, the stone tower and keeper's house still stand.

A few hotels were built to cater to residents of the increasingly industrialized Hamilton, including the Dynes Hotel in 1846, and the Baldry House soon after. Then, in 1875, the Hamilton and Northwestern Railway laid its tracks along the lake side of the beach, ending forever the natural oasis. Almost immediately more hotels began to appear. First the Ocean House, then the Brant House — located in the former home of Joseph Brant — and a few years later, the similarly named Brant Hotel opened nearby. One of the grandest buildings on the spit was that of the Royal Hamilton Yacht Club. Opened in 1891, the two-storey wooden structure boasted wraparound balconies elaborately decorated with fretwork. The club was located next to the lighthouse, but sadly was lost to fire in 1915.

The first bridge constructed over the canal was a swing bridge, the site of a rail accident in 1891 that was all too reminiscent of the Desjardins

Photo courtesy the Ron Brown Collection.

An early view from the Illustrated Historical Atlas of Wentworth County *shows the appearance of Hamilton's beach strip in 1875.*

tragedy thirty-four years earlier. When a fierce gale reduced visibility along the beach, the engineer failed to see the red light signalling that the bridge was open. As the *Hamilton Spectator* of August 31, 1891, recounted:

> [T]he night was dark and a gale was blowing from the east … with a tremendous plunge the engine shot over the brink and disappeared beneath the black water. The cars went tumbling in after it, crash after crash, the lights were extinguished and a terrible silence followed … the engine went down completely out of sight, and then cars popped over on top of it, one after the other until the wreck was piled as high as the top of the water.

Unlike the Desjardins disaster, no lives were lost — the train was a freight, and the engineer and fireman were able to jump to safety before the frightening and near-fatal plunge.

In 1896, a new swing bridge was constructed, this one on the west side of the strip that accommodated road and streetcar traffic. But by the 1950s the streetcars were gone, and a new lift bridge opened, merging rail and car traffic together. By then, traffic on the QEW was on the increase, resulting in major bottlenecks at the bridge. With thirty thousand cars using the highway daily, traffic jams several kilometres long were not uncommon. Clearly, another new bridge was needed. And it came. On October 30, 1958, Ontario premier Leslie Frost officially opened the Burlington Bay Skyway. At nearly seven kilometres long and forty metres high, it was the most ambitious bridge project ever undertaken by the province.

Prompted by the opening of the Beach Road from the east end of Hamilton, and the arrival of the streetcars, Hamiltonians began building summer homes, both simple and grand. Despite a recent intrusion of year-round homes and condos, many early beach homes still stand today. Among the more noteworthy and photogenic are: the 1898 "Sweetheart House" at 935 Beach Boulevard; "Cahill's Castle," built in 1891, at 957 Beach Boulevard; and one-time Hamilton mayor George Tuckett's gothic revival villa at 1008 Beach Boulevard. However, the most acclaimed is the "Moorings." Located at 913 Beach Boulevard, it was built by another Hamilton mayor, Francis Kilvert, in 1891. A designated heritage property, it is noted for its ornate veranda, fish-scale wood shingle siding, and variety of gables. Amongst these grand and glorious summer palaces run small lanes lined with the simpler summer homes of less affluent Hamiltonians.

The Canada Amusement Company opened The Canal Amusement Park in 1903, with a carousel, Ferris wheel, and a funhouse called the Crazy House. After the First World War, the Pier Ballroom opened, and throughout the 1930s and 40s featured the music of Duke Ellington, the Clooney Sisters, and Ozzie Nelson. The railway carried Hamilton's workers to enjoy the amusement park, and made stops at the Beach Road Station, Dynes Hotel, a private mansion known as the "Elsinore," and the Ocean House, as well as at the Brant House near Burlington. But in 1975 the City of Hamilton refused to renew the park's licence. It closed in 1978, and all of its rides were auctioned off.

In 2007, amidst considerable controversy, the ancient Dynes Tavern was taken down, without a demolition permit, to make way for a condominium project. Until then, this beach hangout had been considered by many to be Ontario's oldest surviving operating tavern.

Today, driving isn't the only way to view this historic and much altered Beach Strip. The Hamilton Beach Recreation Trail now follows the route of the old railway right-of-way along the sandy beach. Information plaques recount the days of the amusement park as well as current projects to stabilize the dune formations with such vegetation as Indian grass, rye grass, beach grass, and burr oak. And while it may be a little ambitious to dream of the strip being restored to the condition in which Simcoe found it, at least the endless waves crashing against the grass-covered sand may enhance the illusion.

Aldershot

It's hard these days to figure out just where Aldershot begins and ends. As part of the urban megalopolis known as the Golden Horseshoe, it is indistinguishable from Burlington to the east and Hamilton to the west. Still, it would be reasonable to demark its boundaries as the Queen Elizabeth Way to the east, the CN rail line to the north, Burlington Heights to the west, and Burlington Bay to the south.

The first settlers to arrive in the area, in 1791, were the Applegarth family, whose farmland lay on the north shore of the lake, west of what is today the La Salle Park. The Chisholm family arrived two years later and added gristmills on Grindstone Creek, which tumbles south from Waterdown and then follows an almost hidden valley westerly to Rock Bay. Today that wooded valley forms part of the Royal Botanical Gardens.

In 1806, Colonel Brown, an agent for the North West Company, arrived and established a wharf on Lake Geneva, giving the community its first name: Brown's Wharf. When more settlers arrived, a resident by the name of Ebenezer Griffin built a series of mills around the tumbling water-power sites at Waterdown, a short distance north, and used the wharf to ship flour and wool. By 1823, Aldershot could claim nearly a dozen log homes, and two dozen more substantial dwellings of frame or brick. When the Burlington Canal was completed, larger ships were able to enter the protected waters of the bay more easily. During the 1840s the wharf was enlarged to accommodate steamers and the port was able to provide the ships with a supply of cordwood, used as fuel. By this time the little port was going by the name Port Flamborough.

In 1854, Brown's grandson, Alexander, chose to honour his grandfather's military service by naming the post office Aldershot, after a military base near London, England, where his grandfather had served. Toward the end of the nineteenth century, a large brickyard operation took over Grindstone Valley, located west of the village and along the railway track. The large red kilns remained at the site for years, serving as a visual reminder of the location's history, until they were removed in the 1990s.

But even after the arrival of the railway, and the erection of the Aldershot station, the community remained small, with only a few shops and taverns along Plains Road. The light and sandy soils in the area that had discouraged early wheat farming proved ideal for apples and melons, and Aldershot soon became famous for shipping these products. Hotels were built both by the wharf and along the new road, and included Fenton's Valley Inn, Shorty Biggs's hotel on the lake, and the popular Bayview Hotel.

Now an event venue, the historic La Salle Pavilion, situated in a park of the same name, is the only surviving building from the park's days as an Aldershot pleasure ground.

The Bayview was set on a piece of land known as Carroll's Point, overlooking Rock Bay, the point at which Morden Creek flows into the bay from Cootes Paradise. It was here, in 1836, that Peter Carroll built his baronial "Rock Bay Mansion," and became one of the first farmers in Ontario to cultivate peaches out-of-doors. After his death, the mansion burned, and on this high point of land a man by the name of George Midwinter opened Bayview Park. Vacationers travelled by steamer from Hamilton to stay in the Bayview Hotel, or to ride the new merry-go-round at the park. Disembarking from steamers like the *Lillie*, the *Shamrock*, or the *Maggie Mason*, they could either climb the steep stairs or ride on a two-car incline railway to the summit.

However, by the 1920s, Bayview Park was silent, replaced by a larger park to the east, Wabasso Park. Established by the Hamilton Parks Board in 1912, Wabasso included a dance pavilion, a bathing house, a roller coaster, and a Ferris wheel. In 1923, the name was changed to La Salle Park, and not long after, the rides were removed. But the La Salle Park Pavilion continued to operate, featuring such local bandleaders as Pete Malloy and Eddie Mack.

Today La Salle Park is still a busy green space, now enjoyed largely by local residents. The 1917 pavilion remains, despite being gutted by fire in May 1995. It was rebuilt to its original condition the following year and is now a banquet and event facility called Geraldo's. The site of the dock has been incorporated into a marina and a new park that extends into the bay, while scant ruins of the bathing pavilion lie beneath the underbrush.

Bayview Park and the site of Carroll's mansion are now part of the Woodland Cemetery, although the view from Carroll's Point remains the same as Carroll and the guests at the Bayview Hotel might remember. The site of the Valley Inn is remembered only in the name of the road leading to the location, Valley Inn Drive, which now dead-ends at the location of the former bridge that once spanned across Rock Bay.

Chapter 3
Lake Ontario's "West Coast"

S tarting in the west end of Toronto, the Lake Ontario shoreline bends noticeably. From its east–west orientation east of the city, it angles markedly to the southwest, making that section of the shoreline in effect the lake's west coast. The shore is low-lying and flat. During the last ice age, as the ice lifted from the east end of the developing water body, the bedrock there rebounded, causing the water level at the west end of the lake to rise. As it did, it began to flood the river valleys that had formed as the ice retreated. Such flooding formed several shallow lagoons at the river mouths. These provided shelter for early vessels, and small commercial harbours developed. West of Toronto these lagoons formed at Sixteen Mile Creek, Bronte Creek, and the Credit River. While all three have their sources above the Niagara Escarpment, only the Credit attains any significant size.

According to Chapman and Putnam,[1] the shoreline between Hamilton and Toronto was the result of the earlier and higher Lake Iroquois. The old lake deposited beaches of sand and gravel above the current lakeshore (later used by settlers as building materials). The soil, while light, does not enjoy as long a frost-free growing season as do the lands along the Niagara Peninsula, and therefore tender fruits could not be grown here successfully, though many did try. Apple orchards and strawberry fields, however, were very successful, but in the end could not survive another peril — urban sprawl.

Even as the ports at Dundas and Hamilton were growing and shipping out lumber and wheat, the area between York and the head of the lake remained less developed. Until 1820, the mouths of Sixteen Mile Creek and Twelve Mile Creek remained in the hands of the Mississauga. Only after the Mississauga granted them to the Crown were the vital river mouths opened for settlement.

Although a rough aboriginal trail followed the lakeshore, no route existed for stage travel until 1832, when Ontario's lieutenant governor, Sir John Colborne, ordered the construction of a road along the shore of the lake. By 1836 the river mouths had been bridged, and stages began rolling between Dundas and York, a journey that could take up to two days.

The entire west coast of the lake is now urban; that trend is not new. In 1855, the Great Western Railway laid its tracks toward Toronto from Hamilton, giving rise to a string of stations only a short distance inland. Following the First World War, as Toronto and Hamilton grew, and traffic between them increased, a new highway opened along the shore, the Hamilton Highway. This hard-surface road spurred more development, and the little ports evolved into summer resorts and commuter towns.

The greatest stimulus to sprawl was North America's first limited-access freeway, the Queen Elizabeth Way (QEW), which opened to traffic in 1939. Throughout the 1950s, as car ownership became universal and suburbs took over the farmland, the perils of sprawl and congestion loomed ominously in the future. Today, with no open space left along Lake Ontario's west coast, and with the QEW almost constantly gridlocked, that future has arrived. Still, within that sprawl and traffic, heritage survives: some of it preserved and promoted; some less obvious, or simply hidden.

Wellington Square

Today it is better known as Burlington. In 1798, Mohawk Joseph Brant received a grant of over 1,400 hectares along the shore of Lake Ontario as a reward for his service to the British Army during the American Revolution. Following Brant's death in 1807, his land was sold back to the Crown. One of the early developers of those lands was Joseph Gage, who named the site Wellington Square, after the Duke of Wellington, hero of the Battle of Waterloo (1815). As settlers began to flow into the region,

Wellington Square grew from a cluster of sixteen simple homes in 1817 into a community of four hundred residents by 1845.

With few natural harbours along Lake Ontario's west coast, the three wharves at Wellington Square were exposed to the waves, as were the individual wharves at Port Nelson to the east and that at Port Flamborough in Aldershot. William H. Smith, in 1851, noted:

> Had Wellington Square possessed the advantage of a good and well sheltered harbour, it would have become a place of considerable importance, it being a convenient shipping place for a large extent of back country. As it is its progress is but slow, and property does not appear to have risen greatly in value. For a short time during each spring and fall, while Burlington Bay is locked up with ice, the steamboats run from Toronto to the Square from whence passengers and the mails are conveyed by stage to Hamilton.[2]

In 1855, the Great Western Railway extended its tracks from Hamilton to Toronto, locating its station several kilometres to the north of Wellington Square. In 1875 the Hamilton and Northwestern Railway laid its tracks right along the beach strip and through the centre of the town, bringing with it hoards of vacationers. Joseph Brant's house, which was still standing at that time, became a tourist hotel known as Brant House, which offered croquet, dancing, ice cream, and twenty acres of gardens. Shortly after, the Hotel Brant opened next door and outdid the old Brant House by offering fine dining, electric lights, and elevators.

But the rail age also meant that the ships were now bypassing the west coast ports in favour of the larger facilities at Hamilton, thanks in large part to the improvements on the Burlington Canal. In 1873, when Wellington Square incorporated as a village, the name was changed to Burlington, its population having swelled to eight hundred. Among its industrial assets were grain warehouses, a carriage factory, and a wire factory.

Agriculture changed from grain-growing to the growing of apples and market garden crops, all of which could now be shipped by train, year-round, to the growing urban markets of Toronto. The Canadian Canning Company replaced the grain elevators at the foot of Brant Street. A

Guests relax on the veranda of the popular Brant Hotel in Burlington. The hotel was one of many that lined the lake in the area of Burlington's beach strip

short-lived streetcar line linked downtown Burlington with Oakville and Hamilton, but by the 1930s was gone. The opening of the QEW in 1939 and the post-war boom in suburban growth changed the face of Burlington, from that of a rural community to that of a suburb. The opening of the Ford Motor Plant in nearby Oakville led to more housing, and, in 1974, Burlington became a "city."

Burlington's heritage preservation has been hit and miss. Brant Street contains a few early buildings, such as the Queen's Head and Raymond hotels. Halstead's Inn, now a private home that stands at 2429 Lakeshore Road, may have been operating as early as 1830. And in 1979, a coalition of heritage-minded citizens managed to convince the council of the day to change its mind about demolishing a row of heritage homes along the lakeshore in favour of new development. Sadly, nothing remains of Burlington's waterfront industries, but the area is now benefiting from a massive makeover that includes new walkways, breakwaters, and businesses.

Port Nelson

Situated at the foot of the Guelph Road, Port Nelson offered the backcountry farmers an outlet from which to ship their lumber and wheat. In 1851, William Smith described it as "a mere shipping place, containing about sixty inhabitants, doing but little other business. There are storehouses for storing grain for shipment, and a considerable quantity is exported."[3]

The community was so named for being the port of shipment for Nelson Township (which, like Wellington Square, was named for a British war hero, Horatio Nelson.) The Guelph Line road linked the port to communities farther inland, such as the farm hamlet of Nelson on Dundas Street and the mill town of Lowville on Bronte Creek. It was not unusual during the height of the shipping season for grain carts and lumber wagons to line up along Guelph Line, awaiting their turn at the dock. During one busy season the little wharf handled more shipments than the much larger port of Hamilton.

Port Nelson also had lumberyards, saw and planing mills. A small network of streets was laid out at the intersection of Guelph Line and the Lakeshore Road, comprising Market, St. Paul, 1st, and 2nd streets. Interspersed among the homes of the post-war era are a few older houses that date from the days when Port Nelson was a busy port.

A small lakeside park at the foot of Guelph Line does little to recall the times when the masts of tall ships would tower above the Port Nelson pier. There is no record of whether small piers stood at the foot of either Walkers Line or Appleby Line, although both roads were early farm roads that linked the lake with the farmlands to the north. As access to the lakeshore became easier with the arrival of the auto, wealthy business people began to buy up the shoreline and build some of the period's grandest summer retreats.

East of Port Nelson stands one of the west coast's grandest heritage homes, the "Paletta Mansion." Whoever thought that "money couldn't buy happiness" didn't count on the wealth of Cyrus Albert Birge. It was Birge's Hamilton foundry, the Canada Screw Company, that merged with four other companies in 1910 to form the mighty Stelco. Following his death, his wealth passed to his daughter, Edythe Merriam MacKay.

In 1930, on five and a half hectares at the mouth of Shoreacres Creek, Mrs. MacKay hired architects to design a grand stone mansion that would give her and her family the finest views of Lake Ontario that her father's money could buy. The three-thousand-square-metre palace was designed by Stewart Thomas McFie and Lyon Sommerville. Other structures on the property include a 1912 gatehouse, a child's dollhouse, and a stable. The dollhouse was not your average child's toy either — it came equipped with both electricity and running water.

The mansion was restored by the City of Burlington in 2000 and can be rented from the city for conferences, banquets, and weddings. Now fully modernized, the three storeys still retain seven fireplaces and a grand staircase. A four-hectare "discovery trail" along the creek allows hikers the opportunity to observe birds and rare plant life. The gatehouse now contains a welcome centre and art studio, while the former stable is now the Tim Horton's Learning Loft, offering youth camps and environmental programs.

The history of the property dates back more than two hundred years to the time when a grateful King George III granted the land to War of 1812 heroine Laura Secord.

Bronte

From the "Paletta Mansion," Lakeshore Road traces an historic path, at times offering glimpses of the lake through small waterside parkettes, but for the most part cut off from those views by the endless rows of housing. The view opens up once more at the mouth of Twelve Mile Creek, where the port of Bronte developed.

The port was founded in 1834, and William Smith found Bronte a "stirring" little village in 1846 — one that contained grist- and sawmills, a store, and two taverns, and was home to about one hundred inhabitants. He made no mention of any port activity. Five years later he estimated the population as being about two hundred, and noted four sawmills along the creek. By this time the port had begun to develop, and in 1850 it shipped out six hundred thousand metres of lumber and over eighty thousand bushels of wheat, oats, and barley. More than two thousand cords of cordwood were picked up to fuel the lake steamers. The Bronte Harbour Company was formed in 1856, and shipping and boat-building began to dominate the harbour. Continuing the trend of Wellington Square and

Port Nelson, the post office took the name Bronte in honour of Admiral Horatio Nelson, British war hero, and holder of the Duchy of Bronte.

With the arrival of the Great Western Railway in 1854, the port activity switched from exporting lumber and farm products to commercial fishing. From 1890 to 1950, more than a dozen fishing boats operated in the harbour, where the shore was lined with shanties and net-drying racks. With stonehooking[4] a growing industry, the port also became home to a small fleet of stoneboats. One of the more prolific builders of the stonehookers was Lem Dorland, who between 1880 and 1885 launched five stonehooking schooners, including the *Madeline, Rapid City*, and *Mapleleaf.* By the 1950s, many of the commercial fishermen had moved away, and yachts began to take over the harbour.

Today's urban growth has utterly altered the face of Bronte. Condos have replaced most of the historic storefronts, and new waterfront development has removed most traces of the historic port. Few heritage buildings have withstood the onslaught. One that remains is "Glendella," built in 1845 as Thompson's Hotel. It was originally constructed by Ned Thompson on what was called the Old Lake Road, and served for many years as a stagecoach stop. The arrival of the railway put an eventual end to stage travel in the area, and "Glendella" went on to serve as a grocery store and post office before resuming its role as a summer hotel. In 1987 the building was designated under the Heritage Act, but the act, as worded then, was utterly toothless, and twenty years later the building was threatened with demolition or removal to pave the way for still more condos. Luckily, an agreement was reached, allowing it, along with the old wooden police building and post office, to remain on site. The buildings will form a heritage square within the condo complex.

One of the other structures to survive is "Stoneboats." Built in 1846 out of Dundas shale hauled from the lake, it was originally the home of one of Bronte's prominent stoneboat captains. Today it is a restaurant.

On July 21, 2007, as part of the waterfront redevelopment, a fishermen's memorial was unveiled. The granite stone, two metres high and four metres long, has laser etchings that depict images of a local fisherman named Thomas Joyce and smaller scenes from Bronte's days as a busy fishing port. The new waterfront offers extensive walkways, a replica lighthouse, and a busy marina. On the west side of the harbour (a much more tranquil side)

BRONTE FISHERMEN'S MEMORIAL

Although most of Bronte's heritage buildings have been removed, a monument erected by the municipality in 2007 commemorates the port's fishing days.

stands the Sovereign House. Built in 1825 by Charles Sovereign,[5] it was relocated a short distance from its original site to a wooded promontory known as the Bronte Bluffs. The building, which was occupied briefly (1910–15) by Mazo de la Roche, author of the Jalna series of novels, is open to the public and offers period displays and travelling exhibits. Located at 7 West River Street, south of Lakeshore Road, it also houses the offices of the Bronte Historical Society.

Oakville

Of all the ports along Lake Ontario's west coast, that at "Old Oakville" remains historically the most intact. The oldest part of town, which lies south of Lakeshore Road and east of the harbour, retains an almost intact collection of early-to-mid-nineteenth-century houses and businesses, all lining a shady network of quiet roads, with the waters of the lake and the old harbour on two sides.

In 1827, when then lieutenant governor Sir Peregrine Maitland put the lands formerly held by the Mississauga up for auction, the successful bidder was William Chisholm. For the sum of just £1,029 he acquired 380 hectares. Prior to that, Chisholm had gained prominence through a variety of maritime ventures, having supervised the construction of the Welland

and Burlington canals. Chisholm went right to work to turn the forested riverbanks into a busy port. In 1828 he hired workers who had just finished digging the Burlington Canal, and put them to work building protective piers. The longest, on the east side (the direction from which the most devastating lake storms blew) stretched nearly two metres into the lake.

By 1830 the harbour was ready. Three years later, Chisholm launched the harbour's first steamer, the *Constitution*, and the following year it began a regular run between Oakville and York, a run that took two hours (or about the same amount of time required in today's QEW traffic). Later that year, the *Oakville*, later renamed the *Hamilton*, began steaming between Hamilton and York. In 1852 its schedule showed it departing from Toronto daily at 2:00 p.m., after which it would call at Port Credit, Oakville, Bronte, Wellington Square, and its final port of call, Port Hamilton. By then, a number of shipping lines had been making Oakville their port of call, linking the community with Rochester and other ports along the lake.

Over the next few years, Chisholm added a gristmill and a sawmill. There were two other key sawmills: one operated by a man named Mcraney, and the other the Ransom and Leach mill on Joshua Creek, which flows into the lake near the east end of Oakville. A general store and chandler shop opened in 1827 — a building that still survives today at 115 William Street in "Old Oakville."

The opening of the Lakeshore Road in 1836 brought with it new businesses, as well as hotels such as the Royal Exchange and the Oakville House. It also led to the laying out and sale of 150 building lots. Also in 1836, a new lighthouse flickered into operation. Octagonal in shape, the wooden tower stood twelve metres high. Meanwhile, the harbour continued to undergo repairs and upgrading, and, in the 1850s, was considerably enlarged. In 1888, one of the lake's most vicious storms swept the lighthouse into the lake. The following year, a new one began operation. When finally decommissioned in the early 1960s, the light was saved and moved to the west side of the river mouth.

With the opening of the Great Western Railway's Hamilton to Toronto line, steamer service virtually ended. Vessels carrying passengers to the many amusement parks then lining the west coast shores continued to call, and others would pick up strawberries for which the farmlands of the west coast had become famous. However, after 1904, steamer service into

Now a museum, the Erchless Estate in Oakville was built in 1855 by the town's founding family.

Oakville ended for good. Fishing and stonehooking continued to occupy the harbour for several more years, but by the 1920s the stonehookers were gone and by the 1950s the fishing fleet had sailed off as well. Today the harbour teems with yachts and sailboats belonging to the members of the town's yacht clubs. Shipyard Park contains the 1889 lighthouse (although the plaque reads 1875) and a relocated log cabin.

The town prides itself on its heritage. Along Oakville's first main street, Navy Street, a string of early buildings have been preserved, including the Murray House Hotel, which dates from 1857. Across from the hotel stands the stone Granary, built in 1855 as a grain warehouse, even as the days of the steamships were about to wind down. The William Sumner House dates from 1832, and is located at 65 Navy Street, while the house at 45 Navy Street predates it by a couple of years, having been built in 1830, and the house at number 41 was added in 1833.

But the most compelling of Oakville's heritage homes is the "Erchless Estate." Located on a high bluff overlooking the harbour entrance, it was built by Robert Kerr Chisholm, son of William Chisholm, the town's founder. As the younger Chisholm was also the port's customs officer, he built a customs house here in 1855, also including in it a branch of the Bank of Toronto. Chisholm's own house, "Erchless," was constructed next to the customs house the following year. The brick buildings are now owned by the Town of Oakville and its historical society, and are open to the public as a museum.

Front Street, which lies along Lakeside Park, also contains many of Oakville's oldest homes, including numbers 143 and 176, built in 1834 and 1837 respectively. Within the park itself are a pair of relocated structures, the Merrick Thomas House, built in 1829 on a farm to the west of town, and the 1835 post office, which was moved in 1951 from its first location on Navy to the Lakeside Park.

Lakeshore Road, Oakville's later main street, owes its original prosperity to the arrival of the railway in 1855, and still contains a few commercial structures from that period. Among the earliest in this part of Oakville are: 145 Lakeshore Road, built in 1855 by a cabinetmaker; number 240, now a restaurant, but built in the 1850s as a furniture store; and number 234, which began in 1860 as a hardware store. Buildings at 149 and 155 date from around 1840, while what may be the street's oldest commercial structure stands at 182. It served as a doctor's office from 1835 until 1933, and is currently the location of To Set a Table, a store that sells kitchen tools and baking items.

The West Coast Mansions

Lakeshore Road, which today links Oakville with Port Credit, lies close to the shore, but views of the lake are obscured by homes, many of palatial grandeur. Most have appeared in the past two decades, although a few of them sport designs of another era, including one that from the road appears to be an ancient English baronial castle. Not only do these super-mansions hide the lake, they also hide themselves, privacy being the main concern.

But the aesthetic value of the lakeshore dates back several decades. Following the First World War, much of the rural property that lay along the lake's west coast was bought up by some of Ontario's wealthiest men, who built a string of grand mansions on them. As property values soared through the 1980s and early 90s, many of those grand palaces were demolished, and the property subdivided for new homes, many now palatial in their own right.

One of the few remaining mansions allowing public access is the "Gairloch Estate," one of two with that name. It sits on the south side of Lakeshore Road, about halfway between Trafalgar Road and Winston Churchill Boulevard. Like most of these early estates, it dates from the arrival of the auto age. The house was built in 1922 by Colonel William Mackendrick, a civil engineer from Toronto. Following Mackendrick's death in 1957, the house, along with its 4½ hectares, was bought by James A. Gairdner, an investment dealer from Oakville, who renamed it "Gairloch." Gairdner died in 1971, bequeathing the mansion and the grounds to the Town of Oakville, on condition that it was used as an art gallery. The house and the landscaped gardens offer to today's visitor a view that once was exclusive to its owners, overlooking Lake Ontario from a wooded knoll. An oddity in the garden — what looks to be a large log — is in fact a brass sculpture.

It may seem strange, but there is another "Gairloch" estate; this one, equally grand, sits on the southeast corner of Lakeshore Road and Winston Churchill Boulevard. It was originally built in 1937 by Charles Powell Bell in the modern classical style. Bell died soon after, and his widow, Kathleen Harding, married James Gairdner, who named the property "Gairloch." Kathleen Harding was the daughter of C. Victor Harding, president of Harding Carpets. Gairdner added a studio to the west of the mansion and took up painting, and the lakeside estate soon became a popular focus for the local arts scene. Its bar was well-stocked and its lawns manicured. In 1960, Gairdner divorced Kathleen and moved to the Mackendrick estate, which he also dubbed "Gairloch," and relocated his studio there.

In 1961, Ontario Hydro moved its Canadian Fusion Fuels Technology Centre into the "first" Gairloch, vacating it in 1999 when the City of Mississauga acquired the site. Although the grounds are open to the public, work is still ongoing to the building itself. Unlike most of the west coast estates, this home faces not the lake but toward the road, over the open lawns, gardens, and a gate that marks the entrance. The lakeside, while offering a small patio, overlooks wooded hillsides and a small lagoon.

A short distance to the east of the historic village of Port Credit is the "Adamson Estate." The property dates to 1809, when a parcel of farmland

The Adamson Estate, located just east of Port Credit, was built overlooking the lake and is now home to the Royal Conservatory School's Mississauga Campus, which offers group music and arts classes.

along the lakeshore was sold to Joseph Cawthra,[6] a man who had become immensely wealthy supplying the British Army from his Toronto apothecary shop during the War of 1812. As the farm passed down through the family it became known as the Grove Farm. In 1900 the land was a wedding gift to Mabel Cawthra and Agar Adamson. In 1919, after returning from his wartime service in France, Adamson designed and built a Belgian-style baronial mansion on the property.

In 1943, Anthony Adamson (Agar's son), a noted restoration architect, acquired the home and rehabilitated it, adding a home for himself. The grounds also feature a barn, a pet cemetery, and a "folly" or gatehouse, built in 1904. In 1975 the property was acquired by the Credit Valley Conservation Authority, which now leases the old mansion to the Royal Conservatory of Music. The property is open to the public and lies at the south end of Enola Avenue, south of Lakeshore, a short distance west of Cawthra.

Port Credit

As with other west coast ports like Oakville and Bronte, development at Port Credit had to wait until the Mississauga Nation sold their land to the Crown. Governor Simcoe didn't wait, however. Shortly after his arrival, while sailing along the shore, a fierce storm forced him to seek the shelter of the mouth of the Credit River. Finding no building where he could take refuge, he ordered that the government build an inn on the west side of the riverbank. But the building was not finished until 1798 — two years after Simcoe had returned to England.

In 1805 the Mississauga ceded twenty thousand hectares to the Crown, keeping for themselves a 1.5-kilometre strip of land along each side of the river's mouth. This reserve would allow the tribe to continue to hunt and fish their traditional grounds. In 1820, the government bought these lands as well, and moved the members of the tribe to a log village more than a kilometre upriver. As the government began to improve the conditions along the Lakeshore Road, the river was spanned with a new bridge, and 136 hectares on the west side of the river were surveyed as a town site. In that year the Port Credit Harbour Company began to dig out the river mouth and build protective piers.

In 1845, Hurontario Street opened between Port Credit and Collingwood, on Georgian Bay, allowing settlers to make their way far into what was considered to be a remote backcountry. In 1846, William Smith noted that "[Port Credit] possesses a good harbour which might be improved as to

A shale beach shows the type of construction stones that Port Credit stonehookers were seeking.

A stonehooking boat moored at Port Credit Harbour. Stonehooking, a long forgotten industry, was one in which building stones were wrenched from the shallow lake bottom. By the 1920s the rise of the cement industry meant the end of stonehooking.

be capable of affording refuge to almost any number of vessels.... Several vessels have been built here and five schooners of a good class are owned in this place ..."[7]

Between 1837 and 1844, large quantities of wheat and lumber were loaded onto the schooners for export. But ten years later the arrival of the Great Western Railway would change all that, as it did wherever it went. The shipments through the harbour dwindled as farmers lined their wagons up at the train station instead.

The whole nature of harbour activity changed as the schooners sailed out and the fishermen and the hookers moved in — not the ladies of the evening, although as a bustling port, the place would have had its share. These harbour hookers were the two dozen or so stonehookers, boats equipped to wrench building stones from the lake for shipment largely to the construction industry in Toronto. Although stonehookers operated out of Bronte and Oakville, the fleet was largely centred in Port Credit. Schooners had to be specially adapted for the stonehooking trade. Because of the weight of the stones, ships' sides had to be lower, and the holds shallower. Stonehookers had their own distinctive names: *Reindeer*, *Olympia*, and *Lithophone* were a few of the earlier vessels.

The fishing industry grew after the arrival of the railway. While early fishermen were local settlers who caught and smoked enough for their own needs, the later industry began using larger vessels that could sail farther into the lake. Companies like the Pickards and the Fowlers used the harbour for their fleets. By the 1920s the hookers were gone, replaced by the cement industry. The fishermen remained until 1960, when the government, suddenly and with little warning, sold off the federal lands on which the fishermen had built their net-drying sheds and shanties. Their licences were unceremoniously transferred to more distant fishing grounds at places like Point Traverse in Prince Edward County, and Kingsville on Lake Erie.

During the dark days of Prohibition, in Ontario and the United States, a new, albeit short-lived, industry thrived in Port Credit Harbour — rum-running, or "midnight herring" as it was code-named. The owner of the Lakeview Inn, one Joe Burke, operated a bootlegging operation from the second floor of a shoe-repair shop. He would load his two large fishing boats at the Parliament Street dock of the Gooderham and Worts Distillery in Toronto, and then secretly unload the liquid gold onto cars waiting at the abandoned brick factory in Port Credit.[8]

The harbour's first lighthouse was privately built and began operation in 1863, but was replaced by a government-built structure in 1882. But when the schooners and steamers stopped calling, the harbour began to silt up, and so little traffic was using the port by 1918 that the light was switched off. In 1936 the lighthouse was destroyed by fire. But when more recreational craft began to use the port, a new set of range lights went into operation in 1954. Then, in 1991, an iconic landmark was added to the waterscape — a new light, built in traditional style and mounted beside the bridge next to a new tourist information office.

In 1974 the harbour was enlarged when an unused lake freighter, the *Ridgetown*, was sunk near the entrance, creating a breakwater, and once more the waterway is a busy spot. Although the east side of the harbour has no heritage features to recall Port Credit's early days, having been completely revamped with new docking facilities, condos, marinas, and restaurants, the west side tells a different story. It was here that Port Credit's first streets were laid out, and the names reflect their early association with the water — Front, Bay, and Lake, to name a few.

Many structures here date to the days of schooners and steamers. Lake and John streets in particular offer many examples of early houses. One of the most noted is the inn built by James Wilcox in 1841 at Front and Bay. A two-storey wooden structure, it sported a ballroom on the second floor and was long a refuge for sailors, harbour workers, and farmers who had hauled in their products for sale or shipment. But with the arrival of the railway and the destruction by fire of many village buildings, patronage dwindled, and the hotel became a boarding house, and Wilcox began a new career as a ship's captain. The Wilcox Inn is now a private office building, but retains its original exterior.

Number 42 Front Street was the home of one of the port's stonehooker captains, Abram Block, and dates from 1850; John Thompson's 1852 house at 48 Lake Street was nicknamed the "old fort," as it was rumoured to occupy the former site of a trading post. South of Lake Street, a new park, the J.C. Saddington Park, has opened. Here, walking trails have been built on the landfill where the schooners and fishing boats once bobbed.

Chapter 4
Toronto by the Lake

T he shape of the lake upon which today's Toronto fronts is a far cry from that which greeted the city's first residents. Following the retreat of the last glaciers, twenty thousand years ago, the lake lay at a much higher level. As ice blocked the east end of the lake, forming an ice dam, the lake waters were forming a high beach bluff, marked today by the Davenport Escarpment and its eastward extension to the bluffs of Scarborough. Once the ice dam melted, the lake began to flow through the St. Lawrence River, and the lake level dropped to roughly where it sits today, leaving the old shoreline high and dry as a prominent city landmark.

Little is known about the first inhabitants to wander into the then barren landscape. Archaeologists call them "fluted point people" after the fluted grooves on their arrow and spear points. The first records by Europeans in the 1600s identified the group in this area as the Mississauga. During that time the area was controlled by the French, who built a chain of forts along the lake. On a low bluff they built what they called Fort Toronto to guard the entrance to the Toronto Carrying Place. The Carrying Place, which began at the mouth of the Humber River, followed a series of rivers and portages to Lake Simcoe, and was a vital link in the early fur trade. Since the French were more interested in tapping the fur trade than colonizing the region, Fort Toronto was little more than a trading post, with a fence and a "garrison" of fewer than a dozen men.

But as the Seven Years' War escalated, the British began to capture the Lake Ontario forts. One by one they fell — Frontenac (today's Kingston), Oswego, and Niagara on the American side — but before the British could reach the north shore of Lake Ontario, the French burned Fort Toronto and left. Only a few fur traders remained behind. Overlooking the Humber River, at the Mississauga village of Teiaigon, one James Baby erected a log cabin from which he conducted fur trade deals with the local Mississauga inhabitants. The location is to this day called Baby Point (now a residential neighbourhood in Toronto's west end).

Another trader who remained was Jean Baptiste Rousseau. Closer to the mouth of the Humber River stood the trading post where Rousseau and his father had been given their licence by the Indian Department. The younger Rousseau would later marry Margaret Clyne, who at one time had been held as a prisoner of the Mohawks.[1] It was Rousseau who first greeted the newly arrived Lieutenant Governor Simcoe and his wife and guided them into the Toronto harbour. After being denied a land grant from Simcoe, Rousseau moved to Ancaster (where a home built by Rousseau's grandson still stands), but his cabin remained a local landmark for several years. Today, a plaque marks the site of Rousseau's post.

Following the defeat of the French, the administration of the new territory fell to Sir Guy Carleton, Lord Dorchester. Realizing that a large number of Loyalists were settling in the Bay of Quinte and Niagara areas, he felt that the territorial capital should lie between them, and preferred the site of Fort Toronto. In 1787 he began negotiating to buy the land from the Mississauga, a transaction not finalized until August 1, 1805.

Although Dorchester named the acquisition the "Toronto Purchase," the origin of the name Toronto remains a topic of discussion. Did it originate with the Huron word *toronton*, meaning "a place of meeting," as Henry Scadding concluded in *Toronto of Old*, or did the word mean "a place of plenty," as others suggested. Or did it, in fact, come from the Mohawk word *tkaronto*, meaning "where the trees stick out of the water"? The latter word first appears describing the narrows leading from Lake Simcoe into Lake Couchiching. It was here, over thousands of years, that the early Natives placed their wooden fishing weirs, which indeed did resemble trees sticking out of the water. As a result, French mapmakers called Lake Simcoe "Lac Taronto" for almost a century. Later, the Humber River Portage became known as the "Passage de Taronto," and on the lake stood "Fort Toronto." Because Dorchester was more familiar with his new purchase as "Toronto," it was he who formally applied the name to its Lake Ontario location.[2]

In 1791, Dorchester appointed a deputy for the new province of Upper Canada — John Graves Simcoe. As noted, it was Simcoe's plan to move the parliamentary seat inland from Newark, far from the potential threat of American attack, to the site of today's London, but Dorchester ordered that the capital be at Toronto. Thus, on August 27, 1793, Simcoe sailed into the harbour, heralded by a twenty-one-gun salute. But Simcoe, having distaste for aboriginal names, did away with the traditional name Toronto, and replaced it with York.

He then set about building a fort and devising a town plan for the new capital. Deputy surveyor Alexander Aitkin created a plan of ten square blocks near the east end of the harbour that remains evident in the street pattern of Toronto even today. Although an idealized concept had been created in 1788 by Captain Gother Mann — the captain in the Royal Engineers sent out to survey the harbour and town site for York — the official plan devised by Aitkin was adopted. Simcoe continued changing aboriginal and French place names to those honouring his favourite English heroes or places: Cataraqui thus became Kingston, Niagara became Newark, and Lac aux Claies, Lake Simcoe (after his father). The Wonscoteonach River became the Don.

Simcoe handed out lots of forty hectares to senior officers, while taking eighty hectares for himself on a bluff overlooking his newly renamed Don River. (It was here that he built a summer home and named it Castle Frank in honour of his infant son Francis). Soon, log cabins were beginning to appear around the new fort and farther north on the Don River, where artist-colonizer William Berczy[3] had settled a small band of Germans at a water-power site called German Mills.

One of the earliest first-hand accounts of York is provided by George Heriot in 1807: "Many houses are already completed, some of which display a considerable degree of taste … [visitors] are impressed with sentiments of wonder on beholding a town which may be termed handsome … in the midst of a wilderness."[4] As roads were laid out, York's growth followed — east along Danforth Road (later Kingston Road), west along the Lakeshore Road and Dundas Street, and north along Yonge Street. Activity in the harbour increased and industry arrived. The historic Gooderham gristmill began with a windmill at the mouth of the Don River. Rail lines barged along the waterfront, creating the first of many barriers that Toronto would place between its residents and the lake.

The large lots granted by Simcoe were soon subdivided into small housing lots as throughout the nineteenth century the city pushed ever outward. As it did, and as the air became smokier, wealthier residents began to seek more bucolic rural retreats. Among the earliest escapes were resort hotels near the Humber River, or even farther out. Hotels and resort communities appeared between Etobicoke Creek and the Rouge River, from Lorne Park and Long Branch on the west to Rosebank on the east.

Lorne Park

While it is not a "gated community," Lorne Park might just as well be. Signs proclaiming PRIVATE ROAD and NO TRESPASSING provide just as effective a barrier as any gate or security guard. But this doesn't mean that its history must remain a secret, too.

Lorne Park lies south of Lakeshore Road at Tennyson Avenue. When the land was acquired from the Mississauga in 1805, the government set aside thirty hectares of tall pine forest for use as masts on British ships. The wood proved not to be needed, and in 1831 the property was obtained by half-pay British officer Lieutenant Arthur Jones. In the first of a series of "flips," Jones sold it to Frank C. Capreol, a railway promoter, just two years later. But Capreol's business soured (Peel General Manufacturing Company) and he in turn sold the property in 1839. Over the ensuing four decades, the land changed hands no fewer than ten times, finally ending up with the Toronto Park Association, who established a public park and pleasure ground. Here they built a wharf, gazebo, picnic ground, pavilion, and walkways through the mature pine forest. A refreshment lounge catered to the thirsts of the picnickers — a building that later was converted into a hotel. Opened officially by the Marquis of Lorne, then governor general, the grounds were named Lorne Park. To spend even a few hours in the shady oasis, visitors travelled by steamer from the smoky confines of the city, departing from

York Street in Toronto and landing at the wharf by the park. Others would travel by train and disembark at the flag stop for the Great Western Railway.

The popularity of the site attracted the attention of developers, and in 1886 the Toronto and Lorne Park Summer Resort Colony acquired the property, dividing it into fifty-foot lots that they sold for five hundred dollars each. Their literature promoted a "healthfulness and picturesque surrounding" with a "delightful combination of forest and lawn, lake scenery and landscape." By 1894, seventy-two lots had been sold, many of which were subsequently combined into larger building lots.

Company co-founder William J. Davis commissioned Edmund Burke, a well-known and respected Toronto architect who also designed the Bloor Viaduct, to design two dozen grand summer homes, more than a dozen of which still survive, including that of Davis. Some were given evocative names such as "Buenavista" and "Linstock Villa." Burke also redesigned the hotel, naming it the Hotel Louise in honour of the governor general's wife; it reopened in 1889, with Thomas Anderson operating the popular Bodega Restaurant. It struggled on for another twenty years before being converted into a private club for residents in 1909. It then burned in 1920.

A near tragedy occurred in June of 1903 as a crowd gathered on the dock to await the steamer. Under the massive weight, the dock buckled and collapsed, dampening the spirits and the clothing of the anxious travellers. Fortunately, only one minor injury occurred.

In 1910 the grounds were closed to the public and have remained so ever since. In 1920 the company sold its shares to the residents themselves, and in 1923 more land was subdivided for residential lots, although many would not see a house until after the Second World War. Today the property is administered by the Lorne Park Association, which maintains many of what would otherwise be municipal services. Although off-limits to the general public, the heritage of the estates has not gone unrecognized. In 1980, the Lorne Park Estates Historical Committee published *A Village Within a City: The Story of Lorne Park Estates*, and in 2009 the City of Mississauga designated the 1888 cottage of William J. Davis under the Ontario Heritage Act.

If one were allowed to wander the park-like "village," one would stroll along narrow roads hemmed in by tall pines and maples. Most of the early resort homes cluster on a series of private lanes near the lake, many of them now modernized or upgraded, while only a few, such as that of Davis, retain their original appearance. A small communal park marks the site of the hotel atop a small bluff, while the remains of the road to the wharf are still visible on its slope.

The Long Branch Cottages

The large tract of lakeside land east of Etobicoke Creek was first granted to Colonel Samuel Smith in 1793. Within two years he had added additional property, and by 1795 he owned one thousand hectares. His land included the mouth of the Etobicoke Creek, where Smith built his first house and from which a small amount of shipping occurred — the creek was too shallow to develop into a significant harbour. Today it is the site of Marie Curtis Park.

In 1871, Smith's family sold two hundred hectares of the property to James Eastwood, who in turn sold thirty hectares to Thomas Wilkie. In 1883, recognizing the potential for a summer resort, Wilkie registered the land as the Sea Breeze Park, a 219-lot summer colony. Later renaming it Long

Built in 1884, Long Branch Hotel was a popular destination for city folks who would arrive by ferry. The hotel burned in 1954, and the grounds are now the site of an apartment building.

Branch Park, Wilkie laid out an elaborately landscaped resort with fountains, lawns, walkways, croquet pitches, a pavilion, and a carousel. Overlooking the lake he added the Long Branch Hotel, complete with electricity, speaking tubes in each room, and a telephone line to Toronto. To ensure privacy for the cottagers, Wilkie constructed a wrought-iron fence around the entire site.

The cottage lots were quickly snapped up by Torontonians, who built fanciful dwellings with turrets, gables, and wraparound porches. By 1888, steamships were carrying as many as fifty thousand vacationers each summer to the cottages and hotel or just for a day's outing in the park. Then, with the inauguration of streetcar service in 1894 and the building of Ontario's first concrete road — the Toronto to Hamilton Highway — in 1916, Toronto's urban fringe began to encroach upon the once bucolic resort. By the 1930s, most of the cottages had become year-round homes, or had been demolished in favour of larger, more substantial dwellings. Long Branch expanded into an incorporated village and became visually indistinguishable from its neighbour, New Toronto.

Today, Lakeshore Road is lined with stores, and GO trains take commuters to the city rather than bringing vacationers west. TTC streetcars still rumble along Lakeshore Road, while most automobiles seem content to sit in congestion on the QEW. Still, much of the flavour of that early resort survives. Wilkie's lakeside park still offers walkways and lake vistas, while along the abutting Lake Promenade, several of the old cottages still display their turrets and wraparound porches. Indeed, one of the first such houses is the "Idly Wilde" cottage. It stands at 262 Lake Promenade and was built in 1886 by an architect named Richard Ouge. Other fine examples also still stand along Long Branch Avenue. Unfortunately the old hotel burned in 1954, and the land is now the site of an apartment building. Smith's name does live on in Colonel Sam Smith Park, which sprawls to the east of the old cottage community.

The Mimico Asylum

Many a student will often jokingly refer to their school as an "asylum." But for the students at Humber College's Lakeshore Campus, it's no joke; much of their campus was exactly that. Construction of this remarkable

The spectacular architecture of the former Mimico "Lunatic Asylum" now houses a campus of Humber College. Designed by government architect Kivas Tully, it opened in 1888 and operated until 1979.

assembly of brick and red stone buildings was begun in 1881 as a branch of the Toronto Hospital for the Insane, located on Queen Street, and was called the Mimico Lunatic Asylum.

Placing such as institution outside the city was the brainchild of Dr. Daniel K. Clark, superintendent of the Queen Street facility. As this building was overcrowded, Clark looked farther afield for a new residence, or in this case, residences. A new philosophy was sweeping the mental-health community — that patients would fare better in a rural and communal setting, or "cottage system," as it was called, rather than languishing in a hospital environment. And so it was that Ontario's chief architect, Kivas Tully, and landscape architect Samuel Matheson created a series of dormitories, classrooms, and landscaped grounds on a twenty-one-hectare parcel overlooking Lake Ontario, at the foot of today's Kipling Ave.

In January 1891, 116 of the more troubled patients were transferred from Queen Street, along with forty staff, and placed in three cottages and three general buildings. Two more cottages were added in 1893. In the next year, the asylum became independent from Queen Street, and in 1896 a large brick house was built to house the new superintendent. (In 1936 it would become the Cumberland House, after superintendent Thomas Daly Cumberland.) Two pavilions were added to the grounds, as well. In 1897, patient labour created a new assembly hall for recreation and religious services where patient-run plays were acted out on the second floor. By 1910 the asylum contained 590 inmates and ninety-three staff, housed in ten cottages. After another decade, the asylum had added a nurses' training program and a barn and extra farmland for the inmates to work. And its name changed to the Ontario Hospital, Mimico.

One of the most popular of the asylum's pastimes was cricket, one such match being depicted on a postcard of the facility. But by the 1930s it was described as a "firetrap." In fact, between 1940 and 1950 the inmate population grew to more than 1,300. Overcrowding became a serious problem, so much so that, in 1959, major renovations were needed.

Some treatments sparked concern, as well. In 1971, six hundred signatories presented the Honourable Bert Lawrence, the minister of health, with a petition protesting the treatment and conditions at the Lakeshore hospital. Finally, in 1979, quoting substandard conditions, the Ministry of Health closed the asylum, transferring the remaining 280 patients to hospitals in Whitby and Hamilton. Five years later, the Cumberland House became a centre for treating women with addictions, and was renamed the Jane Tweed House. But the rest of the crumbling buildings would languish until 1991, when they were acquired by Humber College, which began restoring them as part of their Lakeshore Campus. The college undertook extensive renovations and additions, while retaining the spectacular Victorian architecture of the original buildings. Now enjoying a provincial heritage designation, the property has been featured in Doors Open Ontario, and in the movie *Police Academy*. It is today an "asylum" that the Humber students are proud to call their own.

Humber Bay

What this curving indentation on the Lake Ontario shore may lack in visual grandeur, it more than compensates for in its role in the story of Toronto.

A monument to the early French Fort Rouillé stands on the grounds of Exhibition Place on Toronto's waterfront.

The Humber River itself, modest when compared to the Credit, was Ontario's first "highway" to the north. It was along this waterway and its banks that Ontario's aboriginal peoples paddled and portaged to the headwaters of the Holland River and then into Lake Simcoe. In fact, one of their most important villages, Teiaigon, was situated on its banks.

In 1615, French explorer Étienne Brûlé followed the route during his voyages, and was likely the first European to see what would later become the site of Toronto. As the route led to what was once called Lac Taronto (Lake Simcoe), it was called the Toronto Carrying Place, a name that, as noted earlier, migrated to the shores of Lake Ontario and would eventually return the fledgling capital of York to its original and its current name.

Le Magasin Royale, a log fort that had been situated at Baby Point, farther up the Humber River, was built in 1720 under the orders of the then French governor of Canada, the Marquis Philippe Rigaud de Vaudreuil. Little more than a log cabin, it is considered by archaeologists to be the first non-aboriginal building in the Toronto area. The strategic significance of the route, the expansion of the French fur trade, and the increasing competition from the English on the south shore of the lake led the French to build a larger trading post, known as Fort Toronto, near its mouth, as a replacement for Le Magasin Royale. Constructed by Chevalier de Portneuf between 1730 and 1740, Fort Toronto was in turn replaced by an even larger fort, Fort Rouillé, located on what are today's CNE grounds, a site marked today by an historic monument and plaque. After 1759, when the French had destroyed all their Lake Ontario fortifications, the ruins of the earlier Fort Toronto were resurrected by fur trader Jean Bonaventure Rousseau, and run by his son Jean-Baptiste Rousseau, or "St. John," as Lieutenant Governor Simcoe called him.

It was into this bay in 1813 that an invading fleet of American troops landed and made their way to the settlement, which they looted and burned. In response, the British attacked Washington, burning many public buildings in the process, including the White House.

The head of navigation on the Humber extended as far inland as the site of today's Old Mill Inn and Spa. Here, in 1796, John Dennis began a shipyard on the east bank of the river and built the first ship to be constructed here under British control, the *Toronto*, which measured sixteen metres in length. It was one of three launched at that site.

Dennis obtained his lumber from the King's Mill located on the opposite shore. It was here that Simcoe, in 1793, ordered the construction of a sawmill to supply the settlers' needs. In 1835, William Gamble took over the mill and added a nail factory, tavern, and store, and a new five-storey wooden flour mill. After fire destroyed this mill in 1848, Gamble replaced

This early painting depicts the crude wooden bridge, built in 1815, that crossed the mouth of the Humber River.

it with another five-storey mill, this time made of stone. It lasted only ten years, however, and was gutted by fire in 1881. Its shell has survived to the present day and was incorporated into the Old Mill's new Inn and Spa.

After York's first settlers and politicians began to make themselves at home, a road was opened along the shore, following an earlier aboriginal trail. Farther inland, the government had surveyed and constructed Dundas Street to link York with the head of the lake. However, this route had to cross several wide and steep river valleys, and the lake route, although it needed more bridges, was easier to build and to travel.

Starting in 1803, Donald Cameron was ferrying travellers across the mouth of the Humber for six cents each; that is, until 1815, when the first wooden bridge was built to span the river. The rickety structure consisted of simply ten wooden trestles perched nearly ten metres above the river mouth. The ensuing increase in traffic led a Scotsman named MacLean to open a pub in his log home, the only stopping place between York and Port Credit, and Humber Bay began to evolve into what it would remain for several decades — a popular summer playground. John McDowell opened a second tavern in 1854, while Charles Nurse, fisherman and boat-builder, added a hotel to his boatworks.

A short distance west of Nurse's Hotel, John Duck erected what would become the most popular destination in the community, the Wimbledon House. After arriving in Canada in 1872, Duck built a two-storey L-shaped hotel right on the water's edge. He extended an existing wharf into the water far enough to accommodate steamers from Toronto. On the grounds, guests could enjoy ox roasts and dances, or ride the carousel. Duck also kept a small zoo, featuring a wildcat, bear, deer, and raccoons.

A man named O.L. Hicks built the Royal Oak Hotel, which was noted for the oak tree that grew through his veranda. This hostelry was located on a hill on the north side of the road and was popular as a meeting place, banquet hall, and dance hall. In 1882, the hotel owners formed the Humber Steam Ferry Company to coordinate the ferry service from the city.

Closer to the lake, a park known as The Lawn attracted crowds of bathers and picnickers, where, from a row of boathouses, swains who wished to impress their "ladies fair" could rent a rowboat. Today The Lawn's park legacy is reflected in the street name, Park Lawn Avenue. However, many of the old hotels, including Duck's, met their fiery fate in

The sole surviving support of the popular Palace Pier that once stood beside Humber Bay is now a monument to the dance pavilion that hosted such musical luminaries as Louis Armstrong, the Dorsey Brothers, and Duke Ellington. The pavilion burned in 1963.

1912 when flames raced through the aging row of buildings.

The Roaring Twenties brought a new face to this summer playground when Emil Brooker opened a dance hall known as the Rendezvous. Then, in 1926, a Brighton or Atlantic City-style pier was proposed. It would be known as the Palace Pier. Begun in 1929, the pier was to stretch 550 metres into the lake. But the Depression halted the pier at just ninety metres. After sitting empty for a decade, the dance hall finally opened in 1941 and contained the Strathcona Roller Rink and the half-hectare Queensway Ball Room, where dancers would swing to big band sounds of the Dorsey Brothers and Duke Ellington.

For two decades, the CBC aired live broadcasts from the dance hall, often featuring Trump Davidson and his Dixieland combo. The Palace Pier remained a popular dance hall and roller skating rink until 1963 when it suffered an all too common fate — it burned. As with much of the Humber Bay shoreline, the site now contains high-rise condos, behind which a memorial to the venue rests on one of the dance hall's concrete footings.

Although rum-running was more likely to be linked to nearby distilleries during the dry twenties, one small boat, the *Heldina*, would periodically slip away from a Humber River landing at the end of Berry Road with its load of whisky and beer bound for the American shore. If a police raid appeared imminent, a pound of hamburg meat was delivered to the captain as a code that a raid was coming.

But Humber Bay was not without its industry. From 1928 to the 1950s, Hans Sachau, a German immigrant, operated a busy shipyard. While specializing in sailboats and cruisers, including building the largest sailboat on the lake since the *Griffin*, he was commissioned by the Canadian government during the Second World War to construct nine "Fairmiles" — small, lightly armed motor launches built during the Second World War as submarine chasers. At about the same time, automobiles began chugging along Ontario's roads, bringing with them yet another new travel phenomenon, the motor hotel, or simply, the motel. The first on the Humber Bay was the Legg family's tourist cabins, followed by three more in the 1930s.

Throughout the 1950s and 60s, as traffic began using the QEW, Humber Bay's motel strip fell onto hard times. To keep their businesses going, many owners began to allow "hourly" visits, and the area gained a seedy and promiscuous reputation. One of the last to go was the Hillcrest Motel. Used as the locale for a film noir-inspired photo shoot by photographer Finn O'Hara in 2007, the motel was demolished the following day. Its architecture was classic art deco, a style of motel now fast disappearing and little appreciated.

One of the strip's survivors was the Dutch Sisters Inn, built on the site of Hans Sachau's boatyard. It was here that Hans' wife, Anna, opened the original inn, which today houses the popular Casa Mendoza Restaurant that offers patrons a view of the lake and the Toronto skyline.

The Mansions of Mimico

Picnickers and party-goers weren't the only summer sun-seekers who were attracted to the lakeshore's refreshing breezes. Toronto's wealthiest tycoons began eying this prime property as well. As the Toronto and Mimico Electric Railway opened up the area, home builders moved in and created a row of large summer homes on sprawling estates overlooking the lake. Sadly, following the Second World War, as the urban fringe moved ever outward, facilitated by the car craze, many of these wonderful Lakeshore estates were demolished and subdivided, or replaced by apartments. But many elements of that elegance still remain, and even a few of the grand homes themselves.

Courtesy of the Toronto Reference Library, TRL T 33698.

Now gone, the castle-like home of Frederick Featherstonehaugh was one of Mimico's early lakeshore mansions.

One of the first to build in the area was Frederick B. Featherstonehaugh, an attorney and inventor, who built the elegant "Lynne Lodge" and a castle-style guest house in 1899. The grounds included stables, a boathouse, a greenhouse, and a gardener's cottage. Following the death of his wife in 1930, Frederick married a younger woman, who was later granted most of his assets in a divorce settlement. Following Featherstonehaugh's death in 1945, the building became a popular Italian restaurant before being torn down to make way for apartments in 1957. While the main lodge is now gone, the gardener's house still stands at 2669 Lakeshore Boulevard West.

Although hidden from the road by apartments, "Myrtle Villa" is another survivor. In 1906, A.B. Ormsby bought a piece of the lakefront and built a summer home he called "Ormscliffe." A manufacturer of metal doors, Ormsby loved the lure of Hollywood, and produced such films as *Neptune's Bride.* When he retired to California in 1925, he sold his estate to an Italian immigrant named James Francischini. Although he had arrived nearly penniless, Francischini soon amassed a fortune in the construction business — his projects included the Royal York Hotel. He changed the name "Orsmcliffe" to "Myrtle Villa" and erected a stable for his horses. Because of his Italian background, and amid rumours that one of his horses was a gift from Italy's fascist dictator Benito Mussolini, Francischini was sent to an internment camp in Quebec in 1940, and his holdings, including Dufferin Paving and a shipbuilding business, were confiscated. Following his brief detention, he moved to Quebec, and his estate was sold to make way for apartments. Today, along with its formal garden, "Myrtle Villa" still stands, now surrounded by the Amadeo Garden Court apartment. Within this complex are the servants' quarters and the original garage that now serves as a variety store.

One of the grandest among the surviving grand homes is that built in 1927 by the McGuiness family. Today, surrounded by the original wall and guarded by a stern iron gate, the house serves as Toronto's Polish Consulate. Other spectacular homes include the "Ring House" at 2609 Lakeshore, built in 1917; the 1902 home of William Howard Hunter at 10 Lake Crescent, which overlooks the lake just south of Lakeshore; and "Miles Park" at 11 Miles Road, again on the lake. It was built in 1912 by one of the city's leading undertakers, A.W. Miles, who arranged funerals for such dignitaries as Sir Henry Pellatt of Casa Loma fame and William Lyon Mackenzie King. Miles's name remains in the undertaking business at Bayview and Millwood, in Toronto's east end. His extensive lakefront grounds included a dance pavilion, picnic ground, and baseball diamond, as well as a small zoo that his neighbours ultimately encouraged him to move to a country location.

The Western Beaches

Many have lamented that Toronto wasted an opportunity to create a Chicago-style lakeshore boulevard that would follow the curve of the Humber Bay and offer a grand vista as drivers approached Toronto from the west. Blame the Depression. That was exactly the plan of the Toronto Harbour Commission in the 1920s. Their vision would create an avenue that would follow the shoreline and sweep around the south shore of the Toronto Islands. But the Depression halted that plan at Bathurst Street.

In 1939, the QEW opened between the Henley Bridge in St. Catharines and the Humber River in Toronto. Grand, carved monuments marked the two termini. While the one in St. Catharines remains on site (for now), the Toronto monument was relocated when the Gardiner Expressway was widened. The Lion Monument, as it is called (for the face of the lion on its base), was designed by architect William Lyon Somerville and sculptor Frances Loring,[5] and was unveiled in August of 1940 to commemorate the 1939 visit of King George VI and Queen Elizabeth. Its inscription says, in part: THE COURAGE AND RESOLUTION OF THEIR MAJESTIES IN UNDERTAKING THE ROYAL VISIT IN THE FACE OF IMMINENT WAR HAVE INSPIRED THE PEOPLE OF THE PROVINCE TO COMPLETE THIS WORK IN THE EMPIRE'S DARKEST HOUR IN FULL CONFIDENCE OF VICTORY AND A LASTING PEACE.

Three watercourses flow into Humber Bay — Mimico Creek, the Humber River, and Grenadier Pond. Despite its diminutive size, Mimico Creek offers Torontonians an extensive pair of artificial peninsulas that jut into the lake. Created with over 5.1 million cubic metres of landfill, and opened in 1984, Humber Bay Park offers little in the way of a lakeshore heritage, until one notices a pair of historic lighthouses standing in the western portion.

This duo owes their existence to the hurricane of 1858. In that year a vicious storm crashed through the Toronto Island peninsula, forming a new gap wide enough to allow ships an alternative entrance to Toronto Harbour (other than through the precarious western gap). After the channel was widened and deepened in 1895, a pair of wooden range lights was placed on the banks. They provided light until 1973 when the new Leslie Street Spit and a further widening of the gap meant that more modern structures were needed. The old lighthouses were then acquired by the Etobicoke Yacht Club and the Mimico Cruising Club respectively, and placed on their properties in the new park. Although not accessible to the public, they are easily viewed from the walkways that line the park.

The Humber River, which winds its way to the lake for about one hundred kilometres from above the Niagara Escarpment, has historical links with the earliest aboriginal populations, the first French explorers, and the fur trade. Its natural heritage is significant, as well. Of the several marshes that once lay along the Humber's lower reaches, only two survive. One lies close to the Kingsway and can be viewed easily from vantage points nearby. The other is more distant and less visible. Both, however, support a wide variety of plant and animal species, some of which are considered rare. Thanks to the Toronto Field Naturalists, the marshes have been designated as environmentally sensitive.

Although four sets of railway tracks, six lanes of expressway, and twelve lanes of traffic on two roadways now cross the river, the lower reaches of the river remain an idyllic and significant wetland. A gas station overlooking the marshes on the eastern bank marks the seldom celebrated site of what was Toronto's first permanent residence — that of Jean Baptiste Rousseau.

The river is also linked with the deadliest storm ever to lash Toronto. In 1954, a late-season hurricane named Hazel unleashed its unexpected fury on southern Ontario and turned quiet rivers into deadly torrents. The Humber suffered the most. Too many houses lined the banks of the normally placid waterway, and as Hazel's waters boiled downstream, they swept away dozens of homes, along with their terrified occupants. More than eighty people lost their lives that night.

~~

Were it not for the singular benevolence of a wealthy early landowner, Toronto would never have received its most magnificent park, High Park. Here, overlooking the waters of a lagoon named Grenadier Pond, architect John George Howard, in 1873, deeded forty-eight hectares of his sixty-six-hectare estate to the city, on the condition that it be named High Park.[6] When deeding his land to the city, he retained his home and eighteen hectares for himself. Upon his death in 1890, Colborne Lodge and the remaining land became part of the park as well. Built in 1837 in a "regency picturesque" style, the house boasts a near wraparound porch. Toronto operates the site as a museum and the park now contains nearly 160 hectares, including a rare oak-savannah ecosystem. At its heart is Grenadier Pond, named after the famed British military unit, and popular with winter skaters and summer fishers.

Overlooking the west side of the pond was an early and now forgotten village named Windermere. A few small industries, including a bolt manufacturer, and workers' homes, stood near the small wooden station built by the Great Western Railway in 1855 at the foot of today's Windermere Avenue. Urban expansion engulfed the little settlement and it became part of a new housing development known as Swansea.

Who Remembers Sunnyside?

As the years go by, fewer and fewer Torontonians remember "Sunnyside," yet for thirty-three years it remained an iconic amusement park, attracting hundreds of thousands of bathers, strollers, and thrill-seekers every summer.

The name Sunnyside itself originated with a villa of that name erected in 1848 by a prominent local citizen, George Howard, one of many such early estate homes built along this prime stretch of lakefront. The building ultimately became part of St. Joseph's Hospital and was demolished in 1945. But by then the Sunnyside Park was in full swing. Its popularity grew dramatically when Toronto's streetcar service stretched into the area in 1893. Like much of the activity that took place along the shore of the lake, the notion of an amusement park began in 1911 with the newly formed Toronto Harbour Commission (THC). In 1914, Emile Brooker built a bathhouse and shortly after the THC opened a free bathing beach nearby. The Sunnyside Restaurant and dance hall opened in 1917 and remained popular until the park was demolished in 1955. By then it was known as the Club Top Hat.

In the following years, the THC added more landfill and constructed a three-kilometre boardwalk. But the grandest addition came in 1922 with the building of the Sunnyside Bathing Pavilion. Designed by A.H. Chapman, the pavilion was for more than just bathers, as it also provided an open terrace garden, and refreshment and dance areas. Hair dryers, towel rentals, and seven hundred lockers catered to the needs of swimmers, as did manicurists and nurses. Two

Photo by Ron Brown.

Almost Moorish in design, the Sunnyside Bathing Pavilion remains a Lakeshore Boulevard icon and a survivor of the popular Sunnyside Park.

towers overlooked the beach. An enclosed arched area marked the lower level while a spacious upper floor allowed the curious to gaze upon the bathers below. The entrance to the upper level was by way of a grand stairway and soaring archway. On June 28 of that year, Toronto mayor Alfred McGuire cut the ribbon to officially open the Sunnyside Amusement Park, touted as "Toronto's Lakeshore Playground." Its seven original rides were all selected by the THC. Later that year, the park's second iconic building opened, the Palais Royale dance hall, which began life as a combination boathouse and dance hall. (During the 1930s, George Deller took over the lease from Walter Deans, the original operator, and placed the focus on dancing. Through the 1930s and 40s, young and old alike danced to the sounds of the Bert Niosi house band.[7])

Later, more rides were added to the park, including a roller coaster known as the Flyer, and a carousel called the Derby Racer. And in 1925, the park opened what was then called the world's largest swimming pool. Known as the Sunnyside Natatorium, it measured ninety-two metres long and contained 3.4 million litres of water.

But by 1948, with increasing volumes of traffic funnelling into the city along the QEW, the THC decided to demolish Sunnyside Park in favour

An early bird's-eye sketch shows the layout of the Canadian National Exhibition at the close of the nineteenth century.

of a new expressway. By the following year, the park was just a memory.

Two important structures remain from the park's heyday. The Palais Royale dance hall has been refurbished and continues in its role as a dance venue and banquet hall. But the most visible is the Sunnyside Bathing Pavilion. Declared a heritage property in 1975, and now restored, it looms in its Byzantine grandeur beside the Lakeshore Boulevard and the Gardiner Expressway. So distinctive are its architectural features that it is often featured in films.

To the east, the site of what began as a simple agricultural fair in 1846 became the grounds of the Canadian National Exhibition, one of North America's largest seasonal exhibitions. The site still contains the continent's most stunning collection of early twentieth century exhibit buildings, as well as the soaring arches and pillars of the Princes' Gate, built in 1927 to commemorate the diamond jubilee of Confederation.

Old York

In 1787, Lord Dorchester convinced the Mississauga Nation to surrender their traditional lands along the Lake Ontario shoreline, or at least most of them — areas in what is now downtown Port Credit and Belleville remained in their hands. But the lands around Toronto Harbour became British. In 1788, surveyor Captain Gother Mann developed the new town's first plan. Simple and conceptual, his design encompassed a square grid of small streets surrounded by a "common ground," which in turn was surrounded by a series of estate lots fronting on concession roads.

But that plan did not come to fruition. When Simcoe came on shore in 1793, he ordered deputy-surveyor Alexander Aitkin to come up with a new one. Aitkin's plan was of ten city blocks, five each running north and south of King Street. Typically, those early roads sported royal names such as Duke, Frederick, George, Princess, and Berkeley. In 1797, Peter Russell, Simcoe's successor, enlarged the plan to include reserves for a hospital, school, church, gaol, and market. In 1801, surveyor John Stegmann extended the plan yet again, this time from Victoria to Peter streets (names still in use today).

Among the village's first key buildings were those that brought Simcoe here in the first place: the parliament buildings. Located on the lake, between today's Parliament and Berkeley streets, the buildings were erected between 1794 and 1797. They were Georgian in style and consisted of two buildings with colonnaded porches facing the bay. One building was for the Upper House with its seven legislators, the other for the Lower House with its sixteen members. In 1813, the buildings were burned by the invading American forces, who also took many books from the library and the parliamentary mace with them.

By 1810, York was growing slowly and had a population of close to seven hundred. Its buildings consisted of about a hundred houses, equally divided between those constructed of log and those of frame. There were six taverns, yet only a solitary church, a registry office, a customs house and post office, along with the garrison, jail, and the houses of parliament. Industries at the time were simply those of the craftsmen necessary to supply the community's needs.

As early as the 1790s, Simcoe had commissioned the building of a pair of sawmills on the Don and Humber rivers, both at what were then the head of navigation on those streams. On the Don, Aaron and Isaiah Skinner built a sawmill in 1793, and then added a gristmill in 1797.[8] In the 1820s, William Helliwell arrived and added a brewery to the site along with a house made of mud brick. The industrial complex, in 1847, became part of the Taylor milling empire, which included mills farther north in the valley. While all other evidence of the Taylor mills has vanished, the Todmorden Mills were preserved by the Borough of East York in 1967 as a centennial project and include the remains of the one-time brewery and the homes of mill operators the Helliwells and the Skinners. The remains of the Humber River gristmill were incorporated into the Old Mill spa operation discussed earlier.

The most significant heritage feature on the Lake Ontario shore is Toronto's Old Fort York[9]. Not only did it play a major role in the War of 1812, but its stock of structures represents Canada's most complete intact collection of buildings dating from that period. Located near the foot of today's Bathurst Street, it was originally constructed in 1797 where the now buried Garrison Creek entered the lake. Following two subsequent moves, it was reconstructed and strengthened in 1813 on its original site, where it discouraged the Americans from a repeat of their attack some months earlier. In 1841, the old fort's military role was replaced when the New

Fort, or Stanley Barracks, opened on the grounds of today's Exhibition Place. Of this fortification only a single barracks remains.

To celebrate the centennial of the City of Toronto in 1934, the old fort was restored and opened as a museum. Today it offers buildings which date from 1813 to 1815, including two blockhouses, a powder magazine, and a series of barracks. (The lighthouse built in 1857 to protect the fort's wharf also survives.) It is somewhat incredible that such a national historic treasure was threatened with relocation when plans for the Gardiner Expressway were first announced in the 1950s. But saner heads prevailed and today not only has Old Fort York withstood the threat of the Americans, but that of "progress" as well.

After the War of 1812, growth began to shift west. In 1833 a "New Town" was laid out west of Spadina along Wellington. Adopting the new trend in urban planning, this upscale layout was in the form of a wide boulevard linking two open squares. Clarence Square anchored Wellington Place at its eastern end, while Victoria Square lay to the west. The road was wider and the lots were larger and backed onto a bluff — the old Lake Iroquois shoreline — that overlooked the lake.

King Street East was evolving into the town's main shopping street and the warehouses lining Front Street backed onto the wharves on the lake. In

Toronto's finest patrol the grounds of historic Fort York.

1834, York became a city, and reinstated its original name — Toronto. The new municipality needed a city hall. The first was a temporary facility in a market building at the southwest corner of King and Jarvis. In 1844 a new city hall was built south of the market. When the old market burned in the great fire of 1849, St. Lawrence Hall was built on the site. It was designed by William Thomas, who had come to Toronto from England in 1843 and set up an architectural practice. The building was restored in 1967 as Toronto's centennial project. The interior contains an elaborate second-floor great hall. Thirty metres in length, its high, decorated plaster ceiling, chandeliers, and gilt trim make it one of the grandest rooms in Toronto.

In the 1890s a new market building south of Front Street was built literally around the old city hall, the building's dome removed in the process. (By then a new city hall awaited the city fathers at Bay and Queen streets.) Today, while the façade faces Front Street, the rear exterior has been uncovered and looks out onto the vast St. Lawrence food market. On the upper level, the one-time council chamber has been restored and is now an art gallery.

The beginnings of one of Toronto's most important and longest lasting industries took root in the 1830s where the Don River made its way through the Ashbridge's Bay marshland and flowed into the harbour. James Worts, a mill owner from Suffolk, England, erected a windmill to power a gristmill in 1832, and, in partnership with William Gooderham, his brother-in-law, turned the leftover chaff from the gristmill into whisky. The Gooderham and Worts Distillery was born.

Sadly, nearly all of Old York's original buildings are gone, many destroyed in the Great Fire of 1849. Old York's earliest surviving on-site structures, the few to escape the inferno, include the Bank of Upper Canada, built in 1827 at Adelaide and George streets, and to the east, Old York's early post office, built in 1834 and home of postmaster J.S. Howard. The home of Judge William Campbell, built in 1822, stood at Frederick and Adelaide streets until 1972, when a neighbouring card company applied to demolish the historic structure to make way for parking. As the property was built by one of Toronto's leading judges, an association of trial lawyers know as the Advocates Society rescued the building and moved it to a new location at Queen and University, restoring the building for use as a museum. Along with the Grange, now part of the Art Gallery of Ontario, the Campbell House represents the only Georgian-style mansion left in the city. Known as the "Palladian" style, it incorporates elements of classical Greek and Roman influences into its architecture.

Along King Street, very few of Old York's commercial buildings have managed to survive, although the street contains fine examples of later nineteenth-century structures. A series of commercial buildings occupying 167–185 King Street are that street's oldest surviving stores, dating from 1834–43. Other pre-fire survivors stand at 107–111 and 125 King and date from 1841.

But it is Front Street that can boast of the most visually striking structures. Having backed onto the lake's original shoreline, nearly all contained warehouses. Most of the warehouses date from 1860 to 1890, and form a nearly continuous historic streetscape from Church Street east to the St. Lawrence Market. Setting off this streetscape is the picturesque Flatiron Building. Wedged in the gore formed by Wellington and Front streets, it was built in 1891–92 by the Gooderham family, who owned the sprawling Gooderham Distillery complex at Mill and Parliament.

The arrival of Toronto's first railways brought with it a surge of new industries to Old York, forcing out the many grand homes and early hotels. Farther east, Front Street was lined with industries like the Toronto Safe Works (139–145) built in 1866, and the Toronto Street Railway stables and power house at 165 Front Street, now the Young People's Theatre. The Standard Woollen Mills at 223–237 Front now houses the Joey and Toby Tannenbaum Opera Centre. The Toronto Knitting and Yarn Company, built in 1866, still stands at 2 Berkeley Street and contains the offices of architect A.J. Diamond and Partners, who redesigned the building. It is now named the "Berkeley Castle" after an early nearby grand home, demolished in 1904. A fine example of adaptive reuse is the police station at the northeast corner of Parliament and Front. It was built as the Consumers Gas Company in 1898 and had deteriorated badly by the time the Toronto Police Services acquired it in 2000 and converted it into a police station.

But one of the continent's single most outstanding examples of a nineteenth-century industrial complex is the former Gooderham and Worts Distillery, now preserved as a national historic site known as The Distillery District. Although the original wind-powered mill from 1832 is long gone, the property contains more than thirty buildings dating from between 1859 and the late 1890s. The oldest structure is the 1859 gristmill

The Gooderham and Worts industrial complex is one of Canada best-preserved industrial sites and a popular tourist destination today.

and distillery built of limestone at a time when the water's edge was just across the railway tracks beside the mill. In 1863, a cooperage and malting complex began operation on the west side of Trinity Street, while on the east side the pure spirits complex of rectifying stills opened. Between 1884 and 1891, tank-and-barrel rack houses were added along Mill and Cherry streets.

During the dark days of prohibition following the First World War, the complex was sold to Harry Hatch, owner of the Hiram Walker Distillery in Windsor. Hatch put both distilleries to good use, clandestinely supplying whisky to thirsty Americans. Many of the fishermen who lived along the Woodbine beach strip or on Toronto Island were recruited by Hatch to form "Hatch's Navy," which hauled the hooch from the distillery, across the lake to the American shore. It was a choice not without its risks.

On September 30, 1923, during the early lawless years of rum-running, a whisky boat, the *Hattie C*, slipped away from it moorings in Belleville loaded with a cargo of whisky from the Corby Distillery north of Belleville. After stops in Bond Head and Frenchman's Bay, on the night of October 3, she slipped into the safe confines of the Ashbridge's Bay lagoon. Unbeknownst to the crew, an anonymous phone call had been placed to Sergeant Bill Kerr, who, along with four armed constables, confronted the boat and ordered the crew to surrender. When the crew refused, a hail of gunfire erupted. When the smoke had cleared, John Gogo was dead, while his brothers James and Sidney lay bleeding. In all, six men were rounded up and arrested, including Frank di Petro and Rocco Perri.[10]

Finally, in 1990, after 158 years of turning out alcohol, the Gooderham and Worts Distillery closed, and stood vacant for nearly a dozen years. In that interval, Hollywood location scouts recognized the maze of brick lanes and authentic industrial architecture as ideal for the movie industry, and nearly eight hundred movies, including the Oscar-winning *Chicago*, were shot at the site. Then, in 2001, a progressive-minded partnership bought the property and converted it into an arts centre. In addition to the many galleries and studios that now operate in the old buildings, the Distillery District has become a major Toronto tourist destination, offering frequent street and music festivals and a variety of restaurants and cafés. The Mill Street Brew Pub brews its own brand of beer, while the Boiler House's seven-hundred-seat outdoor patio is said to be North America's largest. The Soulpepper Theatre and the George Brown College theatre school specialize in theatrical entertainment, while cafés, including the Brick Street Bakery, SOMA Chocolate, and the Taste of Quebec, cater to a dining crowd. It is difficult to believe when viewing the busy elevated railway tracks and the Gardiner Expressway that run between the site and the lake that this long-lasting industry began on a quiet marsh where the Don River once flowed into the lake.

Immediately to the east of the Distillery District, a former wasteland of rail yards and warehouses is currently undergoing its transformation into the West Donlands Neighbourhood, where a mixture of housing, retail, recreational, and commercial uses are taking shape. Amidst the modern development stands one striking three-storey red brick building with a mansard roof punctured with dormers, and a rounded corner entrance. Built at Front and Cherry streets at a time when Front was called Palace, this Queen Anne-style building began life as the Palace Street School. Built in 1859, it was home to nearly two hundred students. One of the earliest free schools, it is the only surviving example of a school built by the early Toronto Board of Education. In 1890 it was remodelled as the Irvine House Hotel containing forty rooms, an office, and a dining room. Closed in 1910, the building stood vacant until 1922, after which it housed a variety of tenants before opening as the popular Canary Restaurant in 1965. The restaurant is now closed as the new neighbourhood evolves around it.

Toronto's Islands

Each summer, ferries shuttle tens of thousands of sun-seekers across the waters of Toronto Harbour to one of three wharves on the Toronto Islands, as they have for many a year. Although the island grouping has long attracted those seeking recreation, they were not always islands.

Once a narrow sandbar linked the peninsula with the mainland, across the mouth of the Don River, and provided the only access from what would become the village of York. East of that sandbar lay an extensive marsh known as Ashbridge's Bay. Although no aboriginal settlement was known to exist on the peninsula, the local Mississauga would gather there to collect medicinal herbs and breathe in the invigorating lake breezes. As the sun would set, they would embark in their canoes, torches held high, to spear the many salmon.

Years later, John Graves Simcoe recognized that the peninsula offered a strategic military advantage, and ordered a blockhouse built at what he called Gibraltar Point. Simcoe's wife, Elizabeth, spent many of her hours riding on the peninsula while John was off looking for roads to build and towns to create. She would write in her diary:

> Aug. 4, 1793 ... We rode on the Peninsula, so I called the spit of land for it is connected to the mainland by a very narrow neck of ground.... We met with some good natural meadows and natural ponds. The trees are mostly of the Poplar kind covered with wild vines.... On the ground were everlasting peas in abundance.... I was told they were good to eat when boiled.[11]

In 1803, with the growing amount of boat traffic between the old capital at Newark and the new one at York, the government ordered that lighthouses be built at both locations. The structure at York was located near Simcoe's blockhouse on Gibraltar Point, and was completed in 1808. Its original height of sixteen metres was extended to 19.5 metres in 1832 while a new, white revolving light installed in 1878 was considered to be the brightest on the Great Lakes at the time. Its first lighthouse keeper, John Radenmuller, died in 1815, allegedly at the hands of local soldiers to whom

The Gibraltar Point Lighthouse on Toronto Island has been a Lake Ontario landmark since it was built in 1808. Some say it is haunted.

he refused a drink. No one was charged for the crime, if one had been committed, for his remains were not located until many years later by a subsequent keeper. For this reason the building is often referred to as the "haunted lighthouse." In 1945, a fixed green light was installed so that its signal would not blend with Toronto's increasing glare of white lights.

With York's residents increasingly turning to the promontory for summer pastimes, the area's first hotel opened in 1833, owner Michael O'Connor billing it as the "Retreat on the Peninsula." He also started up the first ferry service, bringing hunters and day-trippers on a ferry powered by a pair of horses on treadmills. The *Sir John of the Peninsula* made two trips a day, departing from the main wharf at the foot of Church Street.

More hotels and recreation facilities appeared in the 1840s, and in 1843 Louis Privat opened the Peninsula Hotel, ferrying guests across the harbour on a five-horse paddlewheel ferry, later to be replaced by the steam ferry *Victoria*. Around the same period, a small colony of fishermen was adding shanties near Gibraltar Point and on Ward's Island.

A defining moment in the islands' history occurred in 1858 when a violent storm sent huge waves hurtling against the sandbar that formed the peninsula's narrow eastern neck. The waves crashed relentlessly, and finally broke through the barrier, allowing the lake water to rush into the harbour. Although similar breaches had occurred previously, they were always repaired. This time the government decided to dredge and widen the gap instead, turning the gap into the harbour's most important entrance. And so, in one single storm event, the peninsula became a series of islands.

The fury of the storm was recorded in the *Leader* newspaper of April 14, 1858:

> Between four and five o'clock yesterday morning, the waters of the lake completely swept over a large section of the Island, entirely carrying away Quinn's Hotel … and making a permanent entrance to the harbour, some 500 yards wide. The gale … sprang up about five o'clock on Monday evening and was then of such violence as to cause serious fears that the hotel would be blown down. The lake gained steadily on the Island and the Hotel until about four o'clock in the morning when the Hotel was completely swept away. In anticipation of such an event, Mr. Quinn erected a small building west of the Hotel into which he barely had time to move his family.

Soon cottages were built along the western shore and hotels erected on Hanlan's Point — John Hanlan's in 1862 and that of Patrick Gray in 1866. The next year, the federal government transferred the westerly portion of the islands to the city, which promptly subdivided it into cottage lots and parcels for amusement parks and hotels. Hanlan added a few amusements adjacent to his twenty-five-room establishment, marking the start of one of Toronto's most renowned amusement parks. Following John Hanlan's death in 1872, his son Ned, by then wealthy from his earnings as a famous rower, increased the size of the hotel to three storeys. By this time the city had acquired the islands and had begun improvements that included boardwalks, bridges, and landscaped gardens. Rides and amusements included a switch-back railway and a carousel. Nude bathing is nothing new at Hanlan's Point either, having been officially permitted as early as 1894. The "naked police" arrived in 1930 and prohibited the clothing-optional practice until it was again allowed in 1999.

In 1894, the Toronto Ferry Company bought into Hanlan's resort for an unheard of $250,000 and began to construct one of the city's largest

Courtesy of Archives Ontario, 1000 3746.

During its heyday as an amusement park, from the 1880s until the 1920s, Hanlan's Point on Toronto Islands would entertain visitors by showcasing diving horses.

amusement grounds. They opened a year later with rides that included roller coasters, a "human roulette wheel," and a circle swing. In 1897, a sports stadium was built, one that would house the lacrosse team and the original Toronto Maple Leafs baseball team. A massive fire destroyed many of the park's buildings, including the stadium, in 1909. It was replaced by an eighteen-thousand-seat facility known as Maple Leaf Park. It was from here in 1914 that the legendary Babe Ruth, while playing with the Providence Greys, is said to have launched his first professional home run into the waters of the lake.

The beginning of the end came on April 29, 1929, when the baseball team moved into a new home, the Maple Leaf Stadium, located on the mainland at the intersection of Bathurst Street and Lakeshore Boulevard.[12] The city bought the Maple Leaf Park the following year and began its usual downsizing. In the mid-30s, city council voted to create a new airport by removing the cottages from the Western Sandbar and undertaking a massive landfill off of Hanlan's Point. In 1937, following a struggle by the Hanlan's Point cottagers, in particular the West Island Drive cottagers, Toronto council agreed to move thirty-one homes to what was then Sunfish Island. The original suggestion to move to Mugg's Island was rejected, as the site was too marshy. Streets were laid out and the cottages floated to the new site. The island name was changed to Algonquin.

While Hanlan's was evolving into a major amusement park, the city had acquired much of the property at Centre Island, and, guided by the designs of the park superintendent, John Chambers, had begun to develop Island Park. New wharves were added and a small number of amusements made their appearance. But Centre Island developed into more of a summer resort community than an amusement park. Grand homes were built on leased land along the south shore on Lakeshore Avenue, while on Iroquois Avenue, the city required that homes built there be worth a maximum of two thousand dollars.

Meanwhile, a main street evolved along Manitou Road, running from the new ferry docks to the lake. But rather than rides, the street offered the more practical range of summer services: ice cream parlours, laundries, dairies, and meat markets. Centre Island also echoed to the music from a pair of dance halls: the Park Pavilion and Ginn's Casino.

During the 1950s, most buildings were demolished to make way for grass. The only heritage features to survive that eradication are two enchanting stone bridges, the Manitou Road Bridge, built in 1912, and the Olympic Island Bridge from 1914. The fire station was moved to Ward's Island, where it stands today.

Far to the east of Centre Island is Ward's Island. Early on, in the 1830s, it was the centre of David Ward's fishing operation. In 1882, his son William built the two-storey Ward's Hotel, and in the same year Erestus Wiman opened a bathhouse on the south side of the island, closer to the beach. Here he permitted nude bathing, provided it was done before 9:00 a.m., the hour at which the ladies generally arose. After the turn of the century, Ward's Island became a colony of tents on leased lots just large enough for a family tent. Unlike Centre Island, or Island Park as it was still called, the city had yet to extend electricity or piped water to the tenters' "residences" on Ward's. Finally, in 1931, the city allowed the Ward's Islanders to replace their wind-blown tents with permanent houses, although the buildings could not be larger than seventy-eight square metres — about the size of the tents they had been occupying. In 1937, yearly leases replaced the earlier seasonal ones.

Today, only Ward's and Algonquin islands show the remnants of cottage life. In the 1950s, the Toronto Parks Department had decided that parks meant grass, and little else, and began to systemically cancel the residential leases and demolish the grand homes along Lakeshore Avenue.

This was not going to happen without a fight. In 1980, the council of Metropolitan Toronto voted to evict the remaining island residents and issued writs to do so, with Judge John O'Driscoll ruling that such writs were valid. The high point of the dispute culminated with the showdown on the Algonquin Bridge. It was here on July 28, 1980, that thousands of islanders and their many mainland supporters stared down the sheriffs and won a twenty-four-hour reprieve, long enough for the courts to give them permission to appeal O'Driscoll's ruling.

Meanwhile, the province had set up a commission of inquiry under Barry Swadron, who recommended that the residents could remain for another twenty-five years, but would not be allowed to enlarge their homes. Interestingly, while the Metro government strongly wished the islanders would leave, the City of Toronto supported the group. Yet Metro remained the owner of the land. Eventually Metropolitan Toronto was dissolved and the City of Toronto was enlarged to absorb the five former cities and one borough. The province then passed legislation granting the island residents ninety-nine-year leases on their cottages.

Ward's Island today is one of the more enticing parts of the island complex. Narrow lanes feature tiny cottages, many of them imaginatively sculptured or landscaped. A school, variety store, and restaurant (the Rectory Café, the manse of a now demolished church) make the east end a varied visit. For those wishing to stay overnight, the islands no longer claim any hotels, but Ward's Island does offer a bed and breakfast.

The aging boardwalk that hugs the shore and leads west to Centre Island still shows the scars of the battle with Metro: the concrete foundations of summer homes that once stood hide in overgrown yards, and several barriers of stone or concrete that once warded off waves and high water. Algonquin Island, connected to Ward's by the now famous bridge, offers wider streets and the larger cottages relocated from Hanlan's Point. The walkways continue their way toward Centre Island, the site of the children's village known as Centreville. Adjacent to Centreville is the historic St.-Andrews-by-the-Lake Church. Consecrated in 1884, and relocated from its original site at Cherokee and Lakeshore, its delicate wooden gothic style seems out of place.

Most of the islands' summer fun occurs on or near Centre Island — regattas, dragon boat races, and various festivals all lure crowds to this section. A large formal garden marks the end of the Manitou Road near the shore of the lake. Continuing west, the walkways lead past the former island school, now the Gibraltar Centre for the Arts, a retreat for artists, while nearby the pumping station has a few early buildings with prominent red tile roofs. A new Public and Nature Centre school offers classes to islanders and mainlanders alike. Soon there rises beyond the trees the stone tower containing the Gibraltar Lighthouse. Its distance from the water is due to the ongoing deposits from those easterly currents.

The trails end at the grassy wasteland of Hanlan's Point, a contrast to the raucous heyday of rides, hotels, and sports events. Notwithstanding the presence of an official nude beach, there have been efforts here to restore the dunes of Gibraltar Point by installing protective fencing and planting beach grasses and other native plant species.

The Port of Toronto

Since that time in 1792 when John Graves Simcoe visited the Toronto harbour to establish York as the new seat of government, Toronto has always been a port. The first wharf was naturally located at the mouth of Garrison Creek to serve the garrison stationed there. But the fort was too far west of the new town site to allow convenient trading. As a result, local entrepreneur William Allan, in 1802, built York's first non-military commercial wharf at the foot of Frederick Street. Little more than a landing place for schooners and barges, the wharf had only a small warehouse to store commodities.

When the need for a larger wharf became quickly apparent, Cooper's Wharf was built at the foot of Church Street in 1815. Enlarged in later years, the wharf was purchased in 1828 by William Bergin, another enterprising businessman, and by the 1880s was known as the Maitland Wharf. Following the arrival of the first steamboat, the *Frontenac*, on the lake in 1816, more and larger wharves were added to the shore bluff — the Navy Wharf between John and Peter streets, and the Commissariat Wharf at the foot of Peter. Maps drawn in the 1820s show other wharves, such as the Merchant Wharf on Frederick (formerly Allan's).

In 1840, Richard Tinning built a sawmill and wharf, along with a few houses, between York and Bay streets. In 1872, his son Thomas acquired a

Now buried beneath landfill, Toronto's Yonge Street Market, formerly situated near what is now the corner of Yonge Street and the Esplanade, was once a busy site.

rescue vessel that, along with its volunteer crew, represented Toronto's first marine rescue program. But the natural shoreline had yet to be altered. The wharves were simply built at the foot of the steep shore bluff. In 1842, a map drawn by Sir Charles Bagot shows that by then there were seven wharves: three at Church Street, one at Yonge, another at Spadina, and the garrison wharf by then known as Victoria Wharf.

Dr. William Rees added yet another wharf in 1841, this one at the foot of Simcoe Street. It was at Rees's Wharf that immigrant ships docked, from which new arrivals, many impoverished, others sick, were led to the immigration sheds, a large complex located at the corner of today's King and John streets, which also included quarantine sheds for cholera. But overcrowding threatened the health of the site, and the federal government replaced it with larger facilities elsewhere.

The arrival of the railway age brought with it demands for more land. The wharves once situated at the foot of the shore bluff disappeared beneath landfill for the railway tracks, and a string of new wharves appeared. The railways also brought more industry. One of the port's key industries was

The Polson Iron Works, once located at the foot of Sherbourne Street in Toronto, launches one of its many ships.

the Polson Iron Works, situated on the harbour where Sherbourne and the Esplanade now intersect. Opened in 1886 by William Polson and his son F.B. Polson, the company spent the next twenty-eight years building and launching dredges, ferries, launches, and sandsuckers. But two of its products stand out: one was the country's first steam warship, the *Vigilant*; the other was not so much revered as mocked — F.A. Knapp's ill-fated roller boat. Built in 1897, the strange vessel consisted of two rollers, one outer and one inner. At thirty-eight metres long and seven metres wide, the theory was that the outer roller would roll across the water like a log, while the inner roller would remain stationary and hold the passengers. However, two trial runs proved that it was wildly unstable in windy or wavy conditions and it was quickly scrapped, ingloriously buried, and used as landfill at the Polson site. Incredibly, two of the Polson boats remain in active service to this day — the *Trillium*, which was rescued from a lagoon on Toronto Island, and the *Segwun*, a heritage coal-fired steam vessel that carries tourists around the waters of the Muskoka Lakes.

Over the next half century, landfill projects kept pushing the lake farther and farther away. In 1911, Toronto Harbour's jurisdiction was turned over to the federally created Toronto Harbour Commission, and one of its first projects was to do away with Ashbridge's Bay and the mouth of the Don River. In 1912 they began filling in 250 hectares of what had been the marshland of Ashbridge's Bay. Here they dredged a ship channel from the harbour for more than two kilometres to a large turning basin. In 1931 the massive 750-ton Bascule Bridge was completed over the 120-metre-wide channel, extending Cherry Street to Unwin Avenue and Cherry Beach. With growing traffic both by rail and by water, more elevators and docks were built. In 1927, North America's largest terminal warehouse was built by CN and Harbour Terminal Limited. Situated at the foot of York Street, it covered an area of more than ninety-three thousand square metres.

While today's rail lines are now removed from their original lakeside route (thanks to repeated landfills), the lake's railway heritage survives with Toronto's Union Station, located on the old shore bluff, and in the John Street Roundhouse, now home to a pub, a retail outlet, and a collection of early railway structures.

Air travel was starting to develop in the late 1920s as well, and in

Toronto's second Union Station once stood right by the lake, before the shore was filled in.

1929 the Harbour Commission proposed an airport for the waterfront. To accommodate the need for such an expanse, the commission filled in seventy hectares at the end of Hanlan's Point, narrowing the western gap in the process. In February of 1939, the first airplane flew out of Port George VI Airport. With the Second World War raging, the airport became a training facility for Norwegian fighter pilots, who were housed on the mainland.

After the war, a new airport opened at Malton, northwest of the city. The facility was originally designated to handle freight traffic, while the Port George VI Airport was to handle passenger traffic. But that arrangement wouldn't last. As traffic increased, Malton Airport became the commercial passenger terminal and Port George VI was consigned to civilian traffic. But as Malton, later Pearson International Airport, became busier, short-haul commercial flights resumed at the island airport, and in 1956, Southern Provincial Airlines lifted off on its inaugural flight to St. Catharines, Welland, and Brantford. By 2010, a new airline, Porter, was offering flights to regional destinations both in eastern Canada and the northeastern United States, and Port George airport had become the Toronto City Centre Airport. In 2010, it was renamed again, this time in honour of the Canadian First World War hero, Billy Bishop.

By the 1950s, the port of Toronto was lined with elevators, warehouses, and docks. The opening of the St. Lawrence Seaway in 1958 brought in still more upgrades needed to handle the deeper ocean vessels. At this time Redpath Sugar moved its facilities from Montreal, where it had been since 1854, to the port of Toronto. Here raw sugar was shipped in to the plant on the large ocean vessels and processed into granulated and liquid sugar.[13]

In 1928, the Canada Malting Company built prominent storage silos at the foot of Bathurst Street; the first to be constructed of concrete rather than the flammable wood, the fifteen silos were thirty-seven metres high. They remained in use until 1980 when they were abandoned. At this writing, proposals for a music museum or municipal history museum have been put on hold and the elevators sit weathered and overgrown with weeds, adjacent to a parkette called Ireland Park. Almost like a bookend at the eastern end of the old port area stand the silos of the Victory Soy Mills, built in 1943 by E.P. Taylor, one of the country's leading industrialists and a thoroughbred horse breeder. The silos have been likewise abandoned with no preservation proposal as a yet on the table. Between the two, lies what has been dubbed "the mistake by the lake." In 1972, in a fit of pre-election generosity, the federal government gave twenty-eight hectares of its port lands to the citizens of Toronto. The land lay south of the Gardiner Expressway and between Bathurst and Bay. In determining what to do with the land, the city decided to develop an arts and culture district. In order to finance the proposed events and venues, the city sold off large chunks of the gifted land. To no one's surprise, high-rise condos began springing up like weeds — very tall weeds.

It took thirty-five years, but the Harbourfront development is pretty well complete. Imaginative parks, like the lush vegetation of the Music Garden, the sand-covered "beach" with its aluminum umbrellas, and the city's largest natural outdoor ice rink, now fill in the shoreline. Cruise boats and tall ships bob at the docksides.

Despite the modern developments, the port land's heritage is there, though sometimes not entirely evident. The most prominent of the heritage buildings is the remarkable Queen's Quay Terminal. Once the largest such terminal on the continent, it was renovated and now houses condominiums, offices, shops, and restaurants, earning for its designers an architectural award. Designed originally by Moore and Dunford of New York in 1926, the Toronto Terminal Warehouse served as a cold-and-dry-storage facility for merchandise being transferred from the ships to the rail cars, and was the first structure in Canada to be built using poured concrete.

One of the oldest structures on the waterfront lies immediately east of the Queen's Quay Terminal. This diminutive, blue board-and-batten building was originally the Toronto Ferry Company waiting room and was built in 1907 when the shoreline lay several city blocks to the north of its present location. After serving as the waiting room for the Royal Canadian Yacht Club, it was designated a heritage structure in 2007, and is now a ticket office for harbour cruises as well as a coffee bar.

Farther east, the harbour is utterly obscured by the unsightly towers of a condo and hotel. Watery vistas are only available from a narrow boardwalk hidden behind, and the looming hotel relegates the ferry terminal to a tiny, dark waiting area. This planning defect also hides Toronto's most historic ferry from view — the unsinkable *Trillium*. Built at the Polson Iron Works in 1910, the steamer puffed back and forth, primarily to Centre Island, until 1952. It was retired from service in 1957. Then, in typical Toronto fashion, she was towed to a lagoon at Hanlan's Point, where, neglected and vandalized, she sank rotting into the mud. In 1974, Toronto historian Mike Filey and Alan Howard, curator of the Marine Museum at Exhibition Place, launched a drive to restore the historic vessel. Although too big to fit the current ferry docks, it was restored to a 1910 appearance, retrofitted to run on diesel, and now operates as a charter and on special occasions.

Since 1833, more than forty-six different ferries have seen service between the mainland and the islands. Even the current fleet of Toronto Island ferries might be considered historic. In 1935 the *William Inglis* entered service, followed in 1939 by the *Sam McBride*, and in 1958 by the *Thomas Rennie*.

L.J. Solman, who owned and operated the baseball stadium and amusement park at Hanlan's Point, ran the Toronto Ferry Company until 1926 when the City of Toronto purchased his fleet and turned operation over to the Toronto Transit Commission (TTC). To their dismay, they discovered the dock and Solman's nine vessels were badly deteriorating. Of his vessels, only the *Trillium* and the *Bluebell* operated into the 1950s. In 1927, the TTC opened its new ferry docks at the foot of Bay Street, docks that many older Torontonians remember from their youth, and began ordering the new fleet that operates to this day. Today the ferries are operated by Toronto Parks. It is hoped that short-sighted planning decisions that have blocked the operation of these heritage vessels from public view and confined their passengers to a congested cavern-like waiting area can somehow be rectified and the entry to the ferry operations fully restored to the people to whom it belongs.

In 2010, the area between Yonge Street and the mouth of the Don River was undergoing an extensive transformation, with new parks, walkways, movie studios, and offices destined to line the waterfront. The last vestige of the port's industrial operations is the fifty-year-old Redpath Sugar Refinery.

East of the Don lies the heart of Toronto's active commercial port. Although one of Canada's least busy ports, ships yet glide through the eastern gap, carrying road salt and containers. Most of this land was filled in beginning in 1914 using material dredged from the harbour. In straightening the Don River's watercourse, the aim was to reduce flooding on the lower Don and to provide extra docking. But the new course simply disgorged more pollutants into Ashbridge's Bay, then a wildlife marsh. In 1923, the Keating Channel, a new route to guide the Don into the bay, was opened. Named for E.H. Keating, the city engineer who had proposed the plan fifty years earlier, it was intended to alleviate the pollution by redirecting the dirty Don River waters directly into the harbour. Meanwhile, in one of the port's most extensive landfill projects, Ashbridge's Bay was filled in.

Little in the way of heritage remains here. A bank, a restaurant, and a one-time fire hall near Commissioners and Cherry streets, built during the landfill phase, stand surrounded by vast storage yards. Unwin Avenue follows the old sand spit, once part of the island formation where a colony of fishermen had built shanties and net sheds. That site today is home to a variety of marinas and sailing clubs.

Where the view from Cherry Beach once took in the far horizon of the lake, it now extends only to a five-kilometre, rubble-filled spit known as the Outer Harbour East Headland. Tommie Thompson Park occupies a portion of the headland that became, in the late 1960s, a place to dump the dredging from the eastern gap, and a breakwater to protect ship traffic. Since then, nature has also moved in, bringing with it four hundred plant and tree species and three hundred animal species, including the rare prickly pear cactus and black garter snake. More controversial is the damage being inflicted on the trees by the thousands of cormorants that also have decided to call it home. Still, the headland is touted as being an unusual urban nature park in a car-free refuge.

The Eastern Beach(es)

The "Beach" or not the "Beach," that is the discussion. For many years, coffee shops and cafés were alive with debate over what to call this east-end neighbourhood that lies along the city's longest sand beach. Should the area be called the "Beaches," the area's traditional name, or more simply the "Beach," as more recent residents seemed to prefer. Well, both are correct.

From the 1870s until the 1920s, the beach strip was lined with clubs and amusement parks that went by a variety of names, almost all of them ending with the word "beach." Therefore, "The Beaches" can legitimately refer to the string of recreation facilities. On the other hand, the amusement parks are long gone, and the neighbourhood is more urban. Geographically, the beach itself is a single entity, connected by its famous boardwalk. Therefore, "The Beach" would be more accurate today.

Waves frequently threatened the first homes along The Beach area of Toronto. Photo circa 1920s.

Even as Toronto was growing industrially and railways were puffing in and out of the city's many stations, the sandy beach east of Ashbridge's Bay remained "thickly wooded," as one observer noted, and Queen Street was described as a simple country trail with stumps at random intervals. A few settlers had created farms along Kingston Road, and some fishermen had shanties and net sheds scattered along the beach itself. Among these settlers was the Ashbridge family. Arriving in 1794, the Ashbridges took up land along a trail that later would be followed by Kingston Road. Their land looked out over the waters of a lagoon formed by the mouth of the Don River, a bay that would take their name, Ashbridge's Bay. On their allotment they raised pigs and lived on the waterfowl and fish from the bay. Their first log house was followed in 1807 by a more substantial frame building that they continued to use until an attractive brick home was built farther east.

Designed by architect Joseph Sheard, once mayor of Toronto, the new brick home was completed in 1854 and remains one of the city's finest small homes. Over the ensuing years, landfill and housing subdivisions have filled in the waters of the bay and pushed the shore of the lake well to the south. The shingled mansard roof of the Ashbridge house sits above the fanciful arcaded treillage of the full-width veranda, all set well back from Queen Street amidst sprawling, landscaped grounds. This oasis forms a striking contrast to the congested working-class neighbourhood in which it sits. It is hard to believe that this home, still standing at 1444 Queen Street East, once stood at the water's edge. The house remained in the Ashbridge family until 1972, when sisters Dorothy Bullen and Elizabeth Burton donated the house and 0.8 hectares of property to the Ontario Heritage Trust.

In 1854, well to the east of Ashbridge's Bay, Joseph Williams, a wealthy English immigrant, bought a sixteen-hectare farm lot that he named Kew Farm, after the gardens in his native England. In 1870 he opened a park on the beach he called the "Canadian Kew Gardens." Here, on the airy lakeshore, he offered dancing, food, and accommodation — but no liquor. Although transportation was difficult in the early years, the streetcars only travelling as far as Kingston Road and Woodbine, the park became a popular summer retreat. It was here that he also built an elaborate stone house for his son, Kew. In 1907 the city bought the Kew Gardens and assembled other nearby property to create a city park. They then proceeded to demolish Williams' cabins and other buildings, except, fortunately, Kew Williams' stone house. The park today offers lawn bowling and other sports venues and yet still retains its mature tree cover. In keeping with the Kew Gardens tradition, the grounds are the main site for the annual and wildly popular Beaches Jazz Festival.

In 1874 a tram line was built along Kingston Road, which lay well to the north of the beach. With public access improving, in 1878, Adam Wilson, a one-time Toronto mayor and owner of an estate on the water, subdivided much of his land and opened Balmy Beach as a park for the future residents of his new subdivision. His was the first large property in the Beach to be parcelled up, even before Queen Street was fully opened. In 1903, the town of East Toronto, then a separate municipality, designated the grounds as Balmy Beach Park and its administration was turned over to a separate body whose job it was to enact and enforce park rules. The Balmy Beach Club erected a two-storey clubhouse with a wide wrap around patio by the water. Club members would dance to the latest big-band sounds at night, and during the hot summer days engage in canoe races with their rivals from the Kew Beach Club. Fire destroyed the old dance hall in 1964, although the club still functions, and Balmy Beach Park is yet administered by a separate board of management.

Scarborough Beach Park, its iconic tower lit at night, was one of the many "beaches" along the lake. Photo circa 1920.

Further east, Victoria Park enjoyed its grand opening on June 1, 1878. Situated in seven wooded hectares at the foot of today's Victoria Park Avenue, the grounds offered a pavilion, restaurant, and a lookout tower. Visitors would arrive by steamer from the Church Street docks and climb the hillside, where they would also find a petting zoo and donkey rides for the children. The park never developed into an amusement park, but rather remained a picnic ground.

In 1912 the city took over the park and the Board of Education opened its Forest School for underprivileged children. It closed down in 1934 to make way for the construction of the R.C. Harris Water Filtration Plant. The design for this state-of-the-art public work was inspired by the then works commissioner, R.C. Harris, and displays towers and high arched doorways more typical of a palace than a water plant. It remains one of the most stunning architectural sights on the Toronto waterfront, commensurate with the Queen's Quay Terminal or the Sunnyside Bathing Pavilion.

In 1907, just east of the Kew Gardens and south of Queen, between McLean and Leuty avenues, the Scarborough Beach Amusement Park sprang into existence almost overnight. And, unlike the other more passive parks, this one bustled with a midway and swirling rides, including a roller coaster, a House of Fun, a Tunnel of Love, and something called Shoot the Chutes, a twenty-five-metre water ride. Entertainment included crude "re-enactments" of the San Francisco fire and the Johnstown flood. In the evenings, band concerts took over the brightly lit bandshell. But in 1922, yet another amusement park had opened, this one in the city's west end, known as Sunnyside. With the ease of public transportation to the new park, and with the growing popularity of the automobile, Scarborough Park began to lose business. By 1926, the midway and the rides were gone, and yet another residential subdivision was underway.

Most evidence of the heady days of the roller coasters and the hot dogs has gone — with one exception. At the foot of Fallingbrook Avenue, a set of about one hundred steps leads precariously down the bluff to the beach. Here, by the water, was the Fallingbrook Pavilion. The single building contained a dance hall, boat storage, change rooms, and ice-cream stand. The pavilion operated from the early 1900s until the 1950s, when it developed a troubled reputation following confrontations between the regular east-enders and troublemakers said to be from the west end. The steps were closed by city bylaw and now lie covered in several decades of leaves and debris. At their base, in the trees, still lie the forgotten concrete ruins of the last of The Beach's amusement parks.

All throughout the heyday of the amusement parks, private homes were being built ever closer to the water's edge even though strong easterly

The Leuty Lifesaving Station, located at the foot of Leuty Avenue at Woodbine Beach, is now a popular filming location.

storms often washed away front yards and steps. Still, the residents did not own these homes, but rather were leasing them from the Toronto Harbour Commission. In 1927 their leases expired and the homes were removed. In their place appeared a boardwalk running the length of the beach, with protective groins built into water to retard the huge waves. For the first time, the entire length of the beach was open to all, although not everyone appreciated that. Early anti-Jewish protests sprang up to deny Jewish residents access to the park. These were quickly put down, and the park along the beach is today one of the city's most popular.

Far from the din of the traffic, trees form a canopy over the boardwalk, where visitors, residents, and many fine-looking dogs stroll contentedly, regardless of the weather. A new swimming pool, the Donald D. Summerville Pool, named for a former Toronto mayor, roils with young swimmers. An artificial peninsula now extends far into the lake, catching the sand-filled currents and creating a wider beach, popular now with the city's beach volleyball enthusiasts. As if to recall an earlier era, the white wooden form of the lonely Leuty Lifesaving Station, built in 1928, stands near the water's edge, a popular subject for photographers and occasional movie shoots.

The View from Here: Atop Scarborough's Towering Bluffs

Rising cathedral-like from the waves of Lake Ontario, the Scarborough Bluffs are one of the lake's most spectacular, yet lesser-known natural phenomena. Soaring ninety metres above the lake at their highest point, they have historically been difficult to view. No roads followed their shores, no harbours allowed safe refuge for boats. The bluffs are incised by a series of deep gullies created by the forces of postglacial erosion, few which allowed access to the beach. Only recently have landfill parks, such as Bluffer's Park, with road access, provided water-side vantage points for viewers.

The bluffs also struck one of the area's first European visitors. In 1794, while venturing from the confines of old York, Elizabeth Simcoe, wife John Graves Simcoe, remarked in her diary: "The shore is extremely bold and has the appearance of chalk cliffs, but I believe they are only white sand. They appeared so well that we talked of building a summer residence here and calling it Scarborough."[14] Although the soaring cliffs brought back memories of Scarborough, England, the Simcoes settled on a locale closer to York for their summer home, building Castle Frank on the western cliffs of the Don River instead.

In 1885, the still undeveloped heights enthralled the authors of the *History of Toronto and County of York, Ontario*:

> The scenery in the neighbourhood of Scarborough heights … is extremely wild and romantic. The heights which are about 320' above the lake present an extensive view over the water and surrounding country … it is charming and delightful spot to all lovers of picturesque and natural scenery.[15]

The bluffs formation extends from the foot of Fallingbrook Drive, near the site of the former Victoria Park pleasure grounds, for fourteen kilometres to the mouth of Highland Creek. The lower shoreline cliffs continuing east of that point represent the erosion of the glacial deposits, and not of the prehistoric riverine delta.

The spectacular vistas from the top of the bluffs have resulted in a mix of early grand homes and clifftop parks. During the age of suburban growth, the recreational potential of the bluffs was ignored by urban planners in Scarborough, and typical suburban housing was allowed close to the cliff edge, to the ultimate dismay of many owners eventually forced to vacate as the edge crept ever closer. But what frightens some has attracted others. Near the foot of Fallingbrook Drive sat a number of grand homes. One, built by Sir Henry Pellatt of Casa Loma fame, was demolished in the 1930s to provide parking for a new apartment building. A home of likely equal grandeur is known as the "Chateau des Quatre Vents." The two-storey structure was built in 1891 by Emile Gagnon and boasts a château roof, three turrets, and arched windows and doors on the ground floor facing the lake. It stands on Rockway Crescent, which leads off Queen Street at its intersection with Fallingbrook. The laneway that leads to it is private.

On the east side of Fallingbrook stands "Edgemont House." Here, on the side of the bluff, businessman H.P. Eckardt built a large summer home in the Queen Anne style. It offers a lakeside porch and second-floor bay

Converted into a housing subdivision during the 1920s, Donald Mann's Fallingbrook Estate featured one of the eastern lakeshore's grandest homes. His gatehouse still stands on Kingston Road.

window, although its conical roof was removed early on. Although private, it is visible from Fallingbrook, and reflects the lakeside tranquility that Eckardt must have long enjoyed.

Fallingbrook itself was named after the estate of railway builder Sir Donald Mann. He and business partner Sir William Mackenzie,[16] over three decades, had cobbled together a transcontinental railway empire by acquiring unprofitable short lines and unused charters. Their wealth enabled them to live in grand style and build elegant homes. Mackenzie's summer home still stands in Kirkfield, Ontario, while Mann built his by the bluffs. Although the house is gone, a small Tudor-style cottage on Kingston Road, visually inconsistent with the 1950s bungalows surrounding it, is the century-old gatehouse that once guarded the entrance to Mann's Fallingbrook estate. His grounds were subdivided for housing.

Up until the Second World War, Scarborough remained a rural township where prosperous farms and barns lined Kingston Road. With the 1950s came suburban sprawl, and the wheat fields and pastures quickly disappeared under curving streets and small homes. While the bluff-side homes were somewhat grander than their inland counterparts, they remained nonetheless unexceptional. Rarely did it occur to the township politicians or their planners to provide open spaces along what is Lake Ontario's most spectacular stretch of shoreline, and when they did it was only at infrequent intervals.

One of those open spaces remains solidly in private hands. Located between Kingston Road and the Bluffs, the Toronto Hunt Club was started in 1843 by officers of the Toronto garrison for their equestrian events. In 1898, streetcar service to the area brought with it the demand for cottages and homes, and the garrison moved the facility to Thornhill. In the 1930s, the Hunt Club became a private golf club, and remains so today.

The next open area is the stunning Rosetta McClain Gardens. This surprising floral display, on Kingston Road east of Birchmount, was the creation of Robert Watson McClain and his brother-in-law, Joseph West. The site was originally part of a sixteen-hectare farm bought in 1904 by the owner of Toronto Safe Works, Thomas McDonald West. He divided the land among his four children, including daughter Rosetta, who died in 1940. In 1959 her husband, Robert McClain, deeded the gardens to the City of Toronto in honour of his late wife. With a view from atop the bluffs, the gardens include natural walkways through a wooded area set off by a fountain and formal gardens that include a rose garden and a rock garden. Were it not for the generosity of a private individual, this open space might well not exist.

The Toronto Railway Company streetcar service continued eastward along Kingston Road and reached stop 14, today's Midland Avenue, in 1901. The old Halfway House Hotel, which opened as a stagecoach stop in the 1830s, stood on the northwest corner and served as a boarding point for the streetcars. It was a popular stop, for many of those travelling the route would disembark here and follow a trail to the top of the bluffs. Here the Borough of Scarborough had established Scarborough Bluffs Park from which a stunning vista extended over the craggy buttresses and clay pillars that earned the area the name The Dutch Chapel Gully.

On Kingston Road opposite the Halfway House stood the Scarborough Bluffs Refreshment Room. Built around 1903, this unusual one-and-a-half-storey structure is wedged into a triangular parcel between Kingston Road and Midland and Kelsonia avenues. With the bicycle craze in full swing at that time, cyclists would stop in to quench their well-earned thirst. Once surrounded by farm fields, the refreshment room now stands in the midst of suburbia. Now recognized as a heritage structure, the Scarborough Bluffs Refreshment

Room was undergoing restoration in 2010. Meanwhile, the Halfway House was relocated to Black Creek Pioneer Village where it has resumed its role as a "stagecoach stop." Happily, the foresight of the Scarborough politicians in 1911 has left today's generation with one of the lakeshore's most spectacular lookout points. As in the past, the vista from Scarborough Bluffs Park incorporates the unusual pillars and buttresses of the bluffs, but now also takes in the popular Bluffers Park located below. This new park was created over the past four decades using landfill to provide marinas, beaches, wildlife sanctuaries, wooded walkways, restaurants, and a houseboat colony.

Overlooking the bluffs, a small cottage community was evolving along Chine Drive, east of Midland Avenue. The little arts-and-crafts homes, built in the 1920s, represent a pleasing architectural anomaly among the later more modern post-war homes of neighbouring streets. During its early days, Chine Drive continued beyond its current dead end and followed a small gully onto what are called the "flats" above the bluffs. Here visitors and locals could enjoy the view as well as a race course.

Drivers on Kingston Road are likely used to the dome-topped St. Augustine's Seminary that rises over one of that area's last farm fields. Construction began in 1910, bringing to fruition the notion to train English-speaking priests, a plan that had been underway since 1890. Designed by A.W. Holmes in the beaux-arts style, the large dome topped by a cross is underlain with a high circle of windows. The main building is a four-storey brick structure and one of the first in the Toronto area to employ reinforced concrete. With its long tree-lined laneway, sitting high atop the bluffs, it has been a striking and unaltered landmark both to drivers and to boaters ever since. It is located on the south side of Kingston Road between Chine Drive and Brimley.

Cathedral Bluffs Park is located at the end of Cathedral Bluffs Drive and off Lyme Regis Crescent. This is the highest part of the bluffs, more than ninety metres above the lake below. It is also one of the most rapidly eroding sections of the bluffs, having receded more than fifty metres in the last twenty years. Several homes on the residential streets to the west of the park have been removed lest they face a descent into the gullies below.

Immediately east of Cathedral Bluffs Drive, Scarborough Heights Boulevard celebrates a forgotten clifftop park of the same name operated between 1905 and the late 1920s by the Toronto Railway Company.

The little-known Passages *sculpture created by Darlene Hilton Moore in 2002 stands at the foot of the Scarborough Bluffs as a tribute to artist and teacher Doris McCarthy whose home sits atop the cliffs.*

As the bluffs reach their eastern limits, they take on a decidedly artistic feel, not due to their appearance, which would appeal to any painter or photographer, but rather due to the artists and art lovers who lived there. Hidden away near the foot of Meadowcliffe Drive, between two steep gullies, stands "Fool's Paradise." At least that is what famed artist and author Doris McCarthy calls it.

Born in Calgary in 1910, she moved to Toronto when she was three, and from an early age was enchanted by the beauty of the bluffs. She entered the Ontario College of Art in 1925 at a time when Group of Seven artists Arthur Lismer and J.E.H. MacDonald were on staff. Graduating in 1930 with honours, she went on to combine her painting with her teaching. In 1939 she bought a five-acre property and small cottage atop the Scarborough Bluffs, which her mother dubbed a "fool's paradise," a name which Ms. McCarthy adopted for the cottage.

She continued teaching at Central Technical School until 1972, after which she received such honours as the Order of Ontario and the Order of Canada. She has painted, sculpted, and authored three books on her life and art. In 2002, in honour of Ms. McCarthy, artist and sculptor Marlene Hilton Moore designed a sculpture called *Passages* that was installed at the foot of the bluffs below McCarthy's beloved Fool's Paradise. A walking trail, the Doris McCarthy Trail, starts at Kingston Road at the foot of Bellamy, follows an old mill trail down Gates Gully (named after a well-known Kingston Road tavern keeper), and ends at the beach and the sculpture. McCarthy has decreed that, following her death, her home will be donated for use as an artists' studio and sanctuary.

Lying just offshore from the *Passages* sculpture is one of Lake Ontario's few visible shipwrecks. Here, lying in just two metres of water, protrudes the boiler of the ill-fated *Alexandra*. On August 3, 1915, the *Alexandra*, a forty-eight metre long side wheeler built in 1866, had departed Port Hope and was making its way to Toronto carrying a cargo of general merchandise. Strong winds forced the vessel toward the bluffs where it became stranded and began to break up. Eager onlookers waited for their chance, then began to scavenge the goods and eventually parts of the ship itself. Fortunately, there were no casualties and the ship came to rest in shallow water.

Another artistic endeavour farther east has left a lasting and unique legacy on the landscape of the Scarborough Bluffs. That landscape is the Guild Inn's "garden of ruins," a collection of portions of Toronto's historic buildings that often were recklessly demolished with little thought to their preservation. The Guild Inn was originally known as Ranelagh Park, a thirty-three-room arts and crafts mansion and large clifftop estate built in 1914 for a Colonel Harold Bickford. There was already a log cabin on the property, likely dating back to the 1840s, although some historians have suggested that it might date as early as the 1790s.

After lying vacant for several years, the mansion was bought in 1932 by Rosa Hewetson, heir to the Hewetson Shoe fortune. She later married Herbert Spencer Clark, a Toronto engineer and fellow art lover, and together they established the Guild of All Arts. Around the mansion, the Clarks built cabins and studios and made them available for artists to practise a wide variety of crafts including wood, leather, ceramic, batik, and wrought iron. The Clarks realized that in order to preserve the arts during the Depression, creators needed low-rent space.

Throughout the 1930s, the Clarks added two hundred hectares to their property and also began to collect remnants from Toronto's demolished

The Guild Inn's "garden of ruins" is both a tribute to the Guild's original owners, Rosa and Herbert Spencer Clark, and a testimony to the callous disregard Toronto has shown toward its heritage buildings.

buildings, placing them in the large garden that stretched from the rear of the mansion to the top of the bluffs. Eventually their property would extend from the Bluffs to Kingston Road and from Livingston to Galloway Road. With more and more visitors, the Clarks added guest rooms and a dining room and moved into a nearby mansion known as Corycliff, since demolished. During the Second World War the government took over the building, using it variously as a base for the Women's Royal Navy Service and later as a military hospital.

In 1947, after the Clarks reacquired their holdings, they continued their passion for collecting pieces of Toronto's vanishing heritage buildings. But in 1953 they were forced by high taxes to sell most of the estate to developers, who in turn subdivided the land to create the neighbourhood known as Guildwood Village. In the 1960s, a hotel tower and swimming pool were added, and the Guild Inn became increasingly popular for conferences and weddings. In 1978 the Metropolitan Toronto and Region Conservation Authority purchased the inn and the land. By then newer and better conference facilities were opening elsewhere and the Guild Inn had begun to lose business. In 2001, both the hotel and the popular restaurant closed their doors and many heritage lovers despaired of losing one of Toronto's most intriguing properties. Since then a fire has destroyed one of the original cabins. Happily, in 2008, Centennial College won approval to open a restaurant and conference centre in the historic building as part of their hospitality program. The gardens and remnants continue to be administered by Toronto Parks and are popular for weddings and wedding photography, as well as summer theatre.

The remnants displayed include a brick wall from the Royal Conservatory of Music, the east-wing entranceway from the historic Granite Club, and the lintel block, Corinthian capital, and a pair of columns from the Bank of Toronto.

Chapter 5
The Ghost Ports and the "Newports"

From Scarborough to the Murray Canal the shore of Lake Ontario is gently scalloped. No headlands, no deep bays mark its course. Beyond the soaring bluffs of Scarborough, the shoreline descends to intermittent low bluffs and marshy backshores. When the great weight of the retreating glaciers finally left the eastern end of Lake Ontario, the land rebounded, forcing the waters to flow back into the river mouths near the western end of the lake. This resulted in lagoons forming in the estuaries, many of which formed the basis of small harbours.

In addition to the harbours, several shipping wharves were built into exposed waters, providing shipping opportunities for nearby farmers, who could now export grain and lumber. But many of these tiny ports were doomed when larger steamboats arrived, requiring deeper water and more protected docks, and when the railways provided a faster, year-round means of shipment. Larger harbours that received the railways survived and sometimes even grew into significant towns, such as Port Hope and Cobourg. Others stagnated; many simply vanished.

Port Hope and Cobourg also attracted wealthy industrialists, more often than not from smoky cities south of the border, who built grand summer homes on or near the bracing breezes of the lake, turning the towns into what some labelled "Newport North."

Port Union

In 1847, William Helliwell, along with Daniel Knowles and Will Heatherington, formed the Scarborough Markham and Pickering Wharf Company and built a wharf on a stretch of lake west of the mouth of the Rouge River. As early as 1834, Thomas Adams had been building ships right on the beach. Located at the foot of a road that formed the municipal boundary between the townships of Scarborough and Pickering, they accordingly called their dock Port Union. The company extended the dock more than eighty metres into the lake and added a storehouse for the farmers' grain. Nearby, a small fishing colony grew up along the beach. When the Grand Trunk built their new tracks along the shoreline in 1856, the wharf began to lose money, and, following a damaging storm in 1895, closed entirely.

Meanwhile, the railway had found its own particular use for the location. Being at lake level, the railway tracks were at the bottom of steep grades in both directions. Under such conditions, the railways used "helper" engines to assist trains going uphill. Port Union thus became a storage yard for the helper engines. Yards were laid out and a station built, along with a watering tower. Employees lived nearby in small homes on a grid of streets or in the Laskey Hotel. One of two hotels located in Port Union, Laskey's was built originally in 1861 by a Mr. Stoner. The two-storey frame hotel was Georgian in style and marked by its two-storey full-width veranda. Inside were six guest rooms, a dining room, and tavern, and on the second floor a ballroom.

The community flourished, handling a peak of 511 tons of freight and 2,600 passengers in 1859. During the twentieth century a few summer cottages appeared along the water's edge, even as the remains of the wharf were washing away.

With dieselization of engines in the 1950s, however, the rail yard was abandoned. The automobile brought an end to passenger service, and the station and water tower were demolished in the 1970s. Laskey's Hotel became a private residence, ultimately burning to the ground in 1994. It was then that Scarborough's infamous urban sprawl began making its way into the Port Union area and old Port Union's last building came down in the year 2000. Today, the site of the village has become a park serving the growing new neighbourhood. A short distance east, the Rouge Hill GO station keeps alive the area's railway traditions, while the cottages have been removed to accommodate a shoreline park. The legacy of the old port itself survives only in the name Port Union Road and in the now underwater ruins of the old wharf.

Rosebank

Despite having a sheltered lagoon, the mouth of the Rouge River failed to evolve into a harbour of any description. The Grand Trunk had even built its line on an embankment close to the water's edge. It is likely that the wharf and railway station at Port Union deflected to it any potential that the mouth of the Rouge might have had. On the other hand, had pioneer colonizer William Berczy had his way in the early 1800s and completed a canal to this spot, no doubt the lagoon would have become a bustling port. Despite the failure of the river mouth to become a port, a short-lived shipbuilding operation took place between 1810 and 1856.

The tracks and the scenery did briefly attract a resort operation. In 1862, farmer William Cowan acquired two farm lots and named the property "Rosebank." It was here, above the east bank of the river, that John Pollock established a modest resort known as the Rosebank House. It grew and expanded through the 1880s and 90s and included a dance hall and camping and picnic grounds. A cottage community developed around it. The railway added a small station shelter where as many as seven trains a day would call in the high season. At the station, stages waited to take the vacationers the short distance to the hotel.

By the end of the Second World War, the hotel was gone and many of the cottages were becoming permanent homes. Today, the site of the hotel contains a senior's residence and larger houses have replaced the older converted cottages. Only a small number remain on the nearby streets. Rosebank Village is located at the south end of Rosebank Road, south of the railway crossing. Trains still pass along the tracks, crossing the Rouge on a high trestle. The river mouth, now a conservation area, still attracts visitors, but these are day-use visitors enjoying the beach, trying their luck with the fish, or canoeing through the protected wetland behind the railway embankment.

The Rouge Valley itself forms part of one of Canada's largest urban parks, the Rouge Park.[1] This "wilderness in a city" offers high bluffs, a variety of flora and fauna, and, somewhere (they don't tell you exactly), the archaeological remains of a prehistoric aboriginal settlement known as Ganestiquiagon. With the Rouge being an important early fur-trading route, the strategic hilltop palisaded village was used by the Seneca to control the flow of furs, and no doubt the payment.

Dunbarton/Fairport

East of the Rouge, Kingston Road brushes by what has been called the largest natural harbour between Hamilton and Trenton, Frenchman's Bay, an extensive and marshy lagoon protected by a sand spit along the lake. In 1832, William Dunbar took up a large parcel of land on that well travelled road near the head of the bay and laid out a town site. He built a road that

This image from the Illustrated Historical Atlas of Ontario County, *published in 1877, shows early port activity at Frenchman's Bay.*

ran the short distance to the head of the marsh, and built piers, calling the place Pickering Harbour. During this early period, a steady supply of lumber made its way to the docks, while a sizable village grew along the Kingston Road and took Dunbarton as its name in recognition of its founder. But the head of the harbour proved to be too shallow and the bay too prone to silting for the schooners and steamers to dock reliably.

In the 1840s, a company was created, tasked to extend two piers into the water near the sand spit to reach a depth of four metres. When it did, a rival town site was laid out closer to the sand spit and was called Fairport. But Edward M. Hodder, writing on Lake Ontario's ports and harbours in 1857, was not overly impressed, noting that "due to the foulness of the bottom an anchor will not hold during a hard blow."[2] In the 1870s, Joseph McClellan obtained a bonus of three thousand dollars from the Township of Pickering to dredge the shallow harbour and extend the piers. There he built a large grain elevator and warehouse.

In 1856, the Grand Trunk Railway laid its tracks between Dunbarton and the harbour; however, a limestone culvert under the railway embankment ensured that access to the bay was retained. Further improvement to the harbour followed the building of the railway, with the federal government expending eighty thousand dollars to replace the wharf, further dredge the channel, and add a fifty-thousand-bushel barley elevator. But the depletion of the lumber supply in the 1840s and the end of the barley trade in the 1890s doomed the little port. When the Grand Trunk doubled its tracks in the 1880s, access through the Dunbarton culvert was closed. Although a small colony of fishermen continued to cast their nets, Fairport's days as a commercial port were over.

Its proximity to the growing city of Toronto did attract cottagers, and by the 1920s Fairport had developed into a summer cottage community, restoring its older geographic name, Frenchman's Bay. During the prohibition years, the harbour enjoyed a brief notoriety as a rum-running haven, with one local dealer named Black Jack being gunned down by the authorities.

The last half century has brought more waves of change. Highway 401 barged its way in beside the railway tracks and Kingston Road was altered to bypass the old core of Dunbarton. Cottages were turned into permanent dwellings and were in turn overtaken by condominium developments. The sand spit has become a popular park for day users and fisher-folk, while the entire shoreline is now dominated by the hulking form of the Pickering Nuclear Power Plant and a new wind turbine.

Amidst it all, vestiges of this community's long heritage still peek through. Thanks to the diversion of Kingston Road, old Dunbarton still retains the ambience of a village street. A number of early buildings can be found, including a one-time general store, century old homes, and the old Dunbar family mansion, built by William's son J.T. Dunbarton (although it, too, has condos as neighbours). From Bayley Street, which follows the south side of the railway embankment, the pilings from Dunbarton's old piers can yet be seen peeking above the water, while the limestone railway culvert remains in place beneath the tracks.

Fairport, too, has been utterly transformed. Still, one can follow the old streets like Front and Commerce, where the older homes and early cottages, including a one-time store and post office, remain concentrated. By the water's edge, the pilings of the later piers still poke above the water, while a fragment of the area's marine heritage is on display in the shoreline park in the form of a screw-drive propeller. Bordering the bay, the surviving marsh areas, in spite of the waves of development, have been designated as a Class 2 Provincially Significant Wetland.

Ajax

While the story of the community of Ajax is not old, its lakeshore heritage is significant. The need for a munitions manufacturing facility arose during the Second World War and the government needed a safe location on the lake away from significant population centres. The farmland east of Duffins Creek, halfway between Whitby and Pickering, seemed ideal.

So, in 1941, the Dominion Industries Limited (later CIL) acquired nearly 1,200 hectares of land and established a shell-filling plant. While the TNT magazines and burning areas were located by the lake, a town site was laid out south of the railway tracks. The town was given the name Ajax, for the name of the British ship that had helped disable the German warship, the legendary *Graf Spee*.

Here the company built family homes as well as separate dormitories for men and women. The workers enjoyed the benefits of a hotel, bank, post office, and recreational centre, as well as places of worship. Many other workers were bussed in from Union Station in Toronto. In all, more than ten thousand employees toiled over the duration of the war to fill some forty million shells, making Ajax the largest shell-filling operation in the British Empire.

For three years following the war, the buildings in Ajax provided dorms and lecture halls for the University of Toronto's 2,300 engineering students. But the site was called a "shanty-town" campus, and in 1949 the buildings were acquired by Canadian Mortgage and Housing Corporation. By then, Highway 401 had been opened from Scarborough to Oshawa, and more housing was added north of the highway.

In 1958, CMHC turned Ajax over to developers, who transformed the community into a modern suburb. They added an industrial park and four new residential neighbourhoods. The wartime factories were refitted for new uses or replaced entirely. As growth pressure continued unabated, Ajax grew south to the lake and expanded to the extent that its boundaries are now barely discernable from the GTA's growing urban fringe.

Although most of the factories are gone, examples of wartime housing lie south of the 401 and east of Harwood along Kings Court Circle. Postwar housing fills the streets north of the 401 and west of Harwood, where street names like Windsor, Tudor, York, George, and Mary reflect royalty, while others like Cedar, Maple, Beech, and Elm show a natural bent. Where the TNT and testing facilities once stood, Ajax's waterfront parkland has earned high praise for remaining an accessible park and walkway.

One walkway crosses Duffins Creek to its west bank, where the area's heritage goes back much farther. While no village ever grew here in pioneer times, Simcoe Point, located on a promontory along the river, attracted pioneer settler William Peak and the Greenlaw family. In 1912, as demand for waterside recreation was growing, John Greenlaw built the Simcoe House resort hotel. It remained popular for four decades before burning in the 1950s. Near the hotel site, a plaque adorns a large granite boulder to commemorate the site of the Peak-Greenlaw pioneer cemetery, while an information board recounts the story of the Simcoe House Hotel for trail-users. As the trail winds easterly from Simcoe Point toward the footbridge over the creek, a large concrete slab lies overgrown in the bushes. This slab was used as a gun emplacement to test-fire shells into the lake, a rare visible reminder of Canada's wartime contribution.

Port Whitby

There were once two Windsors in Ontario; one situated on the Detroit River, the other, now forgotten, on Lake Ontario. Better known today as Whitby, the village that grew at the mouth of Pringle Creek was initially called Windsor Harbour. As William Smith wrote in 1851, "in order to distinguish it from Windsor in the Western District, an Act of Parliament was obtained changing the name to Whitby."[3]

As early as 1833, John Walsh had used the marshy lagoon to build a storehouse and tramway for shipping wheat and flour, but the shallowness of the harbour required him to transport the goods on scows to ships waiting in deeper water. During the 1840s the government upgraded the harbour by dredging and building new piers. Smith further observed in 1851 that "The harbour is capacious, but its borders are bounded by a considerable quantity of marsh through a small stream that enters the bay. A number of houses have been erected here, but the principal business transacted is in storing and forwarding good and produce for which purpose there are large warehouses … there is also a brewery and an Episcopal church built of stone."[4]

Activity at the harbour increased when the Whitby, Lake Scugog, Simcoe and Huron Road Company built a plank road from the harbour to Port Perry on the shores of Lake Scugog. With the laying of the Grand Trunk Railway a short distance north of the harbour, the road fell into arrears and was taken over by the county in 1876. By then, another railway had been added to the landscape. The Whitby and Port Perry Railway opened in 1871, running from the harbour to Port Perry and later extended from there to Lindsay. It linked with the Grand Trunk at Whitby Junction, where, in 1904, the GT built an elegant new station.

Early on, a town site was laid out by the harbour, about five kilometres from where downtown Whitby would later develop. Here, a number of early buildings still line the half-dozen streets. At 1751 Dufferin Street is the home of former storeowner Richard Goldring, built in 1893. At 1733

Courtesy of the Ron Brown Collection.

The elaborate towered railway station at Whitby Junction served the port of Whitby and is now an art gallery.

Dufferin, the house of John Watson dates back to 1856. Watson was a grain shipper and partner in the failed scheme to construct the road from the harbour to Lake Huron. Brock Street, the main route connecting downtown Whitby with the harbour, likewise contains a number of early buildings, some of them originally hotels.

At Brock and Victoria, the St. John's Anglican Church was built of stone in 1846, and remains the oldest church in Whitby. The delightful Grand Trunk station, with its three wooden towers, was relocated to Victoria and Henry streets, where it now houses the Whitby Art Gallery. And at the harbour itself, while only a few overgrown and rusty rails recount the abandoned rail link, a new park with a gazebo and walkways offers visitors an opportunity to enjoy the vistas of both the lagoon where the schooners once called and the open waters of the lake. A memorial recounts those early shipping days. The location is connected to the Lake Ontario Waterfront Trail system.

Camp X: Birthplace of Bond?

Set amid massive modern factories and warehouses, a stone cairn with the Canadian, British, and United States flags stands alone in a grassy field. The monument marks the site of the mysterious World War Two spy-training camp known by many as simply "Camp X." However, during the dark days of the war it went by such secretive code names as S 25-1-1, used by the RCMP; Project J by the Canadian military, and Special Training School 103 by British intelligence. No matter who called it what, its purpose was to train secret agents in sabotage, map reading, weaponry, and the art of the silent kill.

The camp was started on December 6, 1941, by Sir William Stephenson, chief of British Security Coordination who quietly had acquired the 110-hectare Sinclair farm on Lake Ontario. At first the facility was intended simply to link British and American intelligence — the United States had not yet entered the war. But that would change the very next day when the Japanese air force furtively swooped in on Pearl Harbor in the Hawaiian Islands, nearly wiping out the American Pacific fleet. The farm site was ideal, as its lakeside location allowed easy reception of radio signals from Britain while communicating by land line with the Americans. Between 1941 and 1944, the Camp trained more than five hundred recruits, of which 273 moved on to assignments in South America or for further training in England. Surrounded by a double row of barbed wire, the simple grouping of buildings was so secret that even Canada's own prime minister, William Lyon Mackenzie King, allegedly knew nothing of it.

Also hidden within the inner sanctums of Camp X lurked "Hydra." This was a highly sophisticated coding and decoding centre used to intercept German communiqués. According to Sir William Stephenson's biographer, author William Stevenson, Ian Fleming, a British naval intelligence officer, spent a period of time at the camp where, some have suggested, his fictional 007 agent, James Bond, was conceived, based possibly on Stephenson himself. Others who trained at Camp X included members of the RCMP, the FBI, and the pre-CIA OSS (Office of Strategic Services). Because of its historic link with Camp X, the CIA still refers to its modern day training facilities as "The Farm."

The site consisted of seven buildings, which included one for administration and lectures, two trainees' and officers' quarters, guest quarters, and the wireless station that included the mysterious Hydra. By

1944, the training facility was no longer needed and was turned over to the Royal Canadian Corps of Signals as a cold-war intercept station. Eventually, in 1969, even that function ceased and the buildings were removed.

Today with a LCBO warehouse as its neighbour, Intrepid Park sits silently overlooking the lake and reflecting upon its vital wartime role. The memorial cairn was erected by the Town of Whitby in 1984. Far north of the lakeside site, near the Oshawa Airport, the curious could at one time visit the Camp X museum. Displays included training manuals, radio receivers, radio tubes, an early fax machine, and a resistance decode box from the Hydra station. Sadly, the museum is now closed, and many of the items (at the time of writing) have been put up for sale.

Of the hidden features along Lake Ontario's shore, Camp X was for many years the most secret of all.

Port Oshawa

While the little creek that empties into the lake at Port Oshawa is but a trickle, the lagoon created by the rising lake waters following the last ice age created a natural harbour. Throughout the eighteenth century, the Mississauga would paddle their furs to the lake and to a short-lived fur-trading post built there by the French. In 1822, a settlement road was opened between the fledgling harbour and Lake Scugog. Where it crossed the Kingston Road, five kilometres north, Edward Skae opened a general store and post office, and the crossroads became known as Skae's Corners. Following a series of community meetings to select a new name, the aboriginal word *Oshawa*, meaning "where we get out of our canoes," was chosen.

In the 1840s, the Sydenham Harbour Company was formed and began to construct a pier and breakwater at the mouth of Oshawa Creek. Soon the port, at first known as Port Sydenham, began to export lumber and grain. In 1853, a federal order-in-council established Port Oshawa as a warehouse and clearing port. Further improvements were undertaken by the Sydenham Harbour Company in 1878. Meanwhile, the Grand Trunk Railway had rolled into town, or more accurately between the town and

Above: Since this view of the harbour at Oshawa was taken in the days of steamer travel on the lakes, there have been many changes to the lakefront.

Below: The original buildings of the Port of Oshawa now form the Oshawa Community Museum.

the harbour, and around the station grew a community known as Cedar Dale. As shippers began to migrate to the railway, the harbour declined, eventually closing altogether. In 1930, upgraded to accommodate larger vessels, the harbour reopened.

In 1899, Robert Samuel McLaughlin relocated his carriage works from Enniskillen, north of Oshawa, into the town, and established the McLaughlin Carriage Works. After making car bodies for Buick and Chevrolet for a decade, the carriage works in 1918 became part of the General Motors empire, an industry that still dominates both the town's landscape and its workforce. In 1920, McLaughlin bought up the lakeshore land to the west of the harbour and deeded it to the City of Oshawa to be used as a park. The Jubilee Pavilion (named in commemoration of Canada's Diamond Jubilee) was opened in the park in 1927 and went on to host such dance bands as the Glen Miller Orchestra. Today, now winterized and enlarged, it retains its historic dance floor and for a number of years was the locale for the TV series *Dancing at the Palais*.

But the most prominent features of the port's legacy are the three original houses that formerly made up part of the old port. Now part of the Oshawa Community Museum complex, they include the Guy House, a one-and-a-half-storey wooden farm-style house that dates from 1835 and was home to harbourmaster James Odgers Guy; the two-storey yellow brick Robinson House built in 1846, which resembled a hotel more than a residence; and the unusual Henry House, built in 1849 by harbourmaster Joseph Wood, who used stone ballast from the arriving ships to build his lower floor. After Wood's death, Thomas Henry moved in and added a second floor using wood, giving the structure its unusual appearance. The museum's archives and gift shop are located in the Guy House.

Lakeview Park stretches west for a kilometre to a high bluff from which vistas extend along the lakeshore in both directions. Across the street from the viewpoint is a pioneer cemetery that was relocated from the eastern bank of Oshawa Harbour to accommodate the harbour's expansion. However, access is not permitted into the cemetery grounds. To the east of Lakeview Park the much enlarged port now has the status of a port authority and on occasion welcomes ocean vessels to its docks.

Port Darlington

By 1837 the community of Bowmanville had grown into a prosperous mill village, thanks to the mill operations of William Vanstone. But there remained no convenient port from which to export lumber or the grain from the fertile farmlands. To correct this deficiency, the local business community decided to form a harbour company and develop a port at the mouth of Darlington Creek. By 1851 William Smith was able to write that "Darlington Harbour, or Port Darlington as it is now called, is said to have the longest pier on the north shore of Lake Ontario."[5] Shipments from the port in that year, according to Smith, included "29 thousand barrels of flour, 27 thousand bushels of wheat and 700,000 feet of lumber."[6] By 1856, two piers had been built, both extending out to a depth of four metres. The older pier contained a lighthouse, a waiting room, and an office for passenger vessels, while the newer pier, which paralleled the first one, held grain elevators, warehouses, and a customs house. Regular steamer service, provided by the Royal Mail Line, transported passengers to Montreal, Kingston, Brockville, and Prescott.

By the 1890s the beach beside the harbour was beginning to attract

Courtesy of the Toronto Reference Library, TRL PC ON – 242.

Most of the elegant cottages shown in this early view of Port Darlington are now gone, the site now vacant land as the municipality undertakes a waterfront improvement project.

the summer crowd. A row of Victorian cottages was built along the sand strip east of the harbour, all connected by a beach boardwalk. By the 1920s a small dance pavilion was offering music, and short-term visitors might camp in "Cotton Town" or spend a few nights at the Grandview Lodge. The pavilion was torn down in the 1970s. Although the west-side beach had no road link, a cottage community began to grow there, with access provided by a cable ferry called the *Marianne*. A dance pavilion operated from the time of the First World War until the 1960s. It sat unused for years after, and finally collapsed in the 1990s.

Today the heritage on both sides of the harbour has dwindled. Many early buildings were removed to make way for a lakeside park, while an eclectic array of uses were found for the east side of the harbour, sadly offering little in the way of aesthetic appeal. A short distance east of the harbour a few of the early Victorian cottages still stand, at least at this writing. The only survivor of the grand summer homes is an Italianate brick home, two storeys high with a prominent gable above a full height bay, flanked by a pair of verandas with delicate fretwork around their edges. It was built during the beach's heyday in 1886. Even less remains on the west beach, where many early cottages sit empty, awaiting redevelopment. The remains of wooden wharves are still visible at the harbour's edge.

Many of the early vacationers arrived by rail to the Bowmanville Grand Trunk station situated at the head of the bay. Although the station was demolished in the 1970s, the Station Hotel still stands, its façade preserved. It was built in 1897 to replace the first hotel, the Arlington, which was destroyed by fire. The two-storey brick building is encircled with a wrap-around veranda with a corner door that formerly marked the entrance to "Shaw's Little Store." William Shaw, who built and ran the hotel, also built a number of Bowmanville's residences and was assistant harbourmaster. The hotel today is a duplex residence that VIA passenger trains speed past, few inside the coaches aware of the heritage nearby.

Bond Head

Despite his being one of Upper Canada's more despised political figures, Sir

"Bond Head" Newcastle, Ont.

Jan. 4th.

This morning like a good one. They have no slughing either. But quite a few young men. Ha! Ha! Hope you have a good holiday. Your friend Emma I. Venner.

A well marked-up postcard shows an early view of the port of Bond Head.

Frances Bond Head has no fewer than two Ontario communities named after him. The Newcastle port of Bond Head is one. Bond Head Harbour, as it was originally called, developed around the mouth of Wilmot Creek and was the shipping point for the town of Newcastle, which grew along Kingston Road, a few kilometres north.

In 1833 Charles Clark built the area's first gristmill on Wallbridge's Creek, near the lake, creating the need for a shipping port. That year, the Bond Head Harbour Company was chartered and began work on a pier on the east side of the creek, and by 1840 a small warehouse had been built. Enthusiasm grew, perhaps too rapidly. Although nearly sixty houses were constructed along the grid network of streets beside the harbour, fewer than a third were actually occupied. Similarly, three hotels were built, but only one opened its doors. As Smith wrote in 1846, "[Bond Head] contains about 50 or 60 homes which are very much scattered; about one third are occupied; no store open; one tavern open, two or three shut up."[7] The condition of the harbour didn't impress him much either, for in 1851 he would write, "[Although] piers have been run out into the lake, and sufficient depth of water thus obtained to allow of the entrance between the piers of steamers and other lake craft … there is no basin within the piers of any useful width, the valley at the mouth of the stream being choked up with marsh."[8]

A short distance upstream from the harbour, a gristmill operated and was one of the few activities in the ghost village. In the 1850s Bond Head was amalgamated with the village of Newcastle, and the Harbour Company was re-chartered as the Newcastle Harbour Company. Improvements were made, the pier extended, and a new lighthouse built. In 1852 John James Robinson built a substantial grain elevator on a wharf just east of the pier. While wheat, flour, and lumber made up the bulk of the exports, Bond Head's growth remained slow as the Grand Trunk, with its station nearby, began to take over shipping. In 1893 the mill dam gave way and washed silt into the harbour; five years later the mill was closed. In 1906 a fire on a moored ship damaged the west pier but it remained unrepaired. The final blow came in 1913 when a vicious spring gale destroyed the lighthouse. Port activity ceased.[9]

Today the old network of streets remains visible, while the former village lots are attracting new homes as this former ghost town gains new life. A small parkette has opened by the pier, and along the Lakeshore Road a number of the early homes remain, including a former hotel building. A two-storey home on Mill Street built in 1846 was once the home of a Mr. Robson, a grain elevator owner and one-time president of the Newcastle Harbour Company. But many of the backstreets remain mere laneways, reminding today's visitor that this town was one that once had failed. It is somewhat surprising, given the small size of the community, to find such an extensive Bond Head cemetery on these back lanes.

Port Granby

Lakeshore Avenue leads east from Bond Head, up onto a headland from which a picturesque vista extends along the shoreline. That avenue also leads to a series of villages, among them a ghost town, forgotten ports, and a ghost rail line.

Port Granby was first settled in 1827 on a small mill stream. In 1832 a Mr. Decker (possibly David) began operating a sawmill; his son Stephen built a gristmill nearby. By 1847 enough grain was being produced in the surrounding farmlands that a port was needed, and the Port Granby Wharf

Company was formed. By 1854 it had built a wharf from the mouth of the creek into the lake. The gristmill added a distillery to its operation (as did most gristmills in early Ontario) and local legend purports that a spigot installed on the outside wall allowed farmers waiting to take their loads to the wharf a short sip.

That might not have sat well with David Decker, who in 1867 was granted a licence to run a tavern. Although the harbour at Port Granby was small relative to those at Bond Head and Port Hope, it had managed to claim three grain elevators and was shipping ten thousand bushels of barley a day. But the harbour could not keep up with its rivals and in all of 1881 managed to ship fewer than forty-eight thousand bushels. Other exports included hardwood shingles and ships' masts from the pine forests on the Oak Ridge Hills to the north. When the wharf ceased operation in 1890, stonehookers removed the cribwork and took the stones to Toronto.

Port Granby also had a church, which was relocated in 1917 to Port Hope, and a school. The school operated until 1966, and stands today as a private residence. As Lakeshore Avenue winds into the scenic little gully that shelters the remains of the village, it passes the school, the former hotel, and a couple of early homes. The mill dam ruins lie beside the rushing waters of the little creek. A glimpse of the diminutive cove where the harbour once lay reveals no evidence of this small settlement ever being a busy grain and lumber port.

A number of early farm homes also line Lakeshore Avenue, especially above the valley west of the village. One of the most striking is an intriguing stone house, likely built in the late 1840s. A storey and a half in height, it is marked by twin front bay and gables at each end of the structure, between which extends the veranda; a small gable also perches above the main door.

Newtonville Station

When the Grand Trunk first laid its tracks between Port Hope and Newtonville in 1856, the rails lay perilously close to the lake. Indeed, high waves were known to carry portions of the roadbed into the water. When the GT undertook its major upgrades in the 1890s, it chose to double the line, which meant relocating the tracks farther inland. With the abandonment of the lakeside alignment, that section became a ghost railway. The original Newtonville Station once stood there, but the single-storey frame building was not one of the GT's major investments and was removed when the tracks were relocated. The only goods shipped from the station were grain and lumber, and only on the few milk-run trains that stopped there. The only evidence of Newtonville Station is a pair of rail-workers homes, lying south of the current CNR crossing on Townline Road, and the laneway following the former right-of-way.

Wesleyville

East of Newcastle Station, along Lakeshore Avenue, lie the remains of the ghost town of Wesleyville. Although near the lake, it never developed a port, serving instead the needs of the growing farm community that had developed nearby.

By the 1850s the community could count Edwin Rice's sawmill, a temperance hotel run by Francis Little, as well as a Methodist church and a school. The railway did add a Wesleyville Siding and possibly a station on the original line a short distance north of the settlement. When the church was built, the community became known as Wesley, but when the post office opened in 1875, it became Wesleyville.

Forests have grown up around Wesleyville now. While the church remains standing and in use, with the cemetery behind it, the school sits empty. A solitary L-shaped house, which for a time served as the Wesleyville post office, lies between the two.

Port Britain

The shore at Port Britain is a quiet wave-washed boulder beach. The little stream that pushes through the stones gives little indication that here was once a port with considerable promise. The stream first attracted mill owner Samuel Marsh, who as early as 1800 built a sawmill on its banks. Marsh had arrived in 1797 and built a shanty on the beach. A year later he added a gristmill as well as a distillery and carding mill. A community grew around the mills, including a hotel, school, a blacksmith, and the businesses of various tradespeople.

In 1845 Joseph Major bought the mill, and two years later built a substantial Georgian-style house on the property. But he soon developed financial trouble and left. The mill burned in 1874, then again while being rebuilt. Its smaller replacement was forced to close when the water supply in the creek dropped too low.

Between 1848 and 1854, William Marsh launched three schooners from his shipyard, and in 1858 he helped fund the Port Britain Harbour Company. The town was laid out in building lots near the harbour, where the Grand Trunk put its line and constructed a station. The prospectus issued by the harbour company in 1856 claimed that Port Britain "presents natural advantages for a harbour unequalled by any Port on Lake Ontario; it is surrounded by hills and heavy bluffs, it forms a secluded bay in which vessels may seek shelter ..."[10] The inner harbour, the prospectus adds, would have "commodious" wharves along each side which would be connected to the lake through a channel two hundred feet wide and twelve feet deep. It goes on:

> Added to these natural advantages the Grand Trunk Railway have erected a station at this point ...it is the only place where the line of a railway comes to convenient grade above the level of the lake... It is estimated that a safe commodious harbour can be made at the above mentioned place with piers running into Lake Ontario to twelve feet depth ... and an inner harbour with wharves, cranes and all necessary erections and rail connections.[11]

Most of the harbourfront lots, however, remained unsold as the focus of the village concentrated along Lakeshore Avenue a kilometre to the north. But the harbour impressed Edward Hodder, who in writing his critique of the lake's various harbours enthused, "[there is] great advantage to be derived from this harbour ... a splendid anchorage afforded by the blue clay bottom entirely free of boulders ... [it is] protected by bluffs both to the eastern and western limit."[12]

He adds that the harbour was

> a natural basin of 15 acres with 12 feet of water where piers
> were projected to extend out 700' and would be 300' apart
> … The progress of these works has been so rapid that the
> harbour will be accessible by mid-June… For all commercial
> purposes it possesses great advantage of ample room for
> wharves, stores, shipyards or lumber yards with the Grand
> Trunk running along its entire length at all points.[13]

Along the beach, little evidence remains of the port today. The GT line
was abandoned as part of its upgrading in the 1890s and relocated inland, and
the road bed now serves as a lane for more recently built cottages and homes.
The historical heart of the port lies not by the water but along Lakeshore
Avenue, where one can find the home that formerly served as a hotel on the
southeast corner of the intersection and the handsome one-and-a-half-storey
stone house on the opposite side of the road, built by Robert Marsh in 1853.

The largest house in Port Britain, constructed in 1847 as the Port
Britain mill house by Joseph Major, now goes by the name "Sora Brook."

A short distance west, the Willow Beach Road leads to old Grand Trunk
right-of-way and the 1850s house known as "Willow Beach." Although
privately owned, it served as a YWCA camp in the 1920s. The right-of-way,
now a lane, passes by the north side of the house.

Port Hope

Even though Port Hope failed to evolve into a major Lake Ontario port, it
does possess some of the lakeshore's most intact heritage districts. Its homes,
large and small, its business district, and its railway heritage all rank among
the best preserved, not just along the lake, but in the entire province.

A focus for the Mississauga, the mouth of the Ganaraska River attracted
the attention of fur trader Peter Smith, who built the site's first European
structure. With the flow of Loyalists into Ontario, the government offered
large land grants of 294 hectares to Elias Smith and Jonathan Walton in return

Courtesy of Archives Ontario, 1000 3514 11872.

The harbour at Port Hope has changed considerably since this early view.

for settling forty such families along the river. After 1798, when Smith built a flour mill on the river, growth remained slow, and by 1817 the settlement, then known simply as Smith Creek, contained a mere fifteen houses and two taverns. At this time the settlement was called Toronto, adopting the name Port Hope in 1819 (after the township in which it was located, named in turn for Colonel Henry Hope, the lieutenant governor of Quebec at the time).

Throughout the 1820s the village began to evolve in two sections. On the east bank of the river, homes and industries were built beside the harbour. Here, one of the port's earliest shippers was Captain John Wallace, who established the first wharf and operated a fleet of three schooners for his exporting business. The port was not among the lake's most favoured, however, for as Edward Hodder wrote in 1857, "this port cannot be made by large vessels drawing over 9 feet of water owing to the swell rolling in from the lake ... there is not room to check the speed of the vessel without danger to itself or to others."[14]

And as William Smith had noted a few years earlier, "A fine harbour might be made at the mouth of this stream, well sheltered from the east, west and north, but at present the basin is choked up with marsh. The channel through which the water now finds vent is not more than five or six feet in depth above the piers ... at present with a stiff breeze blowing from any point a very heavy sea rolls in between the piers."[15] While noting that the scenery was "very pretty," Smith also cautioned that the scenery made "the situation of the building lots more picturesque than convenient."

The town by that time had two gristmills, three foundries, three breweries, two distilleries, and a variety of factories. Despite its limitations, the harbour was nonetheless exporting six million feet of lumber and sixty thousand bushels of wheat, along with beer, whisky, and a range of farm produce. About ten vessels were owned at the port, as noted by Smith.

King Street leads from the lake northward, paralleling the river before rising onto the eastern bluff. Here can be found some of Port Hope's oldest structures. On the west side of the river, a second part of the town was evolving, less tied to the harbour and more to its town hall and main street.

When the Grand Trunk arrived, it laid its tracks close to the shore, bridging the wide river valley with a long stone trestle and placing its station atop a bluff beside the lake. The harbour also became the focus of another rail line, that of the Midland Railway, which ran its tracks from the wharves, northward to Lindsay, then extending them to Beaverton and eventually Midland. The railways brought with them a period of prosperity, which prompted the construction of some of the town's grandest dwellings.

Above the high western bluff, Dorset Street and adjacent streets offer views of some of those early mansions. "Idalia," built in the 1860s, stands at the corner of Trafalgar and Victoria streets, its three-storey Italianate tower, domed turret, and wide veranda making it one of the town's most impressive homes. But it has considerable competition: "Penryn Park," now located in the Penryn Park Golf Course west of Victoria, was built in 1859 by Colonel Arthur T. Williams.[16] The building's details are gothic, dominated by steep gables, pointed arches, and a massive tower. Military heroism runs in the family, for Arthur was the son of John Tucker Williams, who had served under Lord Nelson. To commemorate that link, the street to his 1828 home, also called Penryn, was named Trafalgar. Both "Penryn" and "Penryn Park" still stand.

On Dorset Street, east of Bramly, a row of architectural extravagances include "Homewood," a grand southern-style mansion with a pillared veranda. It was built in 1904 by James Schwartz, an American, as a summer retreat, and became part of what was known as "Newport North," the collection of American summer mansions built in both Port Hope and Cobourg. Opposite "Homewood" stands "Hillcrest." Another pillared mansion in the beaux-arts style, it was constructed in 1874 by lawyer and distiller David Smart. It was purchased around the turn of the century by John Schwartz, also an American, who added the southern plantation-style pillars to the front. As with "Homewood," Schwartz used this grand building as a summer retreat. He later changed his name to Black, and the home remained in that family name until 1974. Today, it is a popular bed and breakfast.

A bit farther east stands the "Cone," a gothic-style Swiss cottage built in board and batten in 1858 by Thomas Clarke. The main retail street, Walton Street, is among the best preserved of Ontario's nineteenth-century main streets. Here stretches a solid line of three-storey commercial buildings, many with pilasters extending the full height. Among the most important is the St. Lawrence Hotel. Four storeys high, it was built in 1853, and the fight to preserve it sparked the preservation of many more. Today the main street is a designated heritage district.

With the arrival of the Midland Railway, hotels appeared along John Street, which included the Carlyle, built in 1857 at the corner of John and Augusta and the Midland Hotel on the east side of John, its back door facing onto the railway tracks. Although the Midland line has long been lifted, the former right-of-way is now a pedestrian path. Long gone, too, are the structures this railway had erected. The same happily is not true of those of the Grand Trunk Railway. The little stone station, built in 1856 in the typical Grand Trunk style, consists of a wide low roof and a series of rounded windows that replaced a set of French doors. It was a pattern adopted from the 1840s station-style in Kenilworth, England, and used in Ontario to promote the railway's English roots. The French doors were later filled partway to form windows, and an operator's bay added. In the 1980s the CNR threatened to demolish the heritage structure, but the history-conscious community raised enough funds to restore the stonework on the building and convince VIA Rail to maintain it as a station stop. Today the residents here will argue that their station is the oldest continuously operating station in the country.

The trestle, too, is a heritage structure, built in 1856 (though in the 1890s, it did undergo some reconstruction and was substantially improved). Standing by the water, almost beneath the trestle, is a small, yellow, wood building. It, too, has railway roots, having been the original freight shed for the Grand

The former Canada House Inn is one of Port Hope's earliest structures, dating from 1822. After serving as an inn and boarding house, it is now a private dwelling.

Trunk station. A trestle that parallels that of the Grand Trunk was added by the CPR in 1912. Regrettably, that railway company removed its brick station in 1978, as it did with all its historic stations along its lakeshore line.

While the mansions of Dorset Street may be grander, the buildings that line King Street are decidedly older. By the wharf stands the Canada House Hotel. It was built on the 1801 site of a home built by Elias Smith, founder of Port Hope. In 1822, Captain John Wallace, grain and lumber exporter, bought the property and built a home on it. In the 1870s it became the Seaman's Inn and then the Canada House. Today it is a private dwelling. Built on the slope leading to the beach, it is distinguished by its full-width veranda.

The Turner House at Peter and Mill streets is also a one-time hotel that served visiting seamen. From the Canada House Hotel, a series of identical two-storey houses line King Street, built by the ships' captains who called Port Hope their home port.

King Street also contains two "bluestones." That standing at the corner of Dorset Street East was erected in 1834 by John David Smith, the wealthy son of Port Hope's founder, Elias Smith. A year earlier, the forty-seven-year-old widower had taken a twenty-year-old bride who was from New York State. The American-style mansion was intended to make his new bride feel more at home. The same year, Smith's son, Elias Peter, also married and built a smaller bluestone a block farther south. The term "bluestone" refers to the blue stucco covering the walls.

A visually unfortunate intruder on Port Hope's harbourfront is the controversial Eldorado Nuclear Plant. Its massive bulk so dominates the scene that it is nearly impossible for the mind to fully appreciate the heritage of the harbour area.

Cobourg

It is surprising that Cobourg would develop into a significant port of entry, exceeding the importance of its nearby rival Port Hope, for no river flowed into the lake at this point. Rather, the backshore consisted solely of a sizable marsh. The first settler to the site was considered to be Eliud Nickerson, who built a cabin on the fringe of the marsh. He was followed in 1808 by Elijah Buck, who opened the first tavern, giving the community the first of its many names: Buckville. A roadside community grew a short distance west and acquired the name Amherst, while Buckville was becoming Hamilton, after the township in which it is situated. In 1819 it finally became Cobourg, to honour the marriage of Princess Charlotte, daughter of King George IV, to Prince Leopold of Saxe-Coburg-Saalfeld.

By 1827, Cobourg could count forty houses, four stores, and two taverns, as well as a gristmill and distillery. The only landing for ships was a crude wharf beside the marsh near the foot of George Street. Before the wharves were built, shallow draft schooners were able to manoeuvre up as far as Midway Creek, which entered the marsh near Albert and First streets. Clearly it was time for a proper harbour.

In 1829 a joint stock company was chartered to turn the lakeside marsh into a functioning harbour. By 1832 the company had constructed a second wharf at the foot of Division Street, measuring ten metres wide and extending 180 metres into the lake. But after control of the harbour was transferred to a

Toronto board, the conditions of the harbour began to deteriorate. In 1851, William Smith was moved to write, "At the time of our last visit (1846) a company had been formed, and a dredging machine was at work, cleaning out the interior of the basin, with the intention of forming a harbour of refuge."[17] Clearly, things hadn't improved much by 1857 when surveyor Edward Hodder commented, "a shifting sand bar renders the entrance to the harbour still more dangerous than Port Hope for vessels of deep draft."[18]

When control of the harbour passed into the hands of the Town of Cobourg, improvements followed. The piers were repaired and the shipping channel was widened and deepened to allow several steamships a day to dock. By then a new railway was being anticipated, and in 1854 trains began running on the Cobourg and Peterborough Railway, from the docks to the shores of Rice Lake and then across a trestle and on to Peterborough.

After the trestle was decommissioned in 1860 following several collapses, the railway began to redirect its attention to the iron mines at Marmora. From there schooners and barges carried the ore to a new landing on Rice Lake and then on to the port at Cobourg, where ferries transported the load to Rochester and on to the steel mills of Pittsburgh and Bethlehem.

Word then began to spread around these smoky mill towns that for the well-heeled, Cobourg was a forested fresh air retreat, accessible by those same ferries. One of the first to promote the destination was George Schoenberger, who, along with his American partners, revitalized the Cobourg, Peterborough and Marmora Railway and Mining Company. In 1873, Schoenberger's son George, along with William Chambliss, built one of the earliest hotels to cater to the new tourists, the Arlington, whose extensive lakefront lawn has become today's Victoria Park.

Chambliss marketed Cobourg by embarking, with a town doctor, on an "ozone tour" to likely American markets, promoting the town's "salubrious climate." Other hotels like the Columbian on McGill Street and the Cedarmere on Ontario Street soon followed. But while many of the Americans stayed a few days, some only a few hours while the ferries unloaded, others wanted more than that and soon began to build their own colony of palatial summer homes, one that would acquire the nickname "Newport North."

Between 1880 and 1920 many grand estates were built, most of them to the east of the main portion of town. Places with names like "Sidbrook," "Ravensworth," "Balmutto," and "Cottesmore Hall" became the town's social centres, as dances, horse races, and regattas dominated the summer calendar. Most homes belonged to Pittsburgh industrialists, but even political figures like Ulysses S. Grant built retreats on the shores of the lake. Perhaps the pinnacle of the colony's social events was the 1902 wedding of Vivian May Sartoris, granddaughter of President Grant, to Frederick Roosevelt Scovel, cousin to President Teddy Roosevelt.

Following many years of such socializing, a harsh reality fell upon the American visitors — the Depression. During that devastating debacle, many of the Newport North elite lost all of their wealth, or at least enough of it to vacate their summer palaces and retreat back to the States to recover their lost fortunes.

Only a few of the grand homes remain. The two most easily viewed are the sprawling "Ravensworth," with its pillared porches, located on King Street East, now a correctional facility, and across the road from it, "Sidbrook," which has served as a hospital for a number of years.

But if iron was going south, something besides passengers should be flowing north — that commodity was coal. In 1905 the Ontario Car Ferry Company was formed by the Grand Trunk Railway and the Buffalo, Rochester and Pittsburgh Railroad Company, who built two massive car ferries, the *Ontario Number 1*, launched in 1907, and the *Ontario Number 2*,

Ontario 1, *a rail ferry, docks at Cobourg Harbour.*

launched in 1915. Each was capable of carrying up to thirty rail cars and one thousand passengers. The ships sailed profitably through the 1920s, but profits plummeted during the Depression. Still, the rail cars and the passengers sailed across the lake. Following the Second World War, however, the end was very much in sight as car travel drastically reduced the number of vacationers. The Pennsylvania coal fields were running out and the Canadian railways looked to Cape Breton for their coal. Eventually the railways would abandon coal altogether in favour of diesel. The *Ontario 1* and *Ontario 2* sailed out of the Cobourg harbour for the last time in 1950, and were scrapped in 1952.

In the last two decades, the harbourfront of Cobourg has undergone a total reconstruction. Gone are the rail tracks, the warehouses, and the old docks. In their place are a new marina, a waterfront walkway, and, set back tastefully from the water, a string of low-rise condos. But throughout the town, much heritage has survived. Besides the American grand summer homes, the town's most dominant structure, visually as well as historically, is the massive, domed Victoria Hall. Designed in 1860 by Kivas Tully, the Ontario government architect, the courthouse reflects Cobourg's role as the seat of Northumberland County.

The building itself rises three storeys above King Street and is topped by a pillared cupola with four clock faces. Arches mark the ground-level entrance and four pillars extend up another two floors to a Greek-style gable. The yellow-brick walls are covered on three sides with sand-coloured free stone. Carvings mark the cornices of the pillars, while the three symbols of the United Kingdom — the rose, thistle, and shamrock — are carved at the main entrance. By the 1970s the building was in a dilapidated state. Amid talk of demolition, the citizens of Cobourg managed to round up $6.2 million to save their historic landmark. Now restored, the interior retains its original use as a courtroom, in Old Bailey-style décor, while the grand ballroom on the second floor is decorated with *trompe l'oeil* murals by Joseph Moser. An art gallery has opened on the third floor.

Behind the courthouse, a wide low-roofed yellow-brick building is the market, also designed by Tully but built ten years earlier. To the west of the market stands the former Northumberland County Jail. It was relocated here in 1905, behind an existing mansion that became the warden's home. Many of the cells have been converted to bedrooms in what is now a combination tavern, inn, and museum.

Of the many heritage homes lining Cobourg's streets, one of the finest lakeside dwellings lies at the south end of Ontario Street and is known as "Illahee Lodge." This Italianate villa was originally built in 1878 for lawyer William Riddell, the first recipient of a bachelor of science degree from Cobourg's Victoria College. In 1899, during the Newport days, it was acquired by the Sorias family of New Orleans who made it their summer retreat from the smouldering climate of the Big Easy. A subsequent owner, Senator William Kerr, renamed it Ilahee, an aboriginal word meaning "house by the water."

Now the main office for a motel complex, "The Breakers" is a regency style lakeside cottage built in 1840 for Judge George Boswell. It was bought ten years later by James Calcutt, a brewer from Mountmelnick, Ireland. In 1832, following threats on his life, Calcutt fled Ireland to Canada. In Cobourg, he continued his beer-making and added a flour mill and distillery to his industrial empire. In the same year, he built a two-and-a-half-storey mansion, "Lakehurst," which still stands at 128 Durham. In an ironic and grizzly twist of fate, the same individual who had threatened

Cobourg's "mystery" building, located on Durham Street, may have been an early War of 1812 military structure. It is nicknamed "The Barracks."

Calcutt in Ireland was on his way to Cobourg to finish the job when the ship in which he was travelling wrecked offshore from Cobourg. His body would later wash up on Calcutt's own land.[19]

But amidst other prominent historic structures, such as the original Victoria College built in 1836, VIA Rail's 1905 Grand Trunk station, and the birthplace of Marie Dressler, there is Cobourg's "mystery" building. Nicknamed "The Barracks," this long, low stone building located behind Calcutt's Lakehurst home may have been built during the War of 1812, and is reputed to have been a military supply depot during that conflict. But little factual information has surfaced about its origins, and others suggest it may have been related to a later brewery operation. What is known is that it stood on government land in 1819 and was sold to Calcutt in 1832. It is now being restored.

Lakeport

Between Cobourg and Colborne the lakeshore offered few ports of refuge. While Grafton had a wharf in a small sheltered cove, it failed to flourish, and few of the early observers even mention it. Hodder simply states that Grafton "has a harbour."

Still, in the barley days, teams of horses lined up to ship grain, flour, and whisky. Smith noted that the harbour could offer "12 to 14 feet of water" and that the Rochester boat would call twice weekly. A steam gristmill had been built at the harbour but had ceased operation by the time Smith visited. As Hodder noted in 1857, there was no "inducement" for lake steamers, only for small schooners carrying wood or produce. The last vessel departed in 1890, and the site today is a residential community.

Farther east, Lakeport developed as the shipping point for Colborne, and was known variously as Colborne Harbour or the Port of Cramahe (the township in which Lakeport is situated). In fact, the port at Lakeport predates most of the harbours along this section of the lake. It was settled as early as 1793 by a group of settlers who arrived from the United States, led by Joseph Keeler. He built one of the port's two wharves, and a Mr. Campbell the other. Steamers would pick up passengers here while en route to Toronto or Kingston. Besides the wharves, Lakeport could boast four taverns, including Grime's Tavern, as well as Southon's general store and Sproule's flour mill. Beside the wharves stood coal docks, a seed house, and a large grain elevator, as well as a shipyard where a number of schooners were built over the years. Also along the network of streets were a blacksmith, an Anglican church, a post office, a grain office, and, in later years, a Dominion Canners plant, which for a time became the community's largest employer. But the harbour was too exposed, and when heavy weather threatened, the vessels would have to weigh anchor and seek shelter elsewhere.

In the town plan, two streets converge on the wharves: Ontario and Front. Here earlier homes mix with the new. At the foot of Front, a few old port buildings yet stand, while on Ontario Street a cairn in a small open area commemorates the "Many brave souls who went down to the sea in ships from here and may God bless them." The cairn was donated by J.A. Coyle in 1982. Here, too, lie the remains of Keeler's wharf, buried under landfill. The site today lies on Lakeport Road, a tranquil back road now that most traffic travels the busier Highway 2 through Colborne to the north.

Gosport

The settlement of Brighton began to develop with the opening of the Danforth Road to Picton in 1796, but quickened when a better and more direct road to Kingston followed in 1816. Although nearby Presqu'ile Bay was well sheltered by its shallow waters and dangerous shoals, it remained little more than a harbour of refuge. The head of the bay remained a wide marsh with no prospects of a port in sight. Any traffic through those waters was small boats that had been hauled over the Carrying Place portage from the Bay of Quinte. But two developments changed all that: the arrival of the Grand Trunk Railway in Brighton in 1856, and the construction of a new lighthouse at Presqu'ile Point, with range lights that could now guide vessels safely between the shoals.

The Brighton area was also developing into an important apple growing region, and, as the bay was among the most fertile fisheries along the Lake Ontario shore, a harbour was needed to facilitate the harvesting of the fish in addition to exporting the local farm crops. In 1854, the Presqu'ile Road and Wharf Company was formed to develop a harbour on the shore closest to Brighton. By 1866, four wharves had been completed, along with warehouses and a grain elevator. Eleven fishing boats employing twenty-five fishermen were operating out of the port by 1875, catching primarily whitefish and salmon. The fleet grew into one of the largest on the lake, matching that at Point Traverse in Prince Edward County. One of the leading fishermen was Grant Quick, who owned a fish-packing house. Originally known as Freeman's Point, the port changed its name to Gosport.

The opening of the Murray Canal between the harbour and the Bay of Quinte to traffic in 1889 brought small excursions steamers such as the *Mandy*, the *Rapids King*, and the *Brockville* into the harbour, with schedules that took them through the Bay of Quinte and on to destinations such as Belleville, Kingston, and the Thousands Islands. A few schooners were built at Gosport by the Bullock Brothers. The port was also a point of departure for excursions headed for the hotel and dance halls on Presqu'ile Point.

Despite the opening of the canal, the depth of the harbour remained too shallow for the increasingly larger vessels plying the lake, and soon became the domain of pleasure craft instead. As fishing declined, the warehouses and grain elevators at Gosport were removed. Today the waters are popular with small craft and sport fishermen. The one-time fishing colony and port has been engulfed by the growth of Brighton, with new suburban roads winding along the shore and large modern homes dominating the landscape. On Price Street, a block inland, a substantial early building, now a residence, once served as a hotel and boarding house. A few early homes still stand on the main road and a few of the side streets. Otherwise, old Gosport is a new Brighton suburb.

Though little evidence remains today to indicate that Gosport was once one of the lakes busiest fishing ports, the waterfront has undergone a renaissance, with a new general store, café, and busy marina.

Presqu'ile Point

Presqu'ile Point would have made an ideal harbour were it not for one thing: the dangerous shoals lurking barely beneath the surface. Following the retreat of the last ice sheet, the currents of a newly emerging Lake Ontario began swirling eastward. Where those currents slowed to meet a series of limestone shoals and islands, they deposited their material. As a result, a long sand spit began to develop into the lake.

In the 1790s, with demand for land increasing for the Loyalists arriving, government surveyors were ordered to lay out a town site on the peninsula that protected the waters of Presqu'ile Harbour. By 1797 the plan was compete and showed three large blocks containing seventy-six lots (0.4 hectares each), with areas set aside for a market square, church, school, jail, and cemetery. When the government created the new District of Newcastle in 1800, it chose to locate the seat of government in the new town site on the shore of the protected bay. In short order they built a courthouse and jail.

But the new location would shortly be put to a severe and tragic test. In 1804, a Native man named Ogotonicut was arrested in the death of a fur trader near Lake Scugog. Although the site of the crime lay in the newly created Newcastle District, the judiciary lived in Toronto. It was therefore necessary to transport all involved to the new district courthouse for trial. On October 7 they boarded a schooner called the *Speedy* and set sail for Newcastle (as the town site was called). As the ship passed the bluff near Lakeport, a gale blew up and the schooner vanished from sight. The *Speedy* was lost with all on board. It quickly became apparent that the new district seat was in a poor location and the government moved it to Amherst, a village that would later become Cobourg.

Although a few squatters, including some boat captains and shipbuilders, remained at the now abandoned town site, the area remained undeveloped until 1869, when surveyor A.B. Perry arrived to resurvey the old town plan. He found that the squatters had been cutting some of the valuable timber, and that the protected bay had attracted a Canadian pirate named Bill Johnson, a deserter to the American side during the War of 1812, who would on occasion seek shelter here while he plundered British ships on Lake Ontario or along the St. Lawrence River.

Following the survey, the land was transferred to the federal government in order to protect the harbour, and many of the squatters were granted leases. Hunters, fishermen, and campers were likewise attracted to the undeveloped reserve. In the 1880s, Presqu'ile's first summer cottage

Hotel Presqu. Isle Point, Brighton, Ont., Canada

Courtesy of the Toronto Reference Library, TRL PC ON 318.

The once busy Presqu'ile Bay Hotel is now only a grassy park, although the dock remains intact, as do the steps.

appeared, followed by campers using the shore near the lighthouse. In 1905, these sites were surveyed into lots to accommodate the campers.

Presqu'ile's first hotel appeared in 1905, when Peter Covell built one large enough to accommodate fifty guests. It stood on the bank between Salt Point and Calf Pasture Point, facing the bay. Guests would arrive, often by train, at the Grand Trunk station in Brighton and then be transported by stage to Gosport, where they would board ferries to the hotel. Ferries such as the *North King* and *Caspean* brought vacationers from as far as Rochester. Covell enlarged the Presqu'ile Hotel in 1912 before selling it to William McCallum and Grant Quick of Gosport. After buying the hotel, Quick opened the Presqu'ile Pleasure Palace, which soon became a popular dance pavilion.

Through the 1930s and 40s, cottagers added summer homes to the shoreline, while campers and bathers frolicked in the shallow sandy waters. On the bay side more cottages appeared while holidayers filled the hotel to capacity and danced the night away in the dance pavilion. In 1955 the province adopted a new vision for the park — a private community on the original town site on the bay side, and a public park with no private

This lighthouse, a fixture in Presqu'ile Point Provincial Park, has prevented many a wreck on the point's hazardous shoals.

holdings on the lake side. When the bayshore cottage community was turned over the Township of Brighton for administration, the government set about cancelling the cottage leases within the new park boundaries and removing the buildings. In 1971, Grant Quick died, and his hotel and dance hall were demolished. The property was subdivided and more homes built.

Today, Presqu'ile Point Provincial Park is one of southern Ontario's most popular. Wide, sandy beaches attract day-use visitors on warm summer days, while the lakeside campsites fill quickly and usually require reservations. The lighthouse at the tip of the point remains the most important heritage feature in the park. Completed in 1838, the twenty-one-metre tower was built of limestone, and whitewashed to increase visibility. The entrance to the tower was an unusual gothic-style doorway, and the lantern, which at first used whale oil, was designed in an octagonal bird-cage pattern with an ogee (or pointed) dome on top. Inside, the tower's five storeys were linked with five ladders of sixteen steps each.

In 1842 a keeper's house was built nearby, and in 1896, to protect the limestone exterior from further deterioration, the tower was sheathed in cedar shingles. A foghorn situated in a wooden house was added in 1906. In 1965 the lantern was removed and the light replaced with an airport beacon. Today the building still stands in its photogenic shoreline setting. The keeper's limestone house was turned over the park and has been enlarged to include an interpretation centre. While nearly all of the park's cottages were removed, one that remains enhances the park's heritage. On the road to the lighthouse, the château-style "Stonehedge" is now reserved for park staff. Built by Jack Wilson in 1938,[20] the one and a half storey limestone house has a recessed roadside entrance, and hip-gable dormers on the second level. A wide window overlooks the lakeside lawn. By the road, a stone fence and gate mark the approach to the building.

Meanwhile, the former town site has become more of a residential suburb of Brighton than a cottage community, although several early buildings yet stand. The site of the old hotel and its wharf is now marked with a small park where the hotel wharf still juts into the now quiet waters of the bay.

Chapter 6
'Round the Bay: The Ports of the Bay of Quinte

The limestone ridges of Prince Edward County rise from Lake Ontario in a series of mesas and valleys. Thanks to the forces of ocean deposits and glacial scouring, the ridges trend southwest to northeast. Into the valleys poured the postglacial waters of Lake Iroquois, which, once lake levels lowered, become Lake Ontario. The bay it created is a curious zigzagging of cliffs and deep bays that offered shelter to water travellers, but created a long, irregular route.

Into the far western end of the bay poured the waters of the Trent River, fed by the many inland lakes and rivers of the Kawartha system. During the 1600s, the river was variously named the Tanaote and the Sagetewedgwam, until 1790 when the name Trent came into use (possibly due to the influence of Simcoe again).

Trenton

With American victory in their war of independence, Loyalist supporters were forced from their homes, and many fled to Canada. The destination for many United Empire Loyalists (UEL) was the shore of the Bay of Quinte. Although the refugee settlers concentrated more along the eastern reaches of the Bay of Quinte and the Lake Ontario shore near Adolphustown, it was one such UEL, Captain John Walter Meyers, who was the first to arrive at the western end of the bay and the mouth of the Trent River.

When his application for a land grant on the Trent was rejected, he chose a site farther east, now Belleville. Hence, John Smith and John Bleeker became the first to settle at the mouth of the Trent River. Following Bleeker's death, his widow, who was Meyers' daughter, moved to the mouth of the river in 1807 and opened a tavern as well as a ferry operation to convey passengers across the river.

Fortunately for the fledgling settlement, the watershed of the Trent River accessed a vast resource of timber, and waterways down which to float logs for processing or for export. Still, growth was slow at first. The only exports were pine masts floated down from the north for export to England. However, the War of 1812 would change all that, as demand for lumber soared.

The first survey for the fledgling town took place on the west side of the river in 1834. Although a handful of log and frame homes, stores, churches, and a school had already been built, the survey opened up the town site for more growth. The east had been previously surveyed under an order from Bishop John Strachan of Toronto in 1829, an area he named Anndale, but it remained largely unsettled. Up until 1837 the settlement remained known as River Trent. That year the lieutenant governor, Sir Francis Bond Head, declared the mouth of the river to be a port of entry, and the name was changed to Trent Port.

In 1846 William H. Smith observed that Trent Port was "principally supported by the lumber trade, immense quantities of timber being brought down the river. An excellent bridge has been constructed across the River Trent at this place. The Toronto and Kingston stage passes through the village, and during the season a steamboat leaves daily for Kingston, calling at Picton, Belleville, Bath, Amherst Island and other landings."[1] Five years later, Smith would add that the town contained 950 inhabitants and had a tannery and distillery: "The river is here a fine sheet of water and a boom is fastened across it to catch the lumber…. A long covered bridge crosses the Trent having a swing bridge near the western extremity for the convenience of vessels wanting to pass."[2]

In 1853, when the settlement was incorporated as a village, it took today's name, Trenton. Efforts to designate the town as the district capital for the then District of Victoria failed. Shortly after, Belleville became the county seat for the newly created Hastings County in which Trenton was located, while Lindsay became the county seat for a separate Victoria County. By then, changes were underway that would alter the destiny of the town dramatically: construction of the Trent Canal began in 1833 with its first lock in Bobcaygeon; and in 1856 the first train of the Grand Trunk Railway puffed into the Trenton station, although the stop was five kilometres north of the town site.

By the mid-1870s, Trenton's industrial base had boomed, adding two steam sawmills, two gristmills, a brewery, and a paper mill, in addition to the usual range of small industries and shops, with "several good hotels," as the county atlas of 1876 duly added. The major industry for much of Trenton's early existence was the Gilmour Lumber Company. From 1852 their mills and docks occupied most of Trenton's waterfront on the east side of the river, where the company employed a workforce of four hundred and turned out two hundred thousand feet of lumber a day. The mills operated for a half a century, finally closing in the early 1900s.

Transportation continued to improve, adding to the town's growth. On October 7, 1879, another railway arrived on the scene — the Prince Edward County Railway, linking Trenton with Picton. In 1884 the railway was renamed the Central Ontario Railway (COR) as it was extended to the iron mines of Coe Hill. The line would eventually reach the remote northern Hastings community of Maynooth, where it would erect a massive concrete station that survives to this day. The Murray Canal was cut through the neck of what had been the Prince Edward County Peninsula in 1889, allowing vessels to avoid the tortuous bends in the Bay of Quinte.

In 1911, William Mackenzie and Donald Mann brought their Canadian Northern Railway (CNOR) to town, buying up the COR in the process. In the centre of the town they erected a magnificent brick station, two and a half storeys in height, with a full gable, six dormers, and a wraparound canopy. They also added a roundhouse of fifteen stalls. Shortly afterward, the Canadian Pacific Railway (CPR) added their tracks to the town's railway landscape, building for themselves a stylish Tudor-*esque* station and a divisional facility, along with a roundhouse of their own that contained forty-four stalls. The crumbling old covered bridge was replaced in 1914 by a steel-truss structure.

While the railways arrived in rapid succession, work on the vital Trent Canal languished. After the first lock was opened at Bobcaygeon in 1833, the remaining work proceeded slowly. By 1911 it still had not reached

Trenton, and encompassed only the 110 kilometres between Washago and Healey's Falls, north of the town. It was not until 1920 that the first vessel left the town dock to finally navigate the completed Trent Severn Canal.

Despite the delays in finishing the canal, steamers and schooners continued to stream in and out of the port, carrying lumber and grain, especially barley, to the American markets on the south shores of the lake. As tourism developed, excursion steamers would carry happy holidayers to the Thousand Islands. A shipyard at the port catered to the buildings and repair of the ships. But Trenton's next major employer did not depend upon the railway or canals. Rather it was the construction of the Royal Canadian Air Force station on the eastern limits of the town in 1931 that employed thousands, even through the Depression. By 1980, more than one thousand civilians were employed at the base.

The years that followed the Second World War would once more transform the face of the town. Cars and trucks became the main means of travel and the steamers no longer called. By the 1960s, Highway 401 was open north of the town, allowing through traffic to bypass Trenton's once congested core. Riverside industries had gone, leaving vast, empty, overgrown lots, while new industries chose larger lots near the new highway.

For the most part, heritage preservation has not fared well in Trenton. Of its important municipal buildings, only the tower of the old post office survives, along with the 1861 town hall and market. The CN tore up the COR tracks in the 1980s after having torn down its attractive station earlier to make way for a supermarket. Even the sturdy iron railway bridge that crossed the river is gone. Only the roundhouse has survived and now contains a variety of businesses. With the end of steam, the CPR removed its divisional facilities, and tore down its station in 1978. The CNR, meanwhile, replaced their elegant Trenton Junction station with a glass shelter that still enjoys daily service from VIA Rail.

No evidence remains along the riverbanks of the lumber industry or the port activities, although an attractive riverside park has been created on the west bank. On the more positive side, many grand early homes have been preserved, especially along King, Dundas, and Victoria streets. Among them are the Second Empire home built for grain merchant William Jeffs in 1884, which stands at 116 King Street, and the "Gable," built in the same year for leather merchant Samuel Squire Young, at 178 Victoria.

The origins of the cannon perched atop Trenton's Mount Pelion remain a mystery.

Overlooking the town is what might be one of the more curious heritage features along the Lake Ontario shore. Mount Pelion rises more than sixty metres above the streets below; on its summit, facing the centre of the town, rests an ancient cannon. Its exact origin is unclear, but many believe it arrived on a British ship during the War of 1812. Shortly after, it was hauled by six teams of horses to the summit of the "mount," where for several years it boomed a royal salute each Victoria Day. The practice ended after 1898 when an unusually loud blast shattered a number of shop windows. Today, a single-lane roadway winds to the summit, where a plaque commemorates the town's early history, and a set of steps lead farther up to the cannon. Behind the cannon, a small lookout tower grants a wide-ranging view of the town, the hills behind, and the Bay of Quinte.

Belleville

Here, where the Moira River tumbles into the Bay of Quinte, a group of

Mississauga had established a small settlement close to their sacred burial ground, calling it Asaukhknosk, or "the place where the rushes end." In 1785, as the Loyalists began moving onto their land grants, Captain George Single-ton opened a trading post near the river's mouth. In 1787, William Bell added a second post in the area. But they still needed to journey to Kingston to pick up their supplies. In September 1789, Singleton set out by bateau for the jour-ney. Before he could make it back to Belleville, he contracted a fever and died.

In 1789, John Simpson arrived and opened the area's first tavern, considered the best between Kingston and York. It became something of a community centre where town hall meetings alternated with town balls. John McNabb took up land beside that owned by the Mississauga in 1803, and built mills and a dock from which he began shipping furs, potash, and lumber. The following year a ramshackle wooden bridge was slung across the river, where Bridge Street now crosses, replacing the precarious and inconvenient small ferries and a floating bridge that connected Dundas Street on the east side of the river with Dundas on the west.

At this time, none of the land had yet been surrendered by the Mississauga. A key impetus to the growth of the river-mouth settlement was the arrival of Captain John Meyers, who built a lumber and gristmill a short distance upriver — the only mill at the time between Napanee and Port Hope. His efforts to locate his enterprise closer to the river mouth had previously been rebuffed by the government, pending settlement of the Mississauga lands.

Finally, in 1816, a deal was reached, and the Mississauga deeded the land to the government. To celebrate the event, the lieutenant governor of Upper Canada, Sir Francis Gore, arrived, accompanied by his wife Annabella, familiarly known as "Bella," and it is alleged that the community in turn named its post office Belleville after Mrs. Gore.[3]

Almost immediately, Sam Wilmot surveyed out a town plot on the east bank of the river and settlers quickly began to take up the lots. Most of the first homes and hotels were built on the south side of Dundas, the east–west route following the shoreline. One of the town's earliest entrepreneurs arrived in the form of a Brockville businessman named Billa Flint. Despite referring to the town as a dirty, dilapidated place, knee-deep in mud, he built a wharf and erected the town's first steam sawmill. His mill expanded, and soon had one hundred saws and a workforce of ninety men, who turned out enough lumber to load a schooner every day.

By 1846, when W.H. Smith visited Belleville to prepare his *Canadian Gazetteer*, he observed: "It is a bustling and thriving town and a place of considerable business. The greater portion of the town lies rather low but it possesses many good buildings. It was incorporated in 1835 and now contains 2,040 inhabitants. The jail and court house is a handsome stone building and is erected on a rising ground in the rear of the town."[4] He also observed that travel was frequent: "The Kingston and Toronto stages pass through the town daily, and during the season a steamboat calls daily on its passage to and from Trent and Kingston."[5] But he expressed frustration on trying to get information on the products shipped from the harbour: "In consequence of the short-sighted policy of some of the merchants in Belleville who refused to allow any account of the products shipped from the place to be published on the plea that the exports were so large that the publication of their amount would immediately cause the town to be inundated with fresh businesses to the loss of the merchants already established there."[6]

When he returned five years later, he was able to claim that the "gentlemen in question have since seen the folly of the advice tendered them and have become awake to their real interest ... we found amongst the inhabitants every disposition to assist us ..."[7] He learned that nearly fifty-three thousand pounds of goods were exported from the harbour, split almost evenly between farm products and lumber, with wheat and flour being the leading farm exports. The government, he noted, had declared Belleville a port of entry and equipped the town with a collector of customs and inspectors of potash, beef, and pork. Four vessels were owned by merchants in Belleville, including a steamer and three schooners.

Had Smith returned a few years later, he would have witnessed the transformation initiated by the railway age. In 1856 the Grand Trunk built their traditional style of stone station some distance north from the lake, as was their custom, in order to avoid competition with the port. Here, too, the railway established a divisional point with roundhouse, offices, and maintenance facilities.

In the 1870s the firm of Flint and Horton built a large grain elevator on the stone foundations of the first mill. By this time, Belleville's waterfront was lined with sawmills and grain elevators, its wharves crowded with tall-masted schooners and steamers. Hugo B. Rathbun was attracted to the Belleville harbour in the middle of the century, and built a one-hundred-saw steam sawmill. The family shipping interests expanded to include grain, cement, and coal. However, high taxes prompted Rathbun to relocate to Deseronto. Today's Victoria Park marks the site of the renowned Rathbun steam sawmill.

Passenger ships called regularly, including the *Hastings*, which plied between Belleville and Kingston, and the *Kincardine*, which carried passengers to and from Oswego in New York State. Ferries shuttled residents back and forth to the shores of Prince Edward County until 1882, when the first bridge to span the bay was opened. The longest bridge in Ontario at the time, it consisted of a dozen steel-truss sections and a swing bridge near the Prince Edward County shore. (It was replaced in 1927 by a causeway that in turn gave way to the Norris E. Whitney High Level Bridge in 1982.) Other ferries carried merrymakers across the bay to the popular pleasure ground at Massassauga Point.

Twenty years would pass before more rails were laid. In 1877 the Grand Junction Railway began running along Pinnacle Street on its way to Peterborough. The line ran from a switching yard on the waterfront, stopping by its station located in a one-time Methodist church near the market square. In 1914 the Canadian Pacific and the Canadian Northern Railway arrived, not only at the same time, but on the same tracks, and using the same station. Their joint line ran close to the water's edge, where they built a two-storey brick station, employing the same Canadian Northern architectural style as that used in Cobourg and Port Hope.

By this time, Belleville had become a raucous port and railway town, with more than twenty hotels and taverns, many by the wharf, while others were gathered around the Grand Trunk railway yards to the north. Thanks to the proximity of the Corby Distillery at Corbyville, a few kilometres to the north, Belleville figured prominently in the rum-running trade during the American prohibition years and those in Ontario as well. Boats would be loaded from boxcars at the Belleville wharf and then sail out to hide behind Cedar Island until after dark. With liquor sales banned in Ontario, as well (although the manufacture and export was not), the smugglers would simply sail down the coast and then land at places like Point Anne or Shannonville to distribute the whisky locally. One of the main purchasers turned out to be the prestigious Belleville Club.

Only medical personnel could legally buy whisky, and that is exactly what Belleville veterinarian Doctor Hedley Wellbanks did. But rather than distribute it to "patients," he simply loaded the cargo into one of his three boats and hoped to avoid capture at the hands of the vigilant American Coast Guard. But in Wellbanks's case, the Americans were a little too vigilant, for, perhaps unbeknownst to them (or perhaps not), they took over one his boats, the *Rosella*, while it was still in Canadian waters and auctioned it off to an American fishing company. Later, while on a fishing operation, the new owners tied the boat, now renamed the *Vespra*, at the nearby fishing village of Gosport. Wellbanks armed himself and convinced the local customs officer to accompany him while he took back his boat. However, it was Wellbanks who was arrested for carrying a weapon and for theft. Eventually the doctor was acquitted, for, as the judge noted, the boat had been illegally seized in the first place.

Prohibition ended and the Second World War began. Following that conflict, Belleville would begin to change. Dundas Street became the busy Highway 2, carrying increasing automobile traffic. As the highway was widened, roadside commerce replaced the trees and early homes. The wharves and grain elevators were dismantled, to be replaced with landfill and parks. Heritage buildings were torn down, or burned, and are now the site of modern stores and offices. With the demise of the Canadian Northern Railway in 1923, only the Canadian Pacific Railway remained to use the lakeside tracks, and in 1978 the handsome brick station was demolished.

While much of Belleville's shoreline heritage has vanished, some survivors linger. The Belleville Animal Hospital still hugs Dundas Street east of Front, much as it did when this stone building opened in 1830 as a stage stop on the road to Kingston. On Dundas West, the Scottish style of Alexander Chisholm's home is unmistakable, and dates from before 1812. While the harbour has been enlarged to include a marina and modern condos, a handful of early wharf-side buildings recall the days of tall masts and steamships. One of those is one of Belleville's oldest structures. Located at 45–47 South Front Street, it is known as the "McIntosh-Ridley" house. A plain, Georgian-style, wood-frame home, it was built in 1817 by Marsha McIntosh, widow of a ship's captain named John McIntosh. The original fireplace, complete with bake oven, still survives in the kitchen.

The Hotel Quinte has been refurbished and is one of the few to remain from the headier days. Opened in 1895, it stands at the corner of Bridge and Pinnacle streets. While much has been lost on historic Dundas Street,

Bridge Street still possesses one of the finest collections of heritage homes on the bay, especially east of the Hotel Quinte. These include the mansion built by lumber merchant David Bogart, which, with its mansard roof, stands at Bridge and John, and the home known as "Glanmire," built in the French château-style by John Phillips in the later 1800s, now a museum. West of the bowstring bridge across the Moira, Bridge Street may contain few grand homes, but it is here that one of Belleville's more unusual houses is found. Wrapped in an elaborately decorated two-storey porch, the stone house has the appearance of a Mississippi riverboat, hence its nickname, the "River Boat" house. The original stone portion dates to 1832, when James McNabb owned the land on the west bank of the river. Later, in 1859, a lawyer, Horace Yeomans, bought the property and added the two-storey veranda with its ornate trimmings. Since that time, the street has filled in with modern homes, apartments, and malls.

Situated on the west bank of the river, opposite the city hall, stands the Billa Flint House. Lumber-merchant Flint built this two-storey brick

Georgian-style home in 1835. All other contemporary buildings around it have been demolished and the Flint House stands alone. However, the most visually prominent of Belleville's lakefront heritage buildings is the grand old city hall. Built in 1873, with red brick and limestone trimming, its clock tower soars more than sixty metres above the street and offers a stunning vista when viewed from the park by the Flint House on the west side of the river.

Belleville's town hall, built in 1873, still casts its reflection on the vital Moira River.

Point Anne Ghost Town

For many years the tall chimneys rising above the treetops assured travellers westbound on old Highway 2 that they were approaching the outskirts of Belleville. While the structures were not part of Belleville itself, they were the sole industry that created the village of Point Anne, and the reason the place died, or nearly so.

The industry was cement, and the single factory belonged to the Canada Portland Cement Company. A new process, using limestone and referred to as Portland cement, had replaced the earlier method that relied on nearby marl deposits. During the closing years of the nineteenth century, the Canada Portland Cement Company bought up many of the older operations, shutting most of them down, preferring to concentrate the manufacturing closer to the limestone deposits.

In 1905 the Belleville Cement Company opened a plant at the west end of Point Anne, while the following year the Lehigh Cement Company opened at the east end. Here, where the limestone bedrock lay at the surface, the cement companies had ready access to the necessary raw materials. Both companies provided housing and facilities for their employees, as Belleville was not particularly accessible. While some of the cement went by ship, most was shipped along a long-forgotten rail line known as the Thurlow or Belleville and Point Anne Railway. Originally electrified, it switched to diesel in 1951 to allow use by the CN and CP.

In 1909 the Canada Portland Cement Company moved in and bought both plants, shutting the Belleville Cement plant down in 1914. Between the two plants, yet another settlement, also called Point Anne, began to evolve, this one independent of either company operation. This section of town had two general stores, two grocery stores, a Roman Catholic and a United church, and an Orange Lodge and two-storey school, both constructed of cement blocks.

The Canada Portland Cement Company operation thrived for sixty years, their stacks long a landscape icon. In 1974 the company was merged with Lafarge, which moved the operations to the Bath area and closed the plant in Point Anne, having sold the site to Point Anne Quarry. Quarrying operations began in 1975, using the Thurlow railway line. However, the rail operations lasted only a few years.

Point Anne's former school is now a residence in this near ghost town situated a short distance east of Belleville.

With the end of the cement works, the tall chimneys came down and most of the company houses were removed. Today, only overgrown yards serve to remind the visitor of the town sites. The St. Anne's Catholic Church was demolished in the 1990s — only the foundation is left to mark its location at the east end of the town site. A small plaque is embedded in the foundation of the United church indicating that it was built in 1925.

Although the school building survives, it is now a residence, as is the former Orange Lodge building that sits close to the school. Much of the independent middle community still survives, with the earlier workers' homes mingling with a few newer homes. Near the former eastern cement plant site, a few of the grander management homes stand out with their larger lots and more elegant landscaping. At the west end, however, cracked sidewalks lead past overgrown foundations.

Shannonville

Shannonville today is nearly surrounded by the Tyendinaga First Nation Territory and thus buffered from the suburban sprawl creeping eastward from Belleville along the busy Highway 2. Upstream from the mouth of the Salmon River, which the Mohawk called Gosippa, Francis Wallbridge and Warren Noble recognized the potential of a waterfall for providing power for a sawmill. But as the land belonged to the Mohawk, the two men had to negotiate a lease. In 1818, they obtained a 999-year lease on eighty hectares, in return for an annual donation of flour. Wallbridge and Noble built a mill with seventy saws on the site, one that was capable of producing five million board feet of lumber a year.

Known at first as Salmon River, the community's postal name was changed to Shannonville to reflect the Irish home of the pioneer Portt family. Because the Salmon River was navigable to its mouth on the Bay of Quinte, the village was declared a port of entry, and a wharf was built. However, the shallowness of the river meant that the schooners had to moor at the mouth while smaller barges shuttled the flour and lumber to them.

In 1851 William Smith visited the village and noted that it was "built on a bed of rock about a mile from the bay. [It] contains about 250 inhabitants, a sawmill containing five circular and three upright saws, two tanneries three asheries and a post office; a grist mill is erecting."[8] The gristmill Smith referenced was a four-storey stone building on the river beside the sawmill, capable of producing two hundred barrels of flour a day. In 1856 the Grand Trunk built a standard stone station a short distance north of the river, and boat traffic dwindled. As *Belden's Illustrated Historical Atlas* would note in the 1870s, "The Salmon River formerly was navigable for the flat bottoms up to the village, but has fallen to such an extent that navigation is rendered impracticable except for a short distance up from the bay."[9]

Because Shannonville has not shared in the growth of nearby places like Belleville and Napanee, its heritage remains relatively unaltered. The mills are gone, but the river still pours over the old mill dam. A pair of early hotels, one of brick and the other of stone, where the name remains visible on the stonework, still stand on the main street. Queen Street follows the river for a kilometre, along which an old beaten sidewalk remains; likely it once led to the wharf. Several simple early homes still line the quiet street.

The remains of Shannonville's main street show that its heyday as a busy port and mill town is long gone.

The station was removed in the 1960s, and the station hamlet that grew around it has become the site of more recently built homes. Still, in the village proper, few new homes have arrived, leaving Shannonville a relic of its once busy days.

Deseronto

Walking the quiet streets of Deseronto today, it is hard to imagine that this bayside community was for many years one of eastern Lake Ontario's busiest industrial towns.

As was happening along much of the Bay of Quinte, the British government in 1784 acquired the land at the mouth of the Napanee River from the Mississauga and offered it to those who had fought for the British during the American Revolution (archaeologists have dated aboriginal habitation back to the 10th century). One of those to receive land was a Mohawk leader named Captain John Deserontyon. After his daughter

Courtesy of the Lennox and Addington County Museum and Archives, N 3901.

The Rathbun Lumber Company's harbour complex once drove the industry at Deseronto, but nothing remains of it today.

married a Scottish fur trader named John Culbertson, she and her husband inherited the land. Here on the water, Culbertson built a wharf from which to ship lumber, and the community obtained its first unofficial name, Culbertson's Wharf. In 1837, Culbertson obtained full title to the land and began to lay out a town site.

In 1848, Hugo B. Rathbun, along with Thomas Howe and L.E. Carpenter, began a sawmill operation that would mark the start of the extensive Rathbun empire. By then, the settlement was known, appropriately enough, as Mill Point. In 1881 it was renamed Deseronto to honour its founder. When Rathbun's son, Edward Wilkes Rathbun, took over from his father, he diversified the operations to include a shipyard, railway car works, gasworks, and chemical works, along with a flour mill, terra-cotta factory, and a sash and door factory — a massive complex that lined the wharves. It was from these wharves that Rathbun launched his railway line, the Bay of Quinte Railway.

After establishing his shipyard in 1867, Rathbun realized that he needed a link to the railway network then extending across Ontario. In 1882 the line was connected with the Grand Trunk Railway at a point west of Napanee. At the end of Mill Street, Rathbun extended a pier into the bay, where he built a railway-ship depot and transfer warehouse. Two parties benefited — Rathbun was happy, as he now had a link to the railway, and the Grand Trunk was happy because it now had access to a port.

Meanwhile, the community leaders in Napanee were beginning to realize the potential of building a rail line to the interior. Such a connection would allow access to newly discovered mineral deposits and provide an alternative to transporting logs using the tedious and seasonal rivers. In August of 1882, the first train of the Napanee, Tamworth and Quebec Railway rolled into the more northern community of Tamworth. By 1890, to access the timber potential to the north, the line was further extended northwesterly into Tweed and Bannockburn, and then easterly to Harrowsmith and into Kingston. At Bannockburn it connected with the Central Ontario Railway, and at Harrowsmith with the Kingston and Pembroke line.

This brought Deseronto to its peak of prosperity. Its population was then four thousand and the town acquired a new town hall and the Naylor Theatre, where audiences of up to 550 would come to watch plays and musicals. But far in the interior, the timber supply was running out, the mines were yielding little, and the cement operation at Marlbank had been superseded by the perfection of the Portland cement process and was abandoned. With little reason to exist any longer, the Rathbun empire went out of business in 1923.

The effect on the town was devastating. In less than ten years its population had plummeted to 1,300. A few other industries filled the gap, in particular the E.B. Eddy Company, a cannery, and Bridgewater Ropes, which became a major employer. But beginning in 1935, the CNR, then operator of the old railway, began abandoning sections of the line until, in 1941, the last link to Napanee was gone.

Today the harbour wharves sit empty. Factories, foundries, and shipyards are now reduced to bare foundations and overgrown pilings. Here and there trees and shrubs encase the relics of rails and rail cars but no sign of the tracks or the station remain. Yet much of the town's heritage has managed to survive, likely due to the irony of being economically neglected. On the main street, the town hall and the post office remain the dominant

Although Deseronto's main street is pretty quiet, the historic Naylor's Theatre may be given new life with recent proposals to rejuvenate theatrical productions.

structures, although many of the stores have long ago closed their doors. The elegant limestone post office with its corner tower and bay windows has been designated as a "national heritage mail facility," one of only five in Canada. Behind the town hall, and equally appealing, is the Rathbun Park, a shady oasis attractively landscaped during the spring and summer.

Naylor's Theatre remains today, posters outside still advertising Betty Boop and Curly Top. It is rumoured that a plan is in the works to once again stage theatrical productions at the historic venue. The home of Edward Wilkes Rathbun graces Dundas Street, the hilltop route where most of the early grand homes were built. Many of the simpler homes of the workers stand at the bottom of the hill.

What is perhaps the town's most significant building is located out of town and had little to do with the Rathbun empire. That building is the Christ Church Tyendinaga. Designed by architect John Howard of Toronto, the stone edifice was completed in 1843. Built by the Mohawk, the church houses a triptych in the Mohawk language, a bell given by King George III, a royal coat-of-arms donated by King George V, a Bible from Queen Victoria, and a royal chalice from Queen Elizabeth II. A silver communion set presented to the Mohawk in 1711 while they still lived in New York's Mohawk Valley survives, kept in a special vault and shared with the Royal Chapel of the Mohawk at Brantford. A stained-glass window in the church recalls the life of Dr. Peter Martin, 1841–1907. Known better by his Mohawk name, Oronhyatekha, he was responsible for transforming the finances of the Order of Foresters and for building a hotel and pleasure ground on Foresters Island. It was here that he also added an orphanage. Sadly, it lasted only a year — 1906 to 1907. No trace of any of these structures remains on Foresters Island.[10]

A visit to Deseronto, or even to its archives website, will show that the town retains much pride in its history and its heritage, even though its glory days are in the past.

Napanee

A short distance upstream from the lake, the Napanee River tumbles down a series of rock ledges. A small parkette beside the falls offers visitors a chance to enjoy the spectacle, many not realizing that the town of Napanee began right beneath their feet.

With United Empire Loyalist refugees fleeing persecution in the post-revolutionary United States and flooding into the shores of the lake, the British government recognized that these settlers needed, more than anything else, a mill nearby. Robert Clark, the man who had erected the area's first mills on the Cataraqui River near Kingston, was tagged to do the job.

Here, beside what was then called the Appanea Falls, Clark built saw- and gristmills. A clutch of workers' homes around them took the name Clarkville. On the opposite shore, Richard Cartwright of Kingston built the community's second sawmill, and here, too, a settlement sprang up. In 1812, Allan Macpherson[11] took over Clark's mill operations and within a dozen years had created a small empire that included the mills, a distillery, a general store, and a lumber business. His frame house, built in 1825, still stands on Elizabeth Street.

Courtesy of Lennox and Addington County Museum and Archives, N 1565.

Napanee's classic town hall is one of its most celebrated heritage buildings.

In 1851 William Smith would write that Napanee "is a flourishing place" with about a thousand inhabitants. "[The river] is navigable to the village for schooners drawing six feet of water. Napanee contains a grist mill with three run of stones, an oatmeal mill, two sawmills, a foundry, distillery, two tanneries, an ashery, carding and fulling mill, cloth factory …"[12] He noted, too, that a canal was being cut through the limestone for hydraulic purposes.

With the town's incorporation in 1855, the new town fathers set out to create an imposing town hall. Now overlooking a small landscaped parkette, the combined town hall and market sports a distinctly Greek façade with four two-storey pillars topped with a full-width gable. A balcony from which John A. Macdonald is said to have addressed an assembled throng sits above the main entrance. The market stalls, however, have long since been replaced. When Napanee became the county seat for the newly created County of Lennox and Addington in 1863, work began on a courthouse and jail. Finished in 1864, the limestone courthouse boasts four pillars and a cupola, and, today, with newer additions, it still serves as county administrative offices, while behind it the jail houses the county museum and archives.

While the mills and foundries have gone and schooners no longer tie up on the banks of the Napanee River, there remains on Napanee's main street one of Ontario's most historic industries. Predating even Toronto's Distillery District, it is the renowned Gibbard Furniture Shop. In 1835, cabinetmaker John Gibbard arrived in Napanee and leased a mill on a canal running beside the river. Here he began manufacturing sashes, doors, and especially furniture that gained a wide reputation for its quality, with "Gibbard solid walnut" becoming a household name. Despite surviving two fires, the iconic red brick factory, still bearing the Gibbard Furniture Shops Ltd. name, dominates the east end of the main street, though the manufacturing operation has ended.

With the arrival of the Grand Trunk Railway in 1856, Napanee enjoyed a boom in prosperity, and many of the main street buildings were built in the ensuing years, displaying two-tone brickwork, stone arches, and decorative pilasters. Just off the main street and close to the town hall square, the red sandstone post office with its elaborate tower was designed by Thomas Fuller, the same person who co-designed the original centre block of the Parliament Buildings in Ottawa. Along Dundas Street, west of the downtown, are some of the town's grandest homes, ranging in style from gothic to Italianate, Second Empire, and Queen Anne. Just one block away, on Mill and Water streets, workers' homes provide a stark contrast with their simple and uniform styles, although only a solitary early house survives east of Centre Street.

The historic train station, one of the GT's original Kenilworth-style stone stations, still exists and continues to serve VIA Rail passengers. It is located at the north end of East Street.

But the most interesting place in the town remains the park by the falls. Mill buildings still stand on the north side, although the first mills on the south side are long vanished. Providing a visual backdrop for the park is the old Grand Trunk railway bridge with its stone arches spanning the roads that once led to the riverside mill. Unlike many Bay of Quinte towns, Napanee retains an authentic and cohesive heritage townscape.

Chapter 7
The Bath Road: A Loyalist Trail

No sooner had the British gained the Canadas from France than the Thirteen Colonies to the south started to become restive. As is often the case, the dispute revolved around taxes. The colonists didn't much care for the English taxes, and in 1765 the Declaration of Rights and Grievances stated in no uncertain terms that only colonies would tax colonists. But violence erupted in 1770, when a group of besieged British troops opened fire on an unruly mob. Although there were few casualties, it was nonetheless dubbed the Boston "Massacre."

In 1772, Britain granted the East India Company a break from taxes on their tea. The Americans saw this as a threat to their smuggling activities, and when three ships laden with tea entered the Boston harbour, a group of locals, disguised as aboriginals, threw some 342 boxes of tea overboard. Another sore point was the Quebec Act that granted the French in Quebec their rights and customs with the Catholic Church. Since at the time the Quebec boundary extended to the Ohio River, the colonists, who stridently opposed any link between Church and State, saw this as yet another threat. Finally, in 1776, the Thirteen Colonies assembled to accept the Declaration of Independence, even though fewer than one-third of the colonists wished to be independent. Fully one-third wished to remain "loyal" while the final third simply didn't care.

In 1783, after several years of fighting, the Loyalists and their Mohawk allies faced defeat, and Britain surrendered to General George Washington (once a British general himself). While most of the Loyalists were part of regiments which had fought the "patriots," many were independent of any military organization and simply wanted to continue to live under the British Crown. To organize the anticipated influx of refugees, the British government laid out a series of townships stretching from the Cataraqui River at Kingston to Prince Edward County. The original names of the townships paid homage to British royalty. Kingston was named in honour of George III; Ernestown for Prince Ernest Augustus, Duke of Cumberland; Fredericksburg for Prince Augustus Frederick, Duke of Sussex; and Adolphustown for Prince Adolphus, Duke of Cambridge. All were sons of King George.

While many of the Loyalist lands fronted on the shore of the Bay of Quinte, others lay farther inland, and roads were needed. While surveyor Asa Danforth was completing his pioneer road to Picton, a road to link Kingston with the important and growing centre of Bath was opened. The Bath Road became an important stage route, following the shore of the lake to Adolphustown, where a crude ferry linked the route with Danforth's road on the west side at Glenora.

Adolphustown

In 1784 a band of Loyalists under Captain Van Alstine, after a bitter winter in Quebec, living only in tents, landed along a creek in what was known simply as Township 4. Farms were surveyed and a town site consisting of one-acre lots laid out. The next bitter winter saw the arrivals once more huddled in their tents, the severe conditions taking their toll, as a child died and was buried in the woods. When subsequent settlers passed away, their plots were located next to that first victim, and the UEL burying ground was thus begun.

Despite the influx of settlers, Adolphustown failed to develop beyond a small nucleus of buildings along the Bath Road. Two general stores faced each other, while a hotel stood across the road from the town hall, and was one of two located on Adolphustown's small main street. Two churches stood on the north side of the road, as well, St. Paul's and St. Alban's, while a sawmill operated on a creek a short distance away. From the Bath Road, a lane led to the village's two wharves.

The historic Hay Bay Church once served as a courthouse and gathering place for the Adolphustown Loyalist settlers.

Loyalist heritage abounds in the area. In 1884 a monument was erected in the UEL burying ground to commemorate the centennial of the Loyalist landing. Today the cemetery is surrounded somewhat incongruously by a recreation park created by the St. Lawrence Parks Commission. On the road to the wharf site stands the house of D.W. Allison, built in 1878 and now the Loyalist Cultural Centre and Museum. The house and burying ground together form the UEL Heritage Centre and Park, created by the Ontario government in 1959. Today on the Bath Road are the parish hall of St. Alban's Church, originally the church itself, and the later but considerably more architecturally interesting St. Alban the Martyr Anglican Church, erected in 1884–85. Built of limestone, it is distinguished by its corner octagonal steeple and circular window above the knave.

Although it is some distance north of the lakeshore, the ancient and historic Hay Bay Church is one of the oldest churches in Ontario. Built as a Methodist chapel in 1792, it was known as the Adolphustown Meeting House. Although enlarged in 1835, it has for the most part remained little altered. Its original entrance faced the water, the route by which most worshippers arrived. When roads became passable, a door was placed on the road side. After the Methodist chapel was finished, it briefly became the courthouse for the Midland District. During the early years, debate ensued as to whether the court facility should be situated in Kingston or in Adolphustown, considered to be the centre of the Loyalist settlement. It was decided that the sessions would alternate between the two locations. After the first session was held in a barn for lack of a proper facility, the second was held in the chapel, and soon a new courthouse was built. When Kingston became the permanent site of the court, the Adolphustown Courthouse was turned over to the township. In 1860, when a new church was built nearby, the Hay Bay Church fell vacant and was used to store grain and farm tools. Eventually, in 1910, the church was re-acquired by the Methodists (later to become the United Church of Canada), restored, and is now maintained as a classic old house of worship. Designated as a National Historic Site, the Hay Bay Church holds a yearly service in the building each August. The church is Canada's oldest Methodist church and the second oldest church of any denomination in Ontario.

Between Adolphustown and Bath lie the forgotten settlements of Conway and Sandhurst, both of which had wharves and churches, but failed to develop much beyond names on a map.

Bath

Few villages in Ontario possess the historical significance and yet are less well-known than Bath. Known originally as Ernestown, the town site was one of the first laid out in anticipation of the arrival of the Loyalist refugees in 1783.

Bath can boast of many "firsts." Lake Ontario's first steamboat, the *Frontenac*, was built here in Finkle's Shipyard; the first library in Upper Canada opened in Bath, as did the first grammar school, the Bath Academy. Some claim that Bath was also the site of Ontario's first brewery, and that the province's first hanging occurred here when a man was tried in Finkle's Tavern, then strung up from a nearby tree.

Population soon swelled to 850, and the streets were lined with forty-six shops and five inns and taverns. Bath owed much of its early prosperity to its important location on the Bath Road linking Kingston to York via

Courtesy of Lennox and Addington County Museum and Archives, N 00049.

Bath's main street was noted for its double-veranda stores. Most of the buildings burned in the 1940s.

the road that Colonel Asa Danforth had commenced in 1793, as well as to its protected harbour and the shelter provided by Amherst Island. But in 1817 a new Kingston Road opened farther north, offering travellers a faster link between Kingston and York, while bypassing the communities on the Bath Road. The Grand Trunk Railway didn't help either when, in 1856, it located its Ernestown station well to the north. Although much vandalized, the old stone station still stands.

Bath's population plunged from a high of around two thousand to less than four hundred. Still, in the 1870s, shipping remained important, as an extensive grain trade saw many thousands of bushels of barley being exported annually to the United States, even though Bath had lost its status as an official port of entry.

Bath's main street was distinctive, noted for its many double-veranda wooden stores. But a devastating fire in 1942 wiped out most. Bath, however, remains proud of its many surviving heritage properties and has produced one of the area's better guidebooks to the community. The main street still contains a few of these traditional double-veranda stores, the best example being the E.D. Priest store at 428 Main Street, which dates back to 1820. The Fairfax store at 394 Main was built in 1818, but has since lost its veranda. While few buildings in Bath were constructed of stone, the W.H. Davy store (1817) at 169 Main Street was one exception. The Davy family was also responsible for a steam-powered gristmill and one of the many wharves on the lake.

The former town hall in Bath boasts a Tuscan-style portico. Built in 1861, it is a smaller version of the Napanee town hall. It stands at 434 Main Street. Other prominent buildings in Bath include the "Fairfield-Gutzeit House." Built in 1796, it is one of Ontario's oldest structures. Facing the lake, then the only means of travel, it was built by William and Benjamin Fairfield, sons of an early Loyalist who had built a grand home farther east three years earlier. The structure has undergone changes from its original appearance, and, now restored, is operated as a museum by the Fairfield-Gutzeit Society.

Perhaps one of the area's most playful buildings is known as "Layer Cake Hall," so named for its highly decorative Gothic-revival windows and board and batten style of woodwork. Built in 1859 by Abraham Harris, the village carpenter, it was occupied by two denominations, the Anglicans who used the upper floor, and the Presbyterians who used the ground level. It now contains a library and museum, and stands at 193 Davy Street, just north of the main street. Finkle's Tavern, built in 1786, was at one time the only stopping place on the Kingston to York road. It was here in 1787 that a court found a man guilty in the theft of a watch and sentenced him to hang. The sentence was carried out swiftly, using a tree beside the tavern. The hasty verdict was unfortunate, as the man was later determined to be innocent. Finkle's Tavern has long been gone, but its legacy is commemorated on a plaque in a lakeside park.

East of Bath stands what is considered to be one of the province's oldest surviving frame houses, "Fairfield House." It was built facing the lake in 1793 by William Fairfield Sr., a Loyalist who served with Jessup's Loyal Rangers during the American Revolution. The wooden Georgian-style house is five bays wide and fronted with a two-storey full-width porch. With the arrival of stage traffic along the lake road, the house was converted to an inn. In 1959 it was donated to the St. Lawrence Parks Commission, although the family remained in residence until 1972. Today the Commission operates it as a museum. Beside Fairfield House are the stone gates marking the eastern terminus of what has been designated as the Loyalist Parkway. Primarily following Highway 33, it represents a Loyalist route with many heritage buildings and sites from that historic period in Ontario's history.[1]

Another early home lies a short distance east at 4423 Bath Road. Similar in style to the Fairfield House, this five-bay Georgian-style house is constructed of stone and was built in 1813 by Joshua Booth, who used the building to watch for American ships. One of the area's first settlers, Booth went on to become a mill owner in Millhaven and one of the region's wealthiest individuals.

Amherst Island

Geographically, sixty-six-square-kilometre Amherst Island is a flat limestone extension of the eastern tip of Prince Edward County. Low-lying and generally flat, the shoreline consists of boulder beaches and low bluffs. The island measures twenty kilometres long and seven kilometres at its widest point.

At first the island had been part of Sieur de La Salle's extensive seigneury,[2] which included today's Kingston and Wolfe Island. One of La Salle's favoured lieutenants was an Italian named Henri Tonti, who served the King of France at the battle of Messina in 1677. In return for Tonti's bravery, La Salle brought Tonti to New France as his second-in-command and named the second largest island in his seigneury Isle Tonti, after him. In the 1790s, however, Lieutenant Governor Simcoe, displaying his usual disdain for non-English names, renamed it Amherst Island in honour of Lord Amherst, commander-in-chief of the British forces in America.

Did Amherst Island come into Crown ownership through a "dream"? The *Historic Atlas for Frontenac Lennox and Addington* recounts this haunting legend of the negotiations between the local Mohawk chief, Hendrick, and Sir William Johnson:

> ... on [Johnson's] receiving from England some finely laced clothes, the Mohawk became possessed with the desire of equalling the baronet in the splendour of his apparel, and with a demure face pretended to have dreamed that Sir William [father of Sir John Johnson] had presented him with a suit of the decorated garments. As the solemn hint could not be mistaken or avoided, the

monarch was gratified and went away highly pleased with his device. But alas for Hendrick's short-sighted sagacity! In a few days Sir William in turn had a dream to the effect that the chief had given him several thousand acres of land. That land said the chief is yours [Amherst Island] but now Sir William, I never dream with you again.[3]

So goes the legend. The real story is that Johnson received the land in 1788 from the British government in gratitude for the services which his father had performed for the British during the American Revolution and for the loss of his possessions to the Americans in the Mohawk Valley. During the War of 1812, gun batteries were established at each end of the island but were never used. Johnson ran the island as a feudal kingdom, the residents being merely leaseholders. Ownership subsequently passed to the Earl of Mount Cashel[4] in 1835, and he carried on Johnson's autocratic ownership.

In the early days many of the island residents were Loyalists, others were Irish immigrants. French Canadians arrived early, as well, and became some of the island's first fishermen. In 1846, the island's population was over 1,100, and it had three shipbuilders, two taverns, and a store, as well as the usual range of craftsmen's shops. Connections to the mainland consisted of steamers calling between Kingston and other Lake Ontario destinations. Docks were situated at the island's two main villages, Stella and Emerald. Mixed farming and logging dominated in the early years. From 1850 until 1883, barley shipment to the United States brought prosperity, but with the collapse in the barley trade, prices plunged, and many farmers switched to dairying. Eventually most residents were able to obtain title to their land, and by the 1900s all but two thousand hectares were individually owned. Still, the island population has continued to decrease, dropping from its high point of 1,270 in 1860 to fewer than five hundred today.

After the arrival of the railways in the 1850s, steamship service along the Lake Ontario shore gradually declined and a ferry service was needed to replace it. In 1928 the first *Amherst Islander* began service between Stella and Millhaven. It was replaced in 1954 with a larger car ferry. The service remained seasonal until 1972 when an underwater-bubble system allowed winter navigation across the channel. The *Amherst Islander II* in turn was replaced by the current vessel, the thirty-three-car *Frontenac II*.

Amherst Island is seldom visited, yet contains much history, as demonstrated by this former blacksmith shop still standing in the village of Stella.

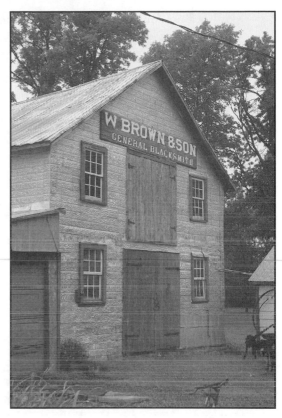

Run by the newly created Loyalist Township, the municipality spent eight million dollars on the boat, but could not set aside enough funds to alter the docks to accommodate it. While the boat is designed as an end-loader, the docks were only sufficient to fit a side-loader. This means that vehicles, rather than driving on at one end and off at the other, must enter by a side ramp and then manoeuvre to exit by the same ramp. Crew members complain that with proper docks they could double the number of runs each day.

Which begs the question, what exactly is there on the island? For the heritage enthusiast, plenty. Much of the island remains little altered from its peak period a century ago. While the industries have gone, many early structures remain. A short walk (or ride) from the current ferry dock, Stella's main intersection contains the island's oldest house (northeast corner) and the island's tiny general store, built in the 1870s as one of the village's five hotels. Across the road stands the well-preserved W. Brown and Son General Blacksmith building. Owned originally by John Robinson, the smithing was taken over by John Brown in 1894. When the first smithy burned in 1913, the present building replaced it.

A short distance east along the village road, the library and ferry office building was originally constructed as a church in 1873. The Easel Arts and Crafts Shop was originally the Neilson Store built by James Neilson, who arrived on Amherst Island in 1869 and opened a small store east of the dock. In 1883 he replaced it with the present store, which operated until 1973. Closer to the present dock, Neilson added a wharf and feed mill. McDonald's Lane to the west of the village leads to the site of the shipyard that operated between 1832 and 1858, where David Tait and his workforce of up to sixty labourers would go on to launch nearly fifty schooners.

Farther west along the shoreline lies the near ghost town of Emerald. From the dock at this location, schooners and steamboats would load cheese, barley, and dairy products. The village could also boast of a gristmill, grain elevator, and general store. Today, only a vestige of the dock is visible, as is the wheel from the mill. The store burned in 1921 but was rebuilt and moved to its present location at the corner.

The road linking Stella and Emerald frequently hugs the shoreline, offering views across to the mainland to the north. In contrast, the South Shore Road follows the lake closely, and from it only the horizon of the lake is seen. At its western tip, the road ends in what was until recently a busy fishing colony. The little cabins built by the fishermen are now mostly cottages.

One of the island's grander homes is now the Poplar Dell B & B. Built by Irish immigrant Isaac Preston in the 1820s, it is also one of the oldest, built of stone to replace an earlier log cabin. A second stone house was added in 1846, and the two connected by a wooden section. Three other B & Bs operate on the island and are the only form of accommodation. The island has no restaurants.

Chapter 8

Quinte's Isle:
The Tranquility of Prince Edward County

I f an island is defined as land surrounded by water, then Prince Edward County is an "island," although artificially so. In 1889 a canal was cut through the neck of land linking this peninsula to the mainland, thereby "surrounding" it with water.

Its shape is unusual. Basically, the entire county is a tilted limestone plain, sloping from lake level on its west coast, to bluffs that soar to eighty metres above the lake on its eastern reaches. Within that plain are long, narrow limestone ridges interspersed with lowlands. On the water's edge the ridges create a series of headlands, while the lowlands become deeply indented bays and marshes. This configuration gives the county an inordinate amount of shoreline for its area, making the early settlers heavily reliant upon the water for shipping and travel.

Belden's Atlas of 1877 noted that

> the coastline being so very great in proportion to the area, and having so many splendid natural harbours along the shore, have given the farmers in this strictly farming community greater advantages as to shipping and marketing their crops, than can be found in any other part of Canada or of America. There is probably not a single farmer's barn in the whole County at a greater distance than seven or eight miles from a good wharf and

storehouse; while the great majority have a half dozen
such to choose from within less than half that distance.[1]

During those early days, the coastline was ringed with little ports and
wharves, many of which were connected to the mainland for many years
by ferry services.

Before all that happened, the land was home to various aboriginal
groups. The first Europeans to visit the region were the French, who in
1668 established the Kente Mission. But by 1680 it had failed and the site
was abandoned, after which the French showed no further interest in a
permanent presence. Following the American Revolution, those Loyalists
who had supported the British during the conflict, and even those who
had remained neutral, were being pushed from their American holdings
and forced to flee northward. In preparation for their arrival, Governor
Haldimand sent his chief surveyor-general, Samuel Holland, to lay out
a series of townships. Over a period of six years, 1783 to 1789, ten such
areas were surveyed between Kingston and Trenton, most eventually
named for King George III and his many friends and relatives, names that
survive in today's townships.

As settlement progressed, towns grew around harbours, landings, and
mill sites. The neck of the peninsula became the focus of transportation,
with a road linking the Bay of Quinte with Wellers Bay. Known as the
Carrying Place, the route followed a long-established aboriginal portage
trail and is known today as Ontario's oldest road. At its western terminus,
the British erected a palisaded blockhouse known as Fort Kente. In
1796, Colonel Asa Danforth surveyed his Danforth Road across the
county, from its northwestern point to beyond Picton. Railways began
to arrive in the 1870s with the construction of the Prince Edward
County Railway, later to become part of the Central Ontario Railway.
In 1882, work began on the Murray Canal, north of the Carrying Place,
eliminating the long and often hazardous shipping route around the
outside of the peninsula.

The county's prosperity depended upon its farms. Its position far out in
the lake meant a mild climate and long growing seasons. While many early
mills provided a market for grain, the peak of prosperity came with the
"Barley Years," a period that began during the American Civil War, when

fund-raising taxes on liquor forced drinkers to switch to beer. The sudden demand for hops and barley sent breweries looking to Prince Edward's farmers for the perceived superiority of their grain. From the 1860s to the 1890s, shiploads of barley made their way to the United States for that country's brewing industry. Not only was the County's barley considered superior in quality, it was a short sail across to the American ports on Lake Ontario, a circumstance that would later prove useful during Prohibition. During the Barley Years, more than a third of the county's acreage was dedicated to the crop, and shipments soared to eight hundred thousand bushels a year. Then, in 1890, the American government, reacting to its own farm lobby, passed the McKinley Act, shutting the door on Canadian barley. Overnight the price plunged by half.

Because of the sizable amount of shoreline, farmers and other landowners who abutted the shore often became their own shipbuilders. Most were small and crewed by the builder's family. The capacity of most seldom exceeded six thousand bushels capacity, while larger boats might have a capacity as great as twenty thousand bushels. Among the earliest shipbuilding centres were Case's wharf and mill near Point Traverse, Port Milford, Black River Bridge, Smith's Bay, Roblins Mills, Rednersville, Wellington, and Hillier, where an estimated fifty vessels were constructed. With the advent of steamers, larger and more sophisticated dry docks were required. The end of the barley trade reduced the demand, and shipbuilding in Prince Edward County slowed to nearly nothing.

However, even as the barley trade was thriving, the county was also becoming the "Garden Capital" of Ontario, and, in 1882, local entrepreneurs George Dunning and Wellington Boulter opened the county's first canning factory. The climate and the soil were ideal for crops such as peas and tomatoes. The industry expanded to include corn, beans, pumpkins, and a variety of fruits. At its peak in 1941, Prince Edward County canneries shipped more than a million and a half cases of tomatoes. But after the war, the industry began a rapid decline. The frozen-food fad was cutting into the market, as were American and other foreign canners. In 1956 the California Packing Corporation, later Del Monte, bought out Canadian Canners Ltd. and shut down its canneries. The last of the county's fabled canneries, the Sprague Cannery in Mountain View, closed its doors in 1996 and moved its facilities to Belleville.

Today, a new agricultural trend is sweeping the county — the wine industry. Since the opening of the Waupoos Winery in 1993, more than a dozen have appeared across the county. Not only has the climate and the soil proved a catalyst, but the growing popularity of wine tourism has brought tour buses by the hundreds to the scenic back roads, where many of the operations are located. As at Waupoos, the wineries, with their restaurants and wine tastings, have successfully been able to combine farming with tourism. In fact, the county has been officially classified as a Designated Viticulture Area (DVA), and is Ontario's fastest growing wine region.

Carrying Place

Not only is Carrying Place the county's oldest transportation focus, it remains the oldest point of land access to the county. The Mississauga called the portage trail *degabunwakwa*, or "the place where I pick up my canoe." The first permanent settler, Asa Weller, opened a tavern in 1783 and began a business portaging small boats across the isthmus using oxen and a wheeled platform. Settlements grew at each end of the portage and the location was briefly considered for the capital of Upper Canada.

It is believed that the British built Fort Kente overlooking Wellers Bay in 1812. The fort was a simple blockhouse about seven metres square and nine metres high. Garrisoned by the Provincial Dragoons, it was situated here to protect the Carrying Place Portage. After the war it was no longer needed, and the site was abandoned. In 1990, with no government funding, local historian Paul Germain led the initiative to build a replica on the site. It soon became a tourist attraction with its blockhouse, palisade, festivals, and military re-enactments; however, following a property dispute, the blockhouse was relocated to the Mariners Park Museum at South Bay in 2000, far from its historic locale.

Today, Carrying Place has become a busy highway village with a gas station and small restaurant. Highway 33 roars through the centre of the community, carrying heavy volumes of traffic to cottages, parks, and wineries throughout the county. The old Carrying Place Portage lies both east and west of the highway. At the east end, the start of the

After Fort Kente was reconstructed near its original site, it was forced to move because of a property dispute.

historic portage is unmarked and lined with more modern homes and cottages. Along the road, a number of early homes remain, including two that belonged to the founding Wellers. One of those houses may date to 1828, possibly earlier. At the opposite end of the portage stands the historic "Robert Young House." Young arrived at Carrying Place in 1795, and in 1808 he built the house that stands today near the southwest corner of the Carrying Place Road and County Road 64. It remained in the family for more than 150 years and is one of the oldest surviving wooden houses in Ontario. On the northeast corner of the intersection stands a large Georgian-style brick home, built in the 1840s to serve as a stage stop and tavern for the Weller stage line. Here a diminutive sign proclaims the road to be Ontario's oldest.

Meanwhile, on Highway 33, a stone cairn commemorates what was known as the "Gunshot Treaty," signed between the Mississauga and the British, whereby the Mississauga would surrender all their land "within the sound of a gunshot." That land ended up being everything between Trenton and Cataraqui (Kingston), and twelve kilometres back from the lake — one loud gunshot. Because of the vague description of the boundaries, that treaty would later be invalidated in 1804 and replaced with one that extended the land surrender as far as Etobicoke.

The Murray Canal

Municipally speaking, the Murray Canal (named after Murray Township) is not actually in Prince Edward County, but rather in Northumberland County — barely. It is, however, the feature that makes Prince Edward an "island."

During the early days of settlement on the shore of the lake, Presqu'ile Bay became a busy harbour, carrying vessels to and from Gosport. But when they needed to make their way around the dangerous headlands on the south shore of the county, dozens sank on the shoals and in the gales that plagued the route. Canal talk began as early as the 1790s. Construction, however, would not begin until 1882, and work went on for seven years. Little or no steam power existed at the time, and most labour was done by hand or by horse. Finally, in October 1889, a steamship carrying Prime Minister Sir John A. Macdonald slowly made its way from Presqu'ile Bay on the western end of the canal to Twelve O'clock Point at the eastern end, where the opening ceremonies took place.

Despite the loss of shipping business to the railways, which by then had made their way along the lakeshore and into Picton, coastal streamers continued to puff through the canal. But with the growth in highway haulage, which began in the 1930s and accelerated through the 1950s, commercial traffic along the canal fell to nothing. Pleasure craft have more than made up the difference, though, and a hundred yachts, sailboats, or simple runabouts might make their way through the waterway on any given summer weekend. Two lift bridges, one at either end of the canal, provide vehicle access across the waterway, both built in 1938. A short distance west of the eastern bridge, the former swing bridge of the railway sits on an angle, no longer used, as the rail line was discontinued in the 1980s. A park, waterside walkway, and picnic tables at the quieter western bridge offer visitors a chance to absorb the tranquility of the canal, fish, or watch the large yachts move through the opened bridge.

Wellers Bay

A short distance south of the Fort Kente Road, Gardenville Road leads to Harbard Road. Along this dead-end lane, the village of Gardenville grew up. Virtually forgotten on the tourist maps, this village first developed as a fishing colony on the lake. When the Prince Edward County Railway laid its tracks in 1873, it placed a small station by the road farther inland, and a cluster of homes were soon built around it. Today, newer housing mingles with the simple frame homes that date from rail and fishing days, although no sign of either activity remains.

There was a time when Wellers Bay was slated to become a major railway hub. When Johnstown Steel and Bethlehem Steel respectively bought the Dufferin and Nelson mines to the north, near Madoc, they needed a location from which to ship the iron, as well as to bring in coal. The protected harbour at Wellers Bay offered a route that would allow the ore to be shipped across the lake twice as fast as if it were shipped from Belleville. Here the railway would build a massive ore dock, proposed to be ten metres high, that would need to be extended roughly six hundred metres into the lake in order to reach water six metres deep, enough to accommodate the ore carriers. In addition, the site would contain a turntable and roundhouse, steel rail mill, and car repair shops. Promoters predicted that five ships at a time could be accommodated at the Wellers Bay dock.

The CPR also showed an interest in the proposed port as a place to import coal and export copper, an initiative that would have involved a new line to Sudbury. But the grand scheme failed. By 1886 the ore supply at Coe Hill was running dry. Siltation and wind exposure created more of a deterrent than had been predicted, and by 1891, except for occasional shipments, the dock sat silent. With the opening of the Murray Canal, any shipping advantage of a dock on Wellers Bay evaporated, and the dock was dismantled.

Smokes Point Road today follows the old road pattern of the town site, but it is now lined with newer homes; no early buildings survive. Although the turntable pit and the dock pilings were visible until the late 1970s, the roadbed is overgrown, and the pilings are little more than a marshy weed bed extending into the lake.

Consecon

Consecon is an aboriginal name that translates as "pickerel." That appellation is somewhat appropriate, as the village became a significant harbour from which fishermen sailed to catch, among other species, the pickerel. But it grew, not as a fishing port, but rather as a mill town when Mathias Marsh arrived in 1804 and built a mill on the creek flowing into the lake.

The village developed into a busy mill town and port, and by 1850 could claim four hundred residents and several stores and small industries. Hotels of the time included Hayes Tavern, Abraham Marsh's temperance hotel, the Prince Edward Hotel (operated by J.M. Wood), and the Commercial Hotel, with R.J. Chute as proprietor. In 1851 William Smith would note, "The village of Consecon is pleasantly situated at the entrance of Consecon Creek into Weller's Bay. It ... contains nearly 400 inhabitants, a grist mill with three run of stone, a saw mill, carding and fulling mill, post office and two churches, Episcopal and Methodist. Large quantities of fish are exported from the village."[2]

The Prince Edward County Railway laid its tracks along shore before swinging inland on the northern outskirts of the village where it built a small grain elevator, freight shed, and a standard country railway station of wood construction. With the railway came new industries — cheese making and canning. Wellers Bay cheese factory was built northwest of the village, while United Canners added a plant in 1929. Fish were brought to the dock, where they were packed in ice, then hauled to the little station for shipment.

During the days of Prohibition, the fishermen were hauling more than fish. Fish-buyer Wes Kaiser coordinated his dozen or so fishermen to load up twenty-five to thirty cases of whisky, bought from the Corbyville Distillery near Belleville, and slip away in the dark to the south-shore beaches near Rochester, where trucks waited to haul the liquor to many a thirsty customer. But lurking in the waters of the American side were the heavily armed cutters of the United States Coast Guard. To avoid detection, the boat captains would paint their vessels a dark colour and submerge the exhaust pipes, making their boats more difficult to see and hear at night. It helped too that United States customs officers could often be bribed to alert the crews as to the whereabouts of the coast guard. Similarly, on the

Canadian side, export officers could often be "persuaded" to sign off on whisky, which the manifest declared was bound for Cuba or Mexico — both legal, if unlikely, destinations.

Few of Consecon's early structures have survived, although a few that have are of note. The mill still stands by the water in the centre of town, now renovated and operating as Cascades Bar and Grill. The former Hayes Hotel has found a new home, near Waupoos, on the county's south shore. The frame United church, built in 1830, remains active, while the fieldstone Anglican church, erected around 1847, is a designated historic site. Of particular architectural note is the church tower with its unusual octagonal stage and its miniature pinnacles that form a "crown of thorns." Today the church houses the local library. The Merchant's Mill fine art and antique shop on Mill Street occupies the "Marsh House," an historic dwelling built by the family of Consecon's first settler, William Marsh. The little country station was the last of its kind to survive in the county, but was allowed to deteriorate to the point that, nearing collapse, it was removed. The freight shed still stands, however, as does the small grain elevator. The railway roadbed is now a trail.

Wellington

Along Highway 33, Hillier and Rosehall are examples of near ghost towns, even though Hillier managed to attract a station on the PEC Railway. Its historic stone town hall still functions as a community meeting hall. South of the village a road sign points to the route of the original Danforth Road, laid out in 1796.

It is rare when a town's first home still survives. This is the case with the community of Wellington, which is strung along the shore of the lake. That settler was a trader named Daniel Reynolds. Sometime around 1792, possibly earlier, he built a solid stone house on the shoreline. According to one theory, it was built as early as 1782 with the help of the aboriginals with whom he traded and who called Reynolds "Old Smoke." Its walls are more than thirty centimetres thick and the small windows testify to its early construction. Inside, hand-hewn beams are still in place, as are the two stone fireplaces that originally heated the building. In the basement, a bake oven and fireplace suggest the location of the original kitchen.

The Danforth Road passed through the village, allowing access for many of the early settlers. Growth began with the usual sawmill, followed in 1815 by Abraham Barker's gristmill. Wharves were soon in place, and the abundance of whitefish and pickerel brought about a busy fishing colony. A large dock provided space for steamers and schooners to call regularly. In 1851, William Smith observed that

> Wellington, which is divided into an upper and lower town is situated on the north shore of West Lake, a bay of Lake Ontario now nearly separated from it by a long ridge of sand hills…. It contains about five hundred inhabitants, a saw mill, two tanneries, a foundry, post office etc. It is a port of entry and has a resident collector of customs. Large quantities of fish are exported …[3]

In 1850, some fifty ships departed the Wellington wharf laden with firewood, fish, and grain. The PEC Railway was built parallel to the main street a short distance north, and a brick station and cannery were built, the latter in 1902 as the Wellington Packing Company. Around this time, the Wellington Fishery closed, putting many out of work. Wellington was also on its way to becoming a tourist destination. With its convenient stop on the rail line, nine hotels opened up to house the influx. A motto was adopted, which is still used to this day: "The coolest spot when the weather's hot." With the constant cooling breezes from the lake, it's no exaggeration.

Although the fishery, the railway, and the cannery have all gone, Wellington is enjoying a resurgence as a destination for retirement living, with new subdivisions appearing to the west of the village. But the core of Wellington yet offers much of its built heritage. The focus without much debate is the ancient Reynolds House, but on the main street you will also find "Tara Hall," one of the county's grandest mansions. It was built in 1839 by Archibald McFaul, an Irish settler who opened a dry-goods business and exported grain and pork. A wide exterior staircase leads to a front entrance with a transom above the door. Inside the door, a vaulted foyer leads to a curving staircase at the top of which was a grand ballroom. Outside, the two-storey brick mansion displays four chimneys, and a pair of French doors flanks the main door. Today, the restored building is a popular bed and breakfast.

Located nearby are the former Orange Lodge, built in 1862, and a Quaker Meeting House dating from the 1880s, now the town museum. In the downtown area, the 1903 Fitzgerald Block retains much of its historic façade. On the lake, at the end of Wharf Street, the Devonshire Inn occupies a former 1860s foundry, extensively renovated to serve as a private home as early as 1897. On Main Street, the Fisherman's Cove Bed and Breakfast is one of the few hotels to survive Wellington's heyday as a port. It was built in 1832 and has been called variously the Wellington Hotel and the Murphy House. Another early hotel at the northwest corner of Main and West streets is now a private home. The western portion of Main Street contains a string of grand Victorian homes built for the better-off residents of the town. Closer to the east end of the main street, an attractive lakeside park fulfills that promise of the town being the coolest spot in the hottest weather.

Beneath the Dunes: Sandbanks

Stretching across the mouth of West Lake, south of Wellington, a mountain range of sand dunes looms above the water, in places reaching a height of nearly fifty metres above the lake. Today they form the backbone of one of Ontario's most popular provincial parks, Sandbanks Provincial Park. On the West Lake side they plunge precipitously into the water, while on their summit, winds have carved sharp ridges and wavy patterns, all the while exposing the roots of the forest that once covered them. On the west, or Lake Ontario side, they slope toward a wide beach that extends 250 metres into the shallow lake waters.

According to the Ontario Department of Lands and Forests,

> The Sandbanks area was less than 180 years ago covered on
> the Lake Ontario side with a forest cover of various species
> of hardwood and softwood, as well as a cedar forest on the
> West Lake side…. The road from Bloomfield extended in
> a straight line through the cedar forest to a point on Lake

Ontario, and it was along this road that a brick factory houses and a hotel were built around the turn of the century. The farmers that located along this road extended their cleared land by cutting the cedar and mixed forest without realizing the danger of such a practice. They were ignorant of the fact that the top soil was very shallow and that the fine sand subject to wind and water erosion lay under this layer of top soil…. The top soil was soon blown away so that sand dunes developed to such an extent that the original road as well as the brick factory and several houses were buried by the advancing sand.[4]

As a result, the Sandbanks Forestry Station was established in 1921 to control erosion.

Two popular resort hotels formerly stood in the Sandbanks area. The Evergreen House, built in 1875, was demolished in 1915 due to the advancing wall of sand. According to the *Picton Gazette*: "Almost at the back door rises a

Only the ruins of the once popular Lakeshore Lodge survive within the Sandbanks Provincial Park. The lodge burned in 1983 while undergoing redevelopment studies.

bank of sand 60' high ... it will not be long before the place will be pointed out to tourists."[5] This was in all likelihood the hotel to which Lands and Forests was referring. The other hotel had a less unusual fate — it burned. Built in 1876, the Lakeshore Lodge occupied a rocky ledge at the tip of West Point on the lake, well out of the way of the sand. It sported a hip roof, and stood three storeys high. A row of cottages provided more private accommodation for visitors. It promoted itself as "one of the finest summer houses in Canada ... where the air is invigorating and the scenery unsurpassed." Rooms in the main lodge cost five dollars per week, while the cottages rented for between a dollar-fifty and three dollars a week. Meanwhile, day visitors could enjoy the ice-cream parlour or the dance floor. But by the 1960s the era of the summer lodge was fading, and in 1972, despite the addition of a golf course, tennis courts, and an outdoor pool, the Lakeshore Lodge closed. While awaiting the outcome of a redevelopment proposal, the lodge burned in 1983, and the cottages were demolished soon after.

But the remains of the lodge can still be seen within the boundaries of the neighbouring Outlet Provincial Park, where the concrete floor and the remains of the shuffleboard and tennis courts lie by the shore of West Point, at the western end of Lakeshore Lodge Road.

The Wild South Coast

The county's longest stretch of exposed shoreline is that extending from Salmon Point on the west to Prince Edward Point or Point Traverse on the east. This rock-strewn shore, battered by the winds and the waves of the open lake, spawned neither port nor town. Fully a third lies within the Point Petre Provincial Wildlife Area. Two lighthouses, similar in style, mark the opposite points.

For many years, the dangerous waters around Salmon Point lacked warning lights of any kind. Finally, bowing to pressure from shippers, the federal government erected a square-shaped wooden lighthouse in 1871. After the lighthouse was decommissioned in 1917 it became a summer cottage and then a campground. Today a solid gate and stern NO TRESPASSING sign prevent its being viewed.

Fishing operations at Salmon Point began in the 1920s with the opening of the Salmon Point Fisheries with its ice house and packing plant. That shoreline today is a popular rural housing retreat. Just south of Salmon Point lies the most southerly peninsula in the county, Point Petre. Built in 1833, the old stone lighthouse at Point Petre was the second oldest in the county. More than eighteen metres high, the tower contained an eighty-seven-step circular staircase. In 1967 the government built a new steel-frame light and entered negotiations with the local historical society to save the grand old light tower. However, even as those talks were taking place, the government clandestinely sent in a wrecking crew and dynamited the historic lighthouse. One of the keepers managed to rescue a brass lamp, which now lies in the Marine Museum at South Bay, a testimony not just to the structure itself, but to the utter insensitivity of a government body to the heritage of the county.

The military base at Point Petre existed for a brief period during the 1950s, the site of test flights for scale models of the ill-fated Avro Arrow interceptor-jet aircraft. Due to lack of proper facilities to test the revolutionary design at supersonic speeds, Avro used Nike missiles to launch the jets over the lake to attain their desired speed. Production of the jet was suspended amid considerable controversy in 1959 and spirited searches continue for those missing models.

On the other hand, the Prince Edward Point Lighthouse, situated on the county's easternmost point, may be difficult to get to but it is at least accessible. Built in the identical style to that at Salmon Point, the lighthouse, including quarters for the keeper, was built in 1881 to guide ships through the shoal-laden passage between the point and the False Duck Islands just offshore. Still, the wrecks of many ships lie in the turbulent waters here, including one that sank as recently as 1965. The light was replaced by a steel tower in 1959, and the lantern removed.

Access to this distant and tranquil point is along County Road 13 and the Long Point Road. While the tip is part of a national wildlife reserve, the highly picturesque harbour at the end still houses a small colony of fishermen. The lighthouse sits at the south end of the bay at the end of a narrow gravel lane.

The Rum-Runners of Main Duck Island

During the years of Prohibition, many of the farmers and fishermen whose cabins and homes dotted the coves and shores of South Bay and Prinyers Cove spent many a night supplying the dry Americans with Canadian liquor. However, Main Duck Island was the home port of many of Lake Ontario's most notorious rum-runners. There, names like "Wild Bill" Sheldon, "Peg Leg" Jones, and "King" Cole are the stuff of legends.

Until the 1450s the 209-hectare island was an important haven for aboriginal travellers crossing the unpredictable waters of the lake. In the early 1800s, European fishermen discovered that the otherwise treacherous waters were also rich spawning and feeding beds for such fish species as lake trout, whitefish, eels, and herring. By the 1900s, a sizable colony of sixty fishermen lived out the summer months in a row of cabins clustered around the shore of Fisherman's Cove. The island had a limited supply of farmable land and a stand of timber, some of which was used in the 1850s in a small boat-building business.

Many a rum-running expedition departed from Prince Edward County's quiet coves during the days of Prohibition.

But one man came to own the island, and that was Claude "King" Cole. He had purchased the entire island from the federal government in 1904 for $1,200, and operated a farm with sheep, racehorses, and hogs that would gorge themselves on the many water snakes living in the island's limestone crevices. For himself, he built a two-storey frame house with a solid stone basement, and rented the cabins to the fishermen.

When the United States passed the Volstead Act in 1917, prohibiting the manufacture, transportation, and sale of alcohol in the United States, Cole realized that his island was perfectly placed to cash in on what would become the notorious era of prohibition. The island lies eighteen kilometres from Point Traverse but only a kilometre from American waters. Out of sight of the Canadian authorities, and within an easy sail of the south shore of the lake, the island would prove ideal for the caching and shipping of booze. With his large boat, the *Emily*, Cole would bring whisky from the Corby Distillery or beer from the Belleville brewery out to the island and stash it in his large home. He would then distribute it to the various fishing crews, who would undertake the dangerous journey across the dark waters of the lake, trying to outrun and outsmart the heavily armed United States Coast Guard cutters. On some occasions he would load the liquor into his own vessel and smuggle it up the New York Barge Canal to Syracuse. Cole was arrested by liquor-licence inspectors after they discovered a large stash of rye whisky and bourbon in the stone basement his two-storey island home. He was acquitted after arguing that it was his personal supply.

One of the most notorious of the fraternity was "Wild Bill" Sheldon. With his large boat, the *Firefly*, he could haul a hundred cases of whisky at a time, and would ride the roads of the South Bay area in a rented Cadillac, with a bottle of bourbon in one hand and a lady in the other. Sheldon, however, came to an appropriately dismal end. While he and his cohort Tony Kane were making their way from Main Duck Island to Oswego in the *Firefly* in the late fall of 1930, they were engulfed in an early blizzard and disappeared. Their bodies were later found washed ashore on the American side. (Other versions suggest that their boat might have hit a submerged log.) One of Sheldon's main partners was Edward "Peg Leg" Jones, another American who ran the rum-running operations of South Bay. He was eventually captured by United States agents while trying to land Canadian beer on the American shore.

Eventually, in 1933, President Franklin Delano Roosevelt repealed the hated legislation, and the rum-runners of Main Duck Island could retire in comfort. In 1941, Cole sold the island to one John Foster Dulles, who would later become the secretary of state to President Dwight D. Eisenhower. Cole retired to his farm in Upstate New York. In 1977, Parks Canada acquired both Main Duck and the nearby but smaller Yorkshire Island, and in 1998 incorporated both into the St. Lawrence Islands National Park. Meanwhile, the home of the hooch-haulers has reverted to the water snakes, now that there are no longer any hogs to gobble them, and to several species of birds. The only evidence of human habitation are traces of the rough road that linked the various buildings and the overgrown foundations of "King" Cole's castle and the Dulles cabin.

Although it no longer has a keeper, the Main Duck Island Lighthouse, built in 1913, still flashes its beam across the waters of the lake, as the keeper's house sits abandoned. There is a public dock at the island.

Point Traverse

The large sheltering confines of Prince Edward Bay lie between Point Pleasant to the north and Point Traverse to the south. Several small shoreline communities sprang up around these shores. With few good roads, the residents of the bay relied on water for their transportation, and many private wharves were built.

At the end of Point Traverse sits a tranquil little bay. Guarded by the ghosts of its now disused lighthouse, its picturesque cove remains the seasonal home of a small colony of fishermen. An advertisement as early as 1848, in which a building was offered for sale, suggested that in addition to the house, the site offered "a convenient wharf with a commodious harbour for steamers" as well as a store, tavern, shipyard, lime kiln, and sawmill. The population in 1873 was estimated at two hundred. The lighthouse was built in 1881 and a lifesaving station added two years later. However, with the end of barley days, and its considerable distance from any rail link, the point's importance declined, and by 1908 it could count only thirty residents.

*The fishing colony at the tip of Point Traverse is the last such operation on Lake Ontario.
Fewer than a half-dozen families still fish from the distant point that at one time was home
to more than two dozen fishing fleets.*

The road to the point was surveyed into the long lot system more typical
of those found in Quebec. While the homes were built on the shore, the
property lines stretched in long narrow parcels, most of them reaching the
south side of the peninsula. Along the coastline, a sawmill, schoolhouse,
and the Point Traverse post office were located. Case's Wharf was the site
of a small shipbuilding operation that saw the launch of such vessels as
the *Ploughboy* and the *Prince Edward*. The Little Bluff Conservation Area,
located on a high limestone cliff overlooking South Bay, also contains the
stone ruins of a grain storage warehouse and wharf used for the shipment
of barley to Oswego during "barley days."

Today the ambience of the entire Point Traverse peninsula remains
refreshingly maritime, with homes, many of them former fishing cabins,
lining the low rocky shore, the open waters of the bay stretching before them.

South Bay

In contrast, the community of South Bay is tucked comfortably into the sheltered head of the bay. The long-lot system prevailed here, as well, along with a community church, post office, cheese factory, and schoolhouse. Vestiges of South Bay's maritime heritage are on display at the Mariners Park Museum. Consisting of both indoor and outdoor exhibits, the museum recounts the story of the county's long legacy with the lake. Among the exhibits are hand-cranked marine radios, a wooden canoe, ship's lifeboat, a rudder from a shipwreck, and model ships, along with photographs of the county's maritime era.

The most photographed display is the light that once beamed from atop the lighthouse of the False Duck Islands. The original light on that distant shoal was erected as an Imperial Tower lighthouse in 1828. The iron superstructure, which contained the lantern and light, was removed in 1967, to sit on top of a new stone tower in the park — a centennial project. Sadly relegated to a corner of the park is what remains of the Fort Kente restoration, relocated from Wellers Bay due to a property dispute and now more of an amusement to children than a link with the past.

Adjacent to the park is the South Bay United Church, where an annual mariner's service is held each August. A maritime cemetery next to it remains the resting place of the many sailors who perished in the turbulent lake waters.

Milford

It may seem odd to link an inland village like Milford with the maritime legacy of South Bay. But when the shallow river that flowed into the bay was made navigable, Milford became in effect an "inland" port. And it played that role as well as any of its small neighbouring ports.

With the water power of the Black River at its disposal, the community began as more of a mill town. After the Loyalists settled into the surrounding area, Joseph Clapp built the first sawmill in 1808, much of the pine coming from the forests on the sandy plains around the great sand hills overlooking West Lake. By the 1830s the growing community contained two mills, stores, and the usual range of craftsmen. But its importance as a shipping point gave the town a population of shipwrights as well as a customs collector for arriving vessels.

That would not have been the case if the village's shipbuilders hadn't decided to convert the place into a port. Using scoop shovels and teams of horses, they cleared the river of logs and dredged it to a depth of three metres, from below the mill dam to the bay at Caldwell (later to be called Black River Bridge). Ships built at Milford could then be hauled down the river from Cole's Landing, where most of the shipbuilding took place, to the lake. Two other small industries at the landing were an ashery and a soap factory. Like most ports, Milford could claim nearly half a dozen taverns to quench the thirsts of visiting sailors (many of whom were also farmers). Shipbuilding started in the 1840s and continued until 1936 with the launching of the *Spray of Milford.* By then, the marsh at Black River Bridge had silted in so much that the ship had to be hauled overland and launched at Port Milford.

A proposal to run a regular steamer service from Milford to Kingston foundered when it was determined that any ship small enough to navigate the river was too small for the open water. Only one ever tried it. While a more recent mill survives in town, and the church now serves as a community hall, the village is a shadow if its early days with a few of the older structures now interspersed with more modern homes.

Port Milford Ghost Town

Although not connected by any water course to its namesake, Port Milford was also a thriving community. It began when James Cooper arrived from Kingston to settle on the north shore of South Bay, where he built a schooner wharf and store. As the boom years of the "barley days" brought prosperity to farmers and shippers alike, A.W. Minaker added a store and hotel to Port Milford. Beginning in 1877, more than a dozen schooners were built and launched here, including the county's first three-masted schooner, the *Huron.*

Even as the barley days ended, the canning industry was beginning to sweep the county. Close to the Cooper wharves, a co-operative canning factory began operation in 1907. Along the lane to the lake stood a string of workers' homes. In 1925, the factory was bought by Canadian Canners, who shut it down in the 1930s and removed the homes. Port Milford became a ghost town.

Today, Colliers Road, a short distance east of the Mariners Park Museum, leads to the shore, where a large brick home built by Earl Collier overlooks the bay. Collier had taken over Cooper's general store, a wooden building which now sits vacant beside it. A short distance away, a field contains the overgrown foundations of the cannery, although no evidence remains of the company homes.

Black River Bridge

Yet another county industry that has come and gone, or nearly so, is cheese-making. From the first factory in Cherry Valley in 1867, the number of cheese factories grew to thirty-six. Black River Bridge's current claim to fame is that it is home to the county's last surviving cheese factory. The first was built by Philip Empry in the 1870s, but he abandoned it in 1901 when a replacement opened on the opposite side of the road. Since that time the site has been making and selling its popular brands of cheddar cheeses. The current building was constructed in 2001 following a major fire that occurred shortly after the factory had celebrated its 100th anniversary.[6]

Beside the cheese factory, the Black River flows into South Bay, and it was here that the first bridge was built on rollers so that it could be pulled aside to allow vessels navigating the river to Milford to pass. Black River Bridge, originally called Caldwell, enjoyed a small shipbuilding industry during the heady barley days, as did many a lakeside community. The view from the modern bridge beside the factory takes in a marsh to the west and a view of the bay to the east. On occasion, a one-man fishing boat may tie up at the Black River dock.

On an old wooden building across the road, a hand-painted plaque commemorates the launch of the cheese industry at Black River Bridge. (A new cheese-making shop opened in the county in 2008 and is called the Fifth Town Artisan Cheese Company.) Close by, a little white wooden chapel, built as a Methodist church in the 1870s, held its last service in 1967. It remains preserved by the local community.

Waupoos/Waupoos Island

Waupoos (named for the aboriginal word for "rabbit") extends from Smith Bay to Cape Vessy, all part of the north arm of Prince Edward Bay. The earliest settlers, unlike the British Loyalists who dominated the rest of the county, were a group of forty Hessian soldiers under Baron von Reitzenstein, a regiment that had fought for the British during the American Revolution. They stayed long enough to build a Lutheran church and school, in which classes were held in both German and English. Most moved on soon after arriving, but a German burial ground remains in the community.

Waupoos remained largely a scattered rural community, the nearest village being Prinyers Cove at the tip of Pleasant Point, where a wharf, store, and post office served the needs of the area. Waupoos had a wharf of its own at which the Waupoos Canning Company operated from the 1880s until 1986 — the second oldest independent cannery in the county. A sawmill, started on Waupoos Creek by Loyalist Joseph Allan as early as 1780 may have been the county's first such industry, although a more likely date appears to have been 1790. The mill was enlarged in 1796 with the addition of a gristmill, which ceased operation in 1932. The remains of the mill have been converted to a private residence.

Vestiges of Waupoos's early heritage endure along the scenic shore road. Among them are the township hall, built in 1872, the Anglican church that dates from 1877, and the Rose House Museum. This simple frame home was built in the early years of the 1800s by a settler named Peter Rose using logs salvaged from the disused Lutheran church. Five generations of the family occupied the dwelling before it was turned into a museum.

Today, the Carl Weese grocery store, built in the 1940s, has become a popular local pub known as the Duke of Marysburgh. Another building that began as a pub, or more accurately a stagecoach tavern, was relocated from its hometown of Consecon and placed in Waupoos. Known as the Hayes Tavern, it was built in 1837–38 by Richard Hayes, an early arrival to

Consecon, according to dates carved in the planks used in its construction. It continued to operate until 1895 as the Porter Hotel, when it fell into disrepair. In 1966 the hotel was rescued and relocated to County Road 8 in the western section of the Waupoos community.

To the east, on a high bluff overlooking the bay, is the 1832 home of Conrad David, son of Loyalist Henry David. The two-storey limestone home sports a hip roof and French doors. The stone barn, also built in 1832, survives, and is now the home of the popular County Cider Company, maker of an award-winning ice cider. The farm produces fifteen varieties of apples on its sixteen hectares of orchard, and offers meals on a patio overlooking the bay.

Of much more recent vintage is the equally popular Waupoos Estates Winery. After experimenting with grape growing as early as 1993, the winery opened in 2001. The county's first, it sparked a trend that has led to the establishment of more than a dozen wineries and the area becoming Ontario's newest wine tour destination. A restaurant on the site overlooks the waters of the bay.

At the busy dock, the Waupoos Marina still contains the frame of the old canning factory, likely the county's only surviving structure of its kind. Just offshore is the tantalizing spectacle of Waupoos Island. It is said that its first inhabitant was a French fur trader from Normandy named Count de Mountenay, who arrived in the 1760s and built a substantial stone château on the western tip of the island. After the land became British, he left the house vacant. Alexander Shannon arrived from Ireland in 1818 and purchased Mountenay's estate. (Other sources suggest that the house was built by Shannon himself after he purchased the land.) His family occupied the grand stone house until 1959 when they sold it to the Oblate Order for use as a retreat. Today it is owned by Harinui Farms, which rents out the home and the nearby Kearney farmhouse (*circa* 1900) for summer vacationers. The island is also home to 1,600 ewes that the farm herds to the mainland on a private ferry. Human access to the island is from the Waupoos Marina. Early transportation was via a horse ferry.

Prinyers Cove

County Road 8 follows the limestone bluff of the bay east from Waupoos and then cuts across the peninsula to become County Road 7, which hugs the shore of Adolphus Reach. Many newer homes and small subdivisions have become intermingled with old stone farmhouses, some dating from the 1830s and 40s. Here and there a small country church or school, no longer in use, remains on the changing landscape.

Prinyers Cove is a sheltered harbour at the eastern tip of Pleasant Point. A surveyor named Collins arrived in the cove in 1783 to begin to lay out lots for the Loyalist influx to follow. Over the following years one such group, led by Lieutenant Archibald MacDonnell, took up land around what was at the time called Grog Cove. MacDonnell, a proud Highlander at a time when kilts were outlawed, brought his group of fellow countrymen to join Sir William Johnson's 84th Highlanders, who were at the time resisting the American revolt in the Mohawk Valley of New York. Such an affiliation represented the only condition under which kilts were allowed. With MacDonnell, in addition to his Highlanders, were English and Irish soldiers and a band of German mercenaries.

The cove was later renamed for MacDonnell's son-in-law and became a busy port of call for schooners hauling lumber and later barley and for a small colony of fishermen. Today the cove is ringed with more modern cottages and homes, while some of the older houses have been converted into bed and breakfasts. Instead of fishing boats and schooners, the waters now fill with pleasure craft. A wharf and a store that contained the Prinyer post office were located a short distance west of the cove. A small dry dock and fishing operation can still be seen here.

Glenora

County Road 7 continues its westerly rise up the limestone cliffs that loom above Adolphus Reach until it comes to what is one of the county's most unusual geological features and one of its most historic sites — the settlement of Glenora and the Lake on the Mountain.

From its perch sixty-two metres above the water, the mysterious lake has spawned many a speculation as to its origin. There were those who believed it to be "bottomless" or that it had a secret source of water from Lake Erie or Lake Superior. The almost circular lake measures one hundred hectares, its waters plunging down the slope to the bay below. Disappointing to those who adhere to the more colourful theories, the lake is in fact nothing more than a collapsed sinkhole in the limestone bedrock and its origins are the underground springs that feed it.

William J. Caniff described it in 1869:

> The Lake of the Mountain is one of the most remarkable objects in the District of Prince Edward.... It is situated on the top of lofty eminence, about one hundred and sixty feet above the level of the Bay of Quinte. The manner in which it is bounded is rather singular. In one direction it is only separated from the waters of the Bay below by a ledge of limestone rock about eighty feet and by a precipitous embankment which extends halfway around it.... Its waters are at present applied to propel only a grist mill and a fulling machine. An artificial canal has been cut along which the water is conveyed to the edge of the embankment from whence it is conducted by a wooden raceway to the mills which are situated on the margin of the bay below. The original outlet of the lake is at a few paces distant from the raceway. At this place the surplus waters formerly escaped through an orifice in the precipice ... dashing over the rocks below.[7]

Caniff was also one of the first to dispel the theory that the lake's source was Lake Erie. Estimating the bottom of the lake at forty-six metres higher than the bay, he reasoned, "Thus then it appears that the Lake of the Mountain does not derive its supply from Lake Erie, that its source is to be found in the immediate neighbourhood ..."[8]

From one of the county's few usable lookout points, largely because it is maintained by Ontario Parks, the view extends down to Adolphus Reach, a panorama that impressed Caniff: "Nothing can surpass the savage grandeur

A view from the ferry shows Glenora's early heritage buildings.

of the scene we look upon from the summit of the limestone rock."[9]

Today, the car ferries, the *Quinte* and the *Quinte Loyalist*, shuttle vehicles and foot passengers alike from Adolphustown to the Glenora landing. This particular spot represents one of the county's most historic locations as well as its most scenic. It was here that Peter Van Alstine landed with the county's first group of Loyalist pioneers. As a reward, Van Alstine was given a parcel of land of more than two hundred hectares. Taking advantage of the water power of the lake's outflow, Van Alstine built a mill near the summit. A stone store was built nearby around 1860 and a small settlement began to develop around what was called the Mountain Mills. While the community atop the cliff remained rather quiet, a rather more robust village was evolving at its base. Here Van Alstine built a substantial five-storey gristmill using limestone. During the 1820s the mill was operated by Hugh Macdonald, father of John Alexander Macdonald, later to become Canada's first prime minister. A plaster mill followed in 1836, and then, in 1872, the Little Giant Turbine Water Wheel Works. Originally a fulling mill, the water wheel works became known far and wide. In effect, the water turbine perfected here replaced the slower and less efficient grindstones and revolutionized the milling industry.

In addition to its importance as a mill centre, the Stone Mills, as the site was then called, was also the location of the one of Ontario's first major roads, the Bath extension of the Danforth Road. Completed in 1802, the road led from Bath, along the shore of the lake, to Dorland's Point at Adolphustown. With the Stone Mills only a kilometre across the channel, a ferry connection of some description was quickly needed. By 1802, two small ferries operated across the bay, one from the eastern shore, run by Captain Thomas Dorland, who owned extensive lands on that side, and from the Prince Edward side by none other than Van Alstine himself. Although little is known about the details of the vessels, they were likely simply rowed across. Canoes likely served the passengers, while scows hauled livestock or freight.

In 1807 Elephalet Adams built the Stone Mills Stage and Ferry Inn on the hill overlooking the landing. It was later acquired by John Green, who took over the operation of the ferry service. (The tap room was said to have been a favourite haunt of a young John A.) Ferry service was hit and miss through most the nineteenth century, usually being the responsibility of the local tavern owner. It was not until the 1880s that a regular service was launched by Joe Thurston, then the owner of the Stone Mills Tavern. Known as a "horse-boat," the craft was powered by a team of horses using a treadmill. A common form of ferry during that period, one similar was used to provide service across Toronto Harbour. The year 1905 saw the first steam-powered ferry puff across the channel, while a diesel ferry began service in 1928. The current ferries, the *Quinte* and the *Quinte Loyalist*, began their runs in 1974.

While the Van Alstine mills atop the cliff were gone by 1839, those at the base form one of the county's most visual and significant heritage landscapes. The water wheel factory became a munitions factory during the First World War, and was then sold to the Department of Lands and Forests in 1922 to become a fish hatchery. It remains in the hands of the Ministry of Natural Resources as a fish-research station. The former gristmill now houses offices of the same ministry. A short distance up the road from the landing, the old frame tavern still stands, now a private home.

Back on top of the mountain, Van Alstine's store remains, as do a few other structures from the community of Mountain Mills. The lake itself lies within the Lake on the Mountain Provincial Park, which maintains the lookout point and offers interpretative information that dispels any of those myths that once surrounded the magical lake.

Picton

From Glenora, Highway 33 retraces the route of Asa Danforth's crude trail into the heart of historic Picton. Logic would dictate that where this strategic route encountered a sheltered harbour, a settlement would grow. And it did — in fact, two settlements. On the north side of the river, which flowed into the bay, the settlement of Hallowell began, while on the south side grew Delhi. Delhi developed later than Hallowell, when a group of settlers led by Reverend William McCauley arrived in 1815. When he laid out a town site in 1823, he named it Picton. Later, when the village of Hallowell incorporated in 1837, it initially wanted to name the new town Port William, but they, too, compromised on the name Picton.[11.] McCauley originally opposed the amalgamation but quickly acquiesced. The harbour soon bustled with schooners and steamers, especially during the busy "barley days." John Tait and A.W. Hepburn were among the leading shipbuilders in the harbour.

Although opposed by the county's shipping interests, in 1879 the Prince Edward County Railway steamed into town, operating at first from a two-storey frame station house. In 1881 the railway was absorbed into the Central Ontario Railway, whose tracks would eventually reach to the far north end

Much has changed in Picton Harbour since this early view was taken. Schooners and sailing ships have been replaced by sleek yachts and pleasure craft.

of Hastings County. A new brick station was built closer to the centre of the town in 1905, and four years later the line became part of the vast Canadian Northern Railway network cobbled together by William MacKenzie and Donald Mann. In 1995, CN, which had assumed the assets of the CNOR in 1923, decided to abandon the line. Despite efforts to turn the line into a tourist train operation, CN lifted the tracks. Outside of Picton, the right-of-way is now a cycling and hiking trail, while both Picton stations survive with new uses. The older building was shifted from its original alignment and is now a real-estate office on Lake Street, while the newer station has become part of a lumber store.

Picton's prosperity is due to a happy coincidence — its selection in 1832 as the seat of the county, its harbour, and the later arrival of the railway. Despite some insensitive architectural intrusions, Picton can brag of a wealth of heritage buildings, from stores, hotels, homes large and small, churches, and even an art deco cinema. Suffice it to say, an inventory of the town's many heritage buildings could fill a book, and has.

The town has been fortunate to retain its earliest hotels: Thomas Eyre's 1835 inn at 64 Bridge Street, the 1835 North American Hotel at the three-road junction at the harbour end of Main Street (303–309), and the later Royal Hotel built in 1881 at 247 Main. Opposite the Royal stands the Regent Theatre, a rare example of a surviving, and operating, art deco cinema. In 1920 George Cook took an early commercial building and converted it into an 1,100-seat theatre. A facelift in 1931 added the current art deco façade complete with a neon crown above the marquee. After more recent renovations, the theatre once again welcomes crowds to see its live performances.

The scenic shoreline of Picton Harbour attracted the town's grandest homes. East on Bridge Street stands the pillared Claramont Inn and Spa, designed in 1906 by Kingston architect William Newlands for cannery owner Edward Young. The residential stretch of Main Street, which runs east from the downtown core, offers a singular row of large mansions. Among the oldest is the 1859 Italianate stone mansion built for local merchant Elisha Sills (346 Main), while the most photographed is the Merrill house with its dozen gables, including three on the steep central tower. It is now a popular inn.

In sharp contrast, the many houses on Mary Street, a backstreet in the old Delhi section, reflect the working-class nature of the neighbourhood. Here you will also find the courthouse and "gaol" that were added in 1832.

Picton has retained one of North America's few original "Crystal Palaces," which still stands on the Picton Fairgrounds.

The individual cells measured a mere one metre by three, and many were below ground. When the facilities were deemed inhumane in 1857, the jail was completely altered. Delhi also contains the home of William Macaulay, built in 1830, and the church he helped to found, St. Mary Magdalene Anglican Church, built in 1825.

Another of Picton's more distinctive structures is found farther east on Main Street: the fairground's "Crystal Palace." While many Ontario fairgrounds could once claim such a feature, such as the CNE in Toronto, Picton's is one of the few in North America to survive. Inspired by Joseph Paxton's original Crystal Palace, built in 1851 for London's Great Exhibition, Frank Wright adopted that design and built the one in Picton in 1887. Even the gatehouse, built in a Tudor-*esque* style in 1920 as a war memorial, is now a designated heritage structure. As in much of the county, there is little public access to Picton's shoreline, with access limited to a small parkette hidden away at the end of Store Street. The rest of the shore remains the domain of condos and yacht clubs. A park lining Hill Street offers limited views from a hill above the harbour. Here the

Fountain of the Tall Ships marks the celebration of the arrival of five tall ships into Picton Harbour in 1984.

On the periphery of Picton, the White Chapel, built in 1809, is one of the earliest Methodist chapels in Canada. Unlike most churches, it is built of wood and painted white, and is square in shape with a low pyramid roof. Inside, the original plank floors remain in place, while a gallery encloses the pulpit on three sides. Now owned and carefully preserved by the United Church of Canada, a yearly service is held there.

Green Point

From the northern outskirts of Picton, county roads follow the cliff-lined shore north to Green Point. It is a route that should be "scenic" but sadly isn't, not because the landscape lacks the power to awe, but rather because the county's decision-makers have decided that it's not to be shared. Lookout points throughout the county are next to non-existent, and the handful that do exist are overgrown or abandoned altogether.

Highway 49 continues to track the clifftop to the community of Roblin's Mills where the old highway, now County Road 35, keeps to the shore, while the new highway forges straight ahead. As you descend the cliff toward Green Point, you can view the shoreline to the east, once the location of the main ferry crossing between Cole's Landing and Huff's Landing (on the mainland). While the road to it is now a private lane on the west side of the channel, on the mainland, Huff's Road still leads to the water's edge, where the stub of the former Huff's Landing wharf yet extends into the water.

Because of the long roundabout journey required between the county and the mainland, a number of ferries linked the two shores. That from Cole's Landing was operating as early as 1795, while another ferry connected Roblin's Mills with Casey's Point beginning around 1817. While these ferries are now but a distant memory, one of the more recently discontinued operations is that linking Green Point with Deseronto. Because of its strategic location, where Long Reach bends suddenly from north–south to east–west into the Bay of Quinte, Green Point was slated to become a major town, and lots were surveyed as early as 1794. Although the new town failed to materialize, Richard Davenport began the point's first ferry. Prior to 1918, a horse-ferry made the run. The most recent ferry, which could accommodate six cars, was built in 1952. When the new Skyway Bridge, carrying Highway 49 across the bay, opened in 1967, Green Point's historic ferry era finally ended.

Northport

From Green Point, County Road 15 follows the now low shoreline west to Northport. The shoreline settlement began around 1791 when James Morden built the first house and his son Richard the first store. During the barley days the wharf was crowded with schooners and steamers, and a small shipbuilding industry took hold, primarily on the C.B. Barker farm. Like many shoreline owners, he both farmed and built small vessels. Here, such vessels as the *Kate* (1850), the *Indian* (1855), and the appropriately named *New Dominion* (1867), were constructed.

By that time Northport could claim three stores, two hotels, a post office, two wharves, and a grain dock. Six steamers called at the wharf each day, linking the port with Kingston, Oswego, and the other Bay of Quinte ports. In 1913 a cannery was built by the wharf. The railways, though, bypassed the little port, and it settled into being a country village. Today it is, like so many of the north shore towns, a bedroom community. Still, despite a devastating fire in 1921 that razed twenty-three homes and businesses, its heritage has not entirely vanished. The streets leading to the wharf site still contain the frame buildings that were once village stores, while by the water the foundation of the cannery has been incorporated into a private residence.

Demorestville

While Demorestville, a short distance west of Northport, was not directly on the water, it benefited from the wharves located to the east and a landing on the nearby Muscote Bay known as the Pitching Place. In its earliest years, its population and prospects were considered greater than places like Kingston and Belleville. During that brief heyday, village streets were laid out, and six stores, three churches, and seven taverns built. Its population peaked in 1824 at nearly two thousand (more conservative estimates put it at four hundred). With its taverns full of boisterous lumbermen and occasional sailors (who likely didn't get along too well with each other) the village acquired the nickname "Sodom."

W.H. Smith visited the place in 1846 and estimated its population at four hundred, but by 1851 he noted it was more like three hundred. "Demorestville," he wrote, "is pleasantly situated.... It contains about three hundred inhabitants who are mostly American or of American descent. A grist mill, with three run of stones, a saw mill, carding and fulling mill ... [and] three churches."[12] Although he also wrote elsewhere that "From the loose manner in which the last census was taken ... it was almost impossible to ascertain the population with any degree of accuracy."[13]

With no railway, no direct water access, and distant from the main roads, the village soon declined and became a near ghost town. Today roads have improved and, being within fifteen minutes' drive of Picton, Demorestville is rebounding. The general store still stands, and now sells crafts; the church dates from 1873 (the oldest portion was built in 1830). A pair of architecturally distinctive houses remain. Known as "temple" houses, they are defined by a single-storey front gable and two wings of equal proportion extending to each side, prompting architects to liken them to Greek temples. The mill site is now little more than a pond with a barely visible ruin, while the once extensive street pattern now ends among overgrown fields.

If there is a "Sodom," then there must be a "Gomorrah." And that is the nickname accorded to the small collection of historic homes that make up Smiths Mills. This former mill village lies along the Gomorrah Road, which leads west from County Road 5. While all evidence of the mill has vanished, the miller's house, built around 1820, is a grand white-frame Loyalist-style house with an enclosed balcony above the full-width veranda. The handful of other homes in the vicinity also date from mill days.

Big Island

From Demorestville, a causeway crosses the Muscote Bay marsh to the farming community of Big Island. With Camp Picton being the site of a major Second World War airfield, pilots used the marsh for low-level bomber training. On the mainland, near the start of the causeway, a school sits on the site of Ontario's first tomato cannery. Although home to more modern rural retreats, Big Island yet offers a few examples of early farm homes, some dating to the 1830s and 40s.

The main road essentially circles the island and there are a couple of side roads and dead-end lanes. Following the route counter-clockwise, the grand white frame house on the left is distinguished by a pair of two-storey bay windows flanking the main entrance. Where Sprague Road heads north to meet the North Big Island Road, a limestone house dates from 1847. The transoms and sidelights mark the main entrance, while the transom set into the wide gable above the door also has decorative sidelights. Midway along this road lies the Baycrest Lodge and Marina, a fishing resort with trailers, cottage units, and a main house that dates to the late 1800s. These, and a one-time township hall nearby, mark the site of an early landing (a small wharf) that was busy during the heady barley days.

Back on the mainland and west of Big Island, County Road 14 leads west along the brink of the limestone escarpment that overlooks Muscote Bay — but one would never know it. Between the road and the rim, a thick row of cedars masks any vista, and the one-time lookout point is now abandoned and overgrown. However, the route does show off one of eastern Ontario's more extensive alvar plains. This rare geographic formation forms in areas where the soil overlying a flat limestone plain is too thin (often non-existent) to support anything but a limited range of vegetation — typically scrub grass and a sparse forest of eastern white cedar.

Massassauga Point

Located only a few hundred metres across the Bay of Quinte from Point Anne lies Massassauga Point. Now a quiet conservation area, this location was once the scene of a major resort complex. The three-storey hotel, originally built in 1877 by early entrepreneur Adam H. Wallbridge, included a two-storey wraparound veranda.

In 1879 George F. Petty, another local hotel entrepreneur, placed an ad in a Belleville paper announcing the grand reopening of the hotel at Massassauga Point. In it he boasted that "pleasure seekers will find this one of the most delightful resorts in Canada. The hotel has been overhauled and enlarged this spring … hot and cold water, swings, dancing platform etc free of charge."[14]

In 1886 Shelley Anderson bought the property and added a dance pavilion. Steamers like the *Annie Lake* puffed back and forth from docks at Belleville every hour and from places like Deseronto and Big Island. The park even attracted visitors from as far away as New York, London, and Toronto. Groups of picnickers from local churches and Grand Trunk Railway employees would sail to the point for an afternoon of games or swimming. The southern portion of the point was sold for a quarry operation in 1914 and a larger dock added. Twenty years later, a legal dispute over the road access ended with the road being closed. Anderson tore down the dance pavilion and salvaged the wood from the hotel to build a house in Brockville. The quarry operated until 1962.

The Prince Edward Region Conservation Authority bought the site in 1971 and opened the Massassauga Point Conservation Area. Once more the point is a popular picnicking and swimming locale. Amid a newly regenerating forest, the cornerstones that once held up the dance hall and portions of the path leading from the dock to the hotel remain visible.

Rednersville

County Road 3 follows the Bay of Quinte shoreline between Highway 62 and Highway 33. Along it, a string of new country homes take advantage of the view over the bay and the proximity to Belleville and Trenton. Halfway along that route lies the historic village of Rednersville.

In 1798 Henry Redner arrived with his family, and in 1810 opened a tavern and built a warehouse and dock. Meanwhile, his son, Henry Jr., acquired title to much of the nearby land. Thomas McMahon came to the

Now an antique store, the Rednersville Country Store was once a general store, one of Ontario's oldest, dating from 1825.

village in 1832 and built his own dock, and for several years the community went by the name McMahon's Corners. The village added four blacksmiths, a brass foundry, a buggy shop, and three general stores. One of those stores still stands at the main intersection in town. It was acquired by James Redner, Henry's son, likely as early as 1825. When Redner became postmaster in 1854, he renamed the place Rednersville. For many years the store was considered to be Ontario's oldest continuously operating general store. Originally built entirely of limestone, a brick façade was added in 1865 following a fire.

The town prospered during the barley days as well as with the arrival of the canning industry (a cannery was opened in the village). Today the village offers up much of its heritage. The main street to the dock is named Barley Street and leads south across the entire county to the village of Wellington. Along Barley Street, the former stone church, established as a Methodist church in 1849, is now a craft gallery. Here a number of early village homes still stand. At the corner of Barley and County Road 3, the store survives, but the Rednersville Country Store is no longer Ontario's oldest general store, as it now features antiques and collectibles. A short distance west of the intersection, James Redner, grandson of the founder, built a solid stone house in the 1840s that stands little altered today.

Chapter 9
The Old Stones of Kingston

L ike a bookend to the beginning of this shoreline adventure, the Kingston end of Lake Ontario mirrors that on the Queenston end. Both were vital military points, both offer heritage features that rank among the oldest to be found in Ontario, and both present landscapes that reflect that historic role. Unlike many of the communities lining the lake's shore, Kingston did not have a strong pre-European aboriginal presence. No First Nation village sites existed as they did at Niagara, Toronto, and Port Hope. Rather, the region was more a key transportation corridor for the fur trade. Because the French colonizers in the seventeenth and eighteenth centuries were more interested in fur than they were in settlement, they chose the Kingston area to establish one of their string of fur forts.

The strategic location, where the Cataraqui River flows into the lake and its confluence with the St. Lawrence River, attracted the attention of explorer Sieur de La Salle who, in 1671, recommended the site for a fort and trading post. Two years later the governor of New France, Count Frontenac, showed up to negotiate with the local Iroquois to secure a site for the fort. In 1674, La Salle was awarded a seigneury that encompassed the area and built a sturdier fort. A small settlement grew around the fort, consisting of fifty French artisans and labourers.

When La Salle's replacement, Governor de la Barre, threw two chiefs in the lockup, the Iroquois burned the fort and the settlers' homes. In response, the next governor, Denonville, vacated the location. Later, when

Frontenac resumed his role as governor, he ordered the fort rebuilt and strengthened. By 1695 the new Fort Frontenac consisted of stone walls up to a metre in thickness. Sturdy bastions marked the four corners, each named after a saint: St. Claude, St. Michel, St. Philippe, and St. Louis. Inside the fort were officers' quarters, a forge, a bakery, powder magazine, and other buildings. Outside, a Native encampment consisted of a dozen longhouses. But the French commander, General Montcalm, was critical of both the construction and the location of the fort, and left only a fifty-man garrison in charge. On August 25, 1758, when the British lieutenant colonel, Bradstreet, arrived with 3,100 troops, it took him a mere two days to force the French to surrender. And with that, the French presence at Kingston ended. The fort lay neglected until 1783, when the British reoccupied it to help prepare for the pending arrival of the Loyalists and for the defence of a new naval dockyard.

Kingston

To prepare for the arrival of the Loyalists, the British government laid out a town site, changing the name in 1788 from Cataraqui to the English Kings Town in honour of George III, and surveyed farm lots around it. But it was the site's military importance that led to much of its early development. The harbour formed by the Cataraqui River was extensive, deep, and well protected from all directions. A high promontory overlooked a second bay, the hilltop ideal for a strategic fortification and the bay well-suited for a naval shipyard. In all, Kingston was considered to rank with Halifax and Quebec for the strength of its military advantages.

With the outbreak of the War of 1812, the British further expanded the area's fortifications, including a new fort on top of Point Henry. Old Fort Frontenac was refurbished and largely replaced in the 1820s with what became known as the Tête-du-Pont Barracks. In 1832, Colonel John By completed construction of the Rideau Canal through swamps and rocky outcrops between Kingston and Bytown (now Ottawa). A seemingly impossible task, it was hailed as an engineering marvel at the time (a compliment reiterated in 2006 when the canal was declared a UNESCO

World Heritage Site). To strengthen the terminus, a new fort, named Fort Henry in honour of Henry Hamilton, the lieutenant governor of Quebec, replaced the older fort.

When Kingston became the capital of the United Province of Canada in 1841, the new status brought with it a boom in housing. It was both before and during this heady time that many of the town's most elegant residences appeared. Throughout its brief existence at Kingston, the legislature met in the four-storey hospital that had been converted for its use. New parliament buildings proposed for what is today City Park, however, were never begun. For the time that the legislature remained in Kingston, the government rented a grand waterfront mansion known as "Alwington House" to serve as a residence for Governor General Sydenham. It had been built in 1834 for Charles Grant, of Wolfe Island,[1] and renovated and enlarged for its vice-regal occupant. The house burned in 1958. Government offices then found a home in the mansion known as "Summerhill," built in 1839 for Archdeacon George Okill Stuart. When the government vacated, it became the site of a new Presbyterian college named Queen's. Employees were quartered in a string of cottages on King Street known as Hail's Cottages.

Buoyed by its status as the province's capital, Mayor John Coulter and his council commissioned architect George Brown to design a large, domed city hall to accommodate the growing city functions — political, economic, and social. Today, its public rooms, Ontario Hall and Memorial Hall, are considered equal to the elaborately detailed galleries found in Victoria Hall in Cobourg and St. Lawrence Hall in Toronto. While its most prominent exterior feature is the dome with its sixteen Doric columns, that structure itself is topped with a sleek cupola. Pilasters, arched windows, and porticos set the building apart from most other city halls in Ontario, and certainly from any other such institution on the Lake Ontario shore. When a fire in 1909 destroyed the original dome, it was rebuilt to include a cupola, clock, and lanterns used to guide ships into the harbour.

When the legislature grew increasingly unhappy with its Kingston location, the city offered them the use of the grand new city hall. In the end the government politicians voted to move Parliament to Montreal.

Despite a downturn in growth after the politicians moved out, industry began to move in. In 1855 John Morton purchased a foundry on the waterfront and began manufacturing locomotives. Within three years it had

Kingston's waterfront has changed dramatically since this photo was taken in the 1920s. At that time the city was largely an industrial centre.

become the city's biggest employer, the largest of five foundries in the city. The "Loco" as it was called, would remain one of Kingston's main employers for the next hundred years, until it finally closed its doors in 1969.

In 1868 James Richardson[2] bought the Commercial Wharf and began operating a fleet of ships, also building many of his own. He added a grain elevator, and, when the Kingston and Pembroke Railway built its yards and station on the waterfront, began to export the many minerals the new rail line was hauling from the iron and mica mines north of Kingston. West of the harbour, the waterfront also attracted many of Kingston's grandest homes. The abundance of limestone near the surface and the influx of skilled stonemasons who had just finished the Rideau Canal gave the town its limestone character. During the heady years of anticipating the town's federal role, more than four hundred houses were built, some of the grandest being located along the lake.

Following Confederation in 1867, the British handed over the role of the military to the new Canadian government and removed its troops from the garrison at Kingston. In 1873, recognizing the need to develop a military training base of its own, the Liberal government of Alexander Mackenzie opted to create a West Point-style military college on the grounds of the now vacated naval shipyards. That new academy was the beginning of the Royal Military College, Kingston's second institute of higher learning, and one of the world's most respected military training schools.

Despite Kingston's growing importance as a military and institutional centre, industrial growth lagged. Not until the outbreak of the Second World War did any major new industries arrive, and those that did were due to the military presence, including Alcan and DuPont. Although Kingston failed to attract new industry, the port managed to stay afloat. Shipbuilders continued to launch new vessels, with forty-nine being completed in the 1880s and another twenty-four during the 1890s. A new dry dock opened in 1890 at Mississauga Point.

Furthermore, Kingston continued to play a major role in the grain trade, with larger lake vessels transferring their loads onto smaller ships capable of navigating the narrower and shallower waters of the St. Lawrence River and its locks. In the late 1890s, two new grain elevators with a combined capacity of more than a million bushels were completed. But with the increasing size of the Great Lakes ships, Kingston's harbour was proving inadequate, and the government and shippers began to search for better harbours at which to tranship their grain loads.

When Kingston was bypassed yet again in favour of new elevators at Prescott, the Canada Steamship Lines decided it would build one there anyway. With its capacity of more than 2.5 million bushels, it opened in the inner harbour on September 15, 1930, and operated until October 17, 1987. By then, port revenue had dropped so low that continued grain handling became no longer feasible. The larger ocean-bound freighters, which could now sail through the new St. Lawrence Seaway and the rebuilt Welland Canal, bypassed Kingston in favour of Hamilton and Toronto.

As the industries were closed, plans were proposed on how to redevelop the waterfront. But when the industrial buildings were demolished, in their place came hotels, apartment buildings, and condominiums. These structures not only blocked the waterfront, but destroyed it. In the entire downtown area only a small park opposite the city hall was set aside to view the harbour. Little or no thought was given to the aesthetic appeal of the new buildings, nor was there any more than a token effort at a walkway along the water's edge. At one time, Kingston could claim not only a fine view *of* the harbour, but *from* the harbour, and views from the Royal Military College or from the deck of any vessel took in a townscape of steeples and domes — one of Ontario's finest vistas, European in its semblance. But, as with the view of the lake, this vista has vanished behind the barrier of new developments.

Ironically, the city's official plan, adopted by council in 1981, recognized the value of a waterside view, stating that "the relationship of this city to Lake Ontario and the Great and Little Cataraqui Rivers is *one of the greatest assets of Kingston* [author's italics], the benefits of which should be exploited to the advantage of the citizens at large as well as those living close to the waterfront … [therefore] it shall be the policy of council to preserve and create views of the water along those streets which terminate at the water's edge."[3] Had council adhered to its own policies, Kingston might yet be able to offer its residents and its visitors what was once one of the finer shoreline vistas along Lake Ontario.[4]

A few steps removed from the "catastrophe on the Cataraqui," Kingston's heritage shines through. On Ontario Street, once a waterside avenue, sit the ruins of the old French Fort Frontenac, exposed within the confines of a busy traffic island at the corner of Place D'Armes, but available for all to visit and read the many interpretative plaques. The newer Fort Frontenac lies within the gates on the east side of the same street, where several current buildings date from 1821–24, including the historic officers' mess located inside the La Salle building. Today, the fort is the Canadian Land Force Command and Staff College.

The dominant building on the waterfront is the remarkable city hall. Renovated during the 1960s and still serving the city, its Greek pillars and dome make it one of the most distinctive waterfront structures in Ontario. Opposite the city hall, in the remnant Confederation Park, the attractive stone KPR station now serves as a tourist information centre. In front sits the old steam engine, The Spirit of Sir John A., which carried the remains of the deceased prime minister from Ottawa to Kingston.

Immediately to the west of the city hall, the Prince George Hotel began life as a simple house. Built by Lawrence Herkimer, son of Loyalist Captain Hans Joist Herkimer, before 1816, it was inherited by his daughter Jane Catherine, who opened it as a hotel in 1838. After surviving a fire and several name and ownership changes, the appearance of the hotel changed significantly when, in 1895, architect William Newlands added a third floor

Kingston City Hall and the Prince George Hotel provide an exceptional heritage streetscape on the city's waterfront. Other parts of the waterfront have not been so fortunate.

with a mansard roof, a full-length balcony, and a prominent central tower. It has since undergone further renovations and is now a boutique hotel.

Along the lake, a string of unusual historic structures include the Marine Museum of the Great Lakes, beside which are the remains of an early dry dock, and the Pump House Steam Museum. Built originally in 1848, the pump house supplied water to Kingston's water hydrants, and was expanded to its the current size in 1887. After sitting vacant from 1944 until 1973, it was restored and its steam engines returned to their original appearance. Near the museum floats a most unusual bed and breakfast, the CGS (Coast Guard Ship) *Alexander Henry*, which served as a Canadian Coast Guard vessel from 1959 to 1985. After its retirement, it was floated to Kingston and converted into tourist accommodation, where, on windy and wavy occasions, guests may well be rocked to sleep.

West of the downtown are some of early Kingston's grandest homes. Overlooking the lake, "Edgewater," at the end of Emily Street, is as a hulking stone mansion built in 1857 for member of the legislature John Hamilton.

The two doors facing the street represent the separate entrances for his two children for whom it was designed. Its neighbouring home was built in 1854 and designed by architect John Power. Its most notable occupant was Sir George Kirkpatrick, one-time lieutenant governor of Ontario. One street inland from the lakeshore, King Street also contains a number of Kingston's finest early homes. One of the most striking is that at King and Gore. The "Cartwright House" dates from 1833, when Reverend Robert Cartwright arrived from Dublin, Ireland, and was appointed assistant minister at St. George's Church. This stone house offers a white pillared portico, servants' quarters, and the original iron-and-stone fence. Even the old stables survive and have been converted into an apartment.

But the military needed space on the water, too. Along the shores of the lake, the British government built a series of six "Martello" towers.[5] These round fortifications were initially strong enough to withstand the onslaught of cannonballs, but, with later, more explosive bombardments, the towers proved to be of little value, and were abandoned.

One of Kingston's Martello towers guards the shoreline at Fort Henry. The tower was one of six built to defend the base against American naval bombardments.

Today, the little round forts remain in place: one just offshore opposite Confederation Square, another at the Royal Military College, two close to Fort Henry, and yet another in City Park on the south side of King, west of Emily. The Murney Tower is now a museum and, along with Fort Henry and Kingston's other fortifications, forms part of the Rideau Canal and Kingston Fortifications UNESCO World Heritage Site.[6]

Portsmouth

West of the growing city of Kingston, a small community was evolving on the sheltering waters of Hatter's Bay. Because of the protection of the bay and the proximity of extensive limestone deposits, the government chose the site as the location for a new provincial penitentiary.

On the east side of Hatter's Bay now stands the stone hulk of the

Parts of the Kingston "Pen" have been around since its opening in 1833. The guard tower in the centre is one of the oldest portions of the prison.

Kingston Penitentiary. Opened in 1833, much of its current configuration was added on in subsequent years. Today, peaking above the stone walls, part of the original octagonal tower can still be viewed. The only clearly visible portion of the prison is the main entrance facing King Street. The solid double doors topped with an arched transom stand between two pillars. The entrance also consists of two wings, each containing a pair of smaller, arched doorways. Topping the entrance is a Tuscan-style portico and a tall cupola with shuttered dormers.

Several nearby buildings were affiliated with the "Pen." On the north side of King Street, a large stone house, added in the 1880s, formerly housed the prison's governor. It is now a penitentiary museum, complete with a recreated cell and torture devices, some used right up until the 1970s. One device on display is evidence that "waterboarding" is nothing new.

Immediately north of the warden's house, the Women's Penitentiary was opened in 1930. Closed in 2000, it has been converted to a university residence. Much smaller than the men's prison, a number of the cellblocks overlook the single-door entrance, where, like the main "Pen," an elegant cupola soars above the building. Farther north, on the west side of Sir John A. Macdonald Boulevard, another stone house represents the 1880s farmhouse of the prison. Between the two stands an odd-looking limestone structure that was built as a water tower for the prison. A pair of arched indentations on each side lends it an unexpected air of grandeur one might not expect from a simple water tower.

To service the facility, a small village (today's Portsmouth), began to evolve by Hatter's Bay. But there was more to Portsmouth's economy than just the "big house." Following a disastrous fire on the Kingston waterfront in 1840, shippers began to look farther afield for more wharfage. On the shores of Hatter's Bay, William Dickinson and Co. built a 230-metre dock that they grandly called the Portsmouth Dock. That year, Hatter's Bay was laid out in village lots, and in 1858 was incorporated as Portsmouth. By 1865 the village contained ninety-five frame houses as well as a collection of stone commercial and institutional buildings. A small town hall was also erected in that year. Designed by William Coverdale,[7] the simple stone structure is two and a half storeys in height and topped with a small tower. On a prominent hill a short distance west, the Roman Catholic Church, using labour supplied by the inmates of the penitentiary, built The Church of the Good Thief (referring not to the prisoners, but to St. Dismas, the thief beside whom Jesus was crucified).

More wharves and storehouses were added to the shore. On the bay stood a brewery, a sawmill, and a shipyard. Boarding houses and taverns crowded Yonge Street, which ran beside the bay. Back from the water, a small network of streets was laid out and other businesses and private homes were soon built. King Street was extended across the marshy head of the bay, giving the community more direct access to Kingston. But it was the opening of the penitentiary that provided most jobs for the village.

Like Barriefield on the opposite side of Kingston, Portsmouth represents a nearly intact collection of early nineteenth-century lakeside village buildings. To recognize this heritage, the Kingston Local Advisory Committee on Architectural Conservation has identified seventy-five buildings as heritage structures, the main concentration being along King, Union, Yonge, and Mowat streets. By 1998 the city had protected many of these structures with a heritage designation.

South of King, narrow streets and laneways contain many of these buildings, including early taverns and the solid stone houses of the workers. Buildings here close in on the busy street, reflecting the early character of the area, many of them pre-dating 1845. As well as the town hall, King Street includes Peter's Drugs, built in 1869 as a grocery store, and the Orange Lodge building that dates from 1869. Indeed, this stretch of King Street, with its concentration of street-hugging stone structures, evokes a decidedly European townscape.

In 1893 the Kingston, Portsmouth and Cataraqui Railway arrived, and although it operated in Kingston until 1940, no evidence remains of its existence. A grain elevator built in 1930 by Canada Steamship Lines was demolished in 1998, replaced by a condo development and new recreation centre. On the western fringe of Portsmouth, Rockwood Cottage was built in the Regency style in 1842 as a summer estate for John Cartwright, president of the Commercial Bank of the Midland District. In 1856 the government bought fourteen hectares of the Rockwood Estate for the building of a "Lunatic Asylum." The villa itself was converted in 1857 to a women's lunatic asylum.

The four-storey main building of the former asylum, vacant as of 2010, overlooks the lake. Designed by architect William Coverdale, it was built between 1859 and 1868, initially to house inmates from the penitentiary who had been driven mad from the harshly enforced codes of silence in that institution. Coverdale's design incorporated the latest thinking on housing the "insane." West of the main buildings, a stone house known as "Leahurst" overlooks the lake and displays a corner tower and wide-pillared porch. It was built in 1902 as a cottage for convalescents. "Beechgrove," a stone building with a central tower, was added in 1893 to house patients with serious diseases. Other heritage structures on the grounds of the asylum include private cottages built for the Cartwrights. The entire complex represents one of the finest collections of private and institutional heritage structures, not just on the lake, but in the province.[8]

Barriefield

On a hill east of Kingston, like a heritage bookend to Portsmouth, the historic community of Barriefield overlooks the harbour. The town was laid out in 1814 to provide services to the shipyard and the fort. In 1820 the site took the name Barriefield, after Commodore Robert Barrie, commissioner of the dockyard. Most of its growth occurred during the 1830s and 40s. In the latter half of the nineteenth century the shipyards closed and activity at the fort decreased; growth stagnated and the housing stock deteriorated. In more recent years, new residents have moved in and the houses have been improved, although the village retains much of its mid-nineteenth-century ambience.

So complete is this historic complex that the entire village was designated in 1980 as a Heritage District under the Ontario Heritage Act, Ontario's first such heritage designation. While every street is lined with heritage buildings — forty-three heritage structures in total — perhaps the most interesting are found along the main street, where solid squat-stone structures and early frame buildings — stores, one-time hotels, and homes — hug the curb, giving the area a decidedly English flavour. Two of the key buildings are the stone town hall, built in 1889 (now the library), and St. Mark's Church, also of stone, built in 1843 and little altered.

Located across the highway from Barriefield is "Old Fort Henry." In 1812 the first fortification was built on a promontory at the entrance to the Cataraqui Creek to guard the vital navy shipyard and the junction of Lake Ontario and the St. Lawrence River. When the Rideau Canal was completed in 1832, a larger stone fort replaced the original. British troops continued to serve the fort until 1870, when the responsibility was turned over to the government of the newly created Dominion of Canada.

During the First World War, the fort became an internment camp for five hundred Ukrainian Canadians whom the government had rounded up as possible "enemy aliens." As the war progressed, the government built camps in more remote locations, and in 1917 the internees at Fort Henry were relocated to a camp at Kapuskasing.[9]

Fort Henry played a similar role during the Second World War, when German prisoners from the Luftwaffe and Kreismarine (merchant marine) were housed here. Escapes were frequently attempted, but seldom succeeded. On one occasion, two officers attempted to sneak out by hiding in grand pianos, while on another, nineteen soldiers fled through an unused privy system, only to be recaptured, most within hours.

Between the two conflicts, the fort had deteriorated, but during the 1930s, as a Depression-era work project, the government had undertaken the restoration of the aging buildings. Anxious to convert the historic fort into a tourist draw, Ontario's minister of highways, Thomas McQuesten, and Ronald Way, the fort's director of restoration, convinced the Department of the Interior and the Department of National Defence to undertake the massive project. On August 1, 1938, Prime Minister William Lyon Mackenzie King walked up the guard at the gate, who demanded, "Who goes there?" to which Mackenzie replied, "The prime minister of Canada." With that, the restored fort was formally opened, and became one of Canada's most popular tourist attractions. McQuesten would then turn his attention to restoring other military sites, such as Fort Erie, and Fort George at Niagara.

After being designated a National Historic Site, Fort Henry was also included in 2007 with the designation of the Rideau Canal as a UNESCO World Heritage Site.[10] Unlike many other military attractions around Ontario, the fort is neither a replica nor a recreation, rather it is a restoration of the real thing. With its massive stone battlements, towers, moats, and drawbridges, it ranks as one of Canada's largest preserved forts.

From the fort's high bluff, views extend west over the Royal Military College, and to the south over the St. Lawrence River. While most visitors spend their time inside the fort watching military re-enactments, others can follow a driveway around the perimeter of the fort to view the sites where the hospital and other ancillary structures once stood. Here can be found the best view of the Cathcart Tower, one of six Martello towers built to defend Kingston.

While the fort remains a busy tourist attraction, the historic Royal Military College (RMC) just across the bay is often overlooked for its historic features. The RMC was created in 1874 on the site of the Kingston Royal Navy Dockyards, which operated from 1788 until 1853. Among the heritage structures located here are the Commandant's House, of which the oldest portion was built around 1820 as part of the dockyard, and the dormitory known as the Stone Frigate, built in 1820, originally to house remnants of the dismantled British fleet. The earthwork remnants of Fort Frederick still survive from 1790, beside the Martello Tower, now the RMC Museum, on Point Frederick. While the original fort was established in 1790 to protect the navy yards, the tower was added in the 1840s. Other early structures on the campus include the Hewitt House, built in 1876, and the Mackenzie Building that dates from 1878.

Although the planners and politicians who decide what goes and what stays of Kingston's heritage have made costly mistakes, the area, as the UNESCO designations shows, offers one of Ontario's oldest and most extensive collections of heritage buildings and features. Much has been lost, yet, as with the Niagara area, much history, both hidden and well-known, remains for all to celebrate.

Epilogue
If You Go

A s those of us who live on or close to the Lake Ontario shore fully know, not very much of that shoreline is accessible to us. Some communities have made much progress in rectifying that failure — Hamilton, for example, which has resurrected much of its western harbour and established a system of parks and trails. Communities like Burlington, Oakville, Bronte, and Port Credit likewise have refurbished waterfronts, although sometimes at the cost of losing heritage features.

Along the way, Lakeshore Road or Boulevard as the case may be, passes by grand homes and striking institutions such as the former Mimico Asylum. Toronto's mixed results are well-documented, but overall, more and more of that city's harbourfront is being opened up and redeveloped, offering an often surprisingly eclectic array of sights and experiences.

With much of Scarborough, it is a little too late to offer the spectacular bluff tops to much more than the folks who were lucky enough to buy bluff properties (though their homes are getting closer and closer to the cliff's edge). Roadways and protective groins at the base of the bluffs have seriously detracted from the natural ruggedness of that remarkable landscape, yet do little to slow down erosion. The few access areas, however, such as the park at the Guild Inn, Scarborough Bluffs Park, and the Rosetta McClain Gardens, are quite stunning in their beauty, grandeur, and even oddness.

Industrial intrusions do little to attract waterfront aficionados, and that is the case with the Highland Creek Water Treatment Plant, the Pickering and Darlington nuclear plants, the Lafarge Quarry at Bowmanville, and the Eldorado nuclear facility in Port Hope. And then there is the Wesleyville hydro plant, which never operated at all.

Still, many of the lakeside communities east of Toronto have worked to return the waterfront to Ontario residents: Pickering, Ajax, Whitby, and Oshawa have all created appealing lakefront access, some, such as Port Whitby and Oshawa, with considerable heritage, as well. East of here, little development obscures the water's edge and the road itself presents many scenic and historic vistas — at Port Granby, Bond Head, and Port Britain, for example.

While Port Hope has little to offer at its water's edge, the appeal in that community lies with its many heritage homes and businesses. Cobourg happily has both — a newly restored waterfront with a heritage main street, and some of Ontario's more stunning architecture located nearby. Presqu'ile Park with its forests, beaches and historic lighthouse offers the first geographic break in an otherwise plain shoreline.

Prince Edward County, while containing a great many heritage buildings and streetscapes, has kept much of its shoreline off-limits. Private property interests trump public access in most areas, while roadside lookouts from the many clifftops are few and often poorly maintained. The exception is the unusual ridge of sand dunes protected in the Sandbanks and Outlet Provincial Parks. And the county contains many of Ontario's oldest and most interesting structures, many dating to the earliest days of European settlement in this province.

Quinte's north shoreline passes through Trenton, Belleville, Shannonville, Deseronto, and Napanee, where, while little effort has been made to enhance the shoreline, many heritage features still survive and make a visit here worthwhile. The Bath Road, which follows the historic pioneer trail along the shore of the lake, needs little work to enhance its appeal as stretches of it hug the waterline. Some of the province's oldest buildings and most historic sites are located here, saved by the fact that railways and major highways have bypassed the area.

It's not quite true to say that in Kingston the best comes last, for that town does not get very high marks for its waterfront work, having given much of it over to hotels and condos. Still, the place has designated many of its buildings as heritage structures, and thanks to its military and institutional heritage, contains one of the finest concentrations of historic buildings along the shore.

Travelling along Lake Ontario's historic shoreline presents many options. Outside urban areas, the automobile offers the most flexibility; however, for those who may be more active, there is often the opportunity to cycle or walk. The Ontario Waterfront Trail is a mixture of roads, bike lanes, and hiking trails that follow as much of the shoreline as property owners will allow, and can be followed from Queenston to Kingston.

Exclusive bike lanes are not consistent, however. A bike path parallels the Niagara River between Queenston and Niagara-on-the-Lake, but ends there. Only at Hamilton does it resume, along the beach strip and from Pier 4 Park to the Desjardins Canal. Burlington offers a bike and hike lane along its beach strip and its downtown waterfront. The next opportunity for bike or hike only routes comes in Toronto, where the Martin Goodman Trail connects the Palace Pier area with the eastern Beaches. It is necessary to skip ahead to Port Whitby before picking up another bike trail, which leads to the foot of Thickson Road near Oshawa. East of that point, although many quiet lakeside roads lend themselves to easy cycling, exclusive lanes are elusive.

One of the favourite means of travel for this author is by rail, and for the Lake Ontario shore, it works well. Unlike other Great Lakes shorelines — such as Erie and Huron — that of Lake Ontario has for a century and a half been the site of a railway line. These lines still provide travellers the opportunity to experience the shoreline communities as others have done for the past 150 years.

VIA Rail connects them all. While its stops at Niagara and St. Catharines are well away from the shore, the Grimsby station lies within walking distance of the historic Grimsby Park with its decorative Chautauqua style cottages nearby. While passenger service is no longer available at Hamilton's downtown CN station, the train ride does offer a lakeside experience around the head of Hamilton Harbour. Between Hamilton and Toronto, GO Transit provides a stop at Aldershot, a lengthy stroll from La Salle Park, while the GO stations at Port Credit, Long Branch, and Mimico are within walking distance of lakeside parks, as is the seasonal stop at Exhibition Place in Toronto.

The Guildwood GO station is a short distance from the odd collection of building ruins at the Guild Inn, while the station at Rouge Hill lies

close to the marshland at the mouth of the Rouge River. Between these
two stops, both GO and VIA hug the shore of the lake and offer close-up
views of waves washing on the beach. While VIA has no station in Whitby,
the GO station is within a short stroll of historic Port Whitby and the
waterfront park, as well as the historic Grand Trunk train station gallery.

VIA carries on to Port Hope, where the ancient stone station overlooks
the lake and is within blocks of heritage homes and the remarkable historic
main street. Cobourg station is farther from the lake, but still only a ten-
minute stroll to the waterfront. Between the station and the lake, George
Street reveals a row of early mansions, many related to the railway. The
station itself was renovated by VIA to incorporate heritage features such as
the original high ceiling and historic wooden benches.

Though VIA makes no stops between Cobourg and Trenton, it does pass
the original Brighton Grand Trunk station, now preserved as the Memory
Junction Museum. Here, the work of a single concerned individual, Ralph
Bangay, rescued the 1857 building from possible demolition and has turned
it into a museum of railway memorabilia, complete with a steam engine,
caboose, and freight cars.

VIA's stations in Trenton and Belleville are a considerable distance from
the waterfront, but only a short cab ride. The station structure at Belleville
is, like that at Port Hope, one of Ontario's oldest. Although it sees only four
stops a day, the old stone station in Napanee is close enough to both the river
and downtown for an easy visit. The main street, the riverside park and the
jailhouse archives are all close by. Meanwhile, the Kingston station is one of
VIA Rail's newest and busiest. The waterfront is a long way away, though, and
it will require a ride on one of Kingston's public buses or a taxi ride to get to.

Got a yacht? The shoreline now has many new marina facilities at
which to dock and visit the waterside heritage. To list them, however,
would be like listing the towns and villages all over again. Suffice it to
say that communities as large as Toronto and as small as Gosport provide
waterside berths from which to experience the heritage of the Lake Ontario
shoreline, much in the same way as it was seen originally — all the way
from Queenston to Kingston.

Notes

Introduction: The Shaping of a Lake

1. The Neutrals were a member of the Algonkian linguistic group known to themselves as Attirondawonks. The French labelled them "Neutrals" because they appeared not to take sides in the various intertribal wars. Their traditional territory lay between the Niagara River and the Grand River. Ironically, despite their neutrality, their members were either killed off or absorbed by other Native groups during the 1600s.
2. A useful summary regarding these villages appears in *Kingston: Building on the Past* by Brian Osborne and Donald Swainson, published in 1988 by Butternut Press of Westport, Ontario.
3. During the Seven Years War in Europe (1756–63) between England and France, the English were also determined to drive the French from North America. In 1758 the British defeated the French at Louisbourg in Nova Scotia, and the following year General James Wolfe defeated the French General Lois Joseph Montcalm de Gozon on the Plains of Abraham outside the ramparts of Quebec City. The Treaty of Paris, signed in 1763, ceded France's North American territories to England.

Chapter 1: The Niagara Frontier

1. Father Louis Hennepin, a Récollet priest, travelled on La Salle's 1679 Mississippi expedition. His published account of this voyage contains the first recorded description of Niagara Falls.
2. In 1807, George Heriot, the deputy postmaster general of British North America, published an account of his extensive travels through the Americas.

Although his work is titled *Travels Through the Canadas*, it includes description of the scenery and aboriginal customs of Central and South America, as well. The two-volume set was published by Richard Phillips of London, England, in 1807.

3. Born in Scotland in 1753, Robert Hamilton moved to Queenston, where he became a successful merchant and shipbuilder, as well as a lieutenant in the regional militia. He later became a justice of the peace and member of Parliament in Upper Canada.

4. John Norton (Teyoninhokarawen), son of a Scottish mother and Cherokee father, and the friend and protégé of Joseph Brant, was an adopted war chief of the Six Nations. He led a band of warriors in the defence of Upper Canada during the War of 1812.

5. Major Thomas Ingersoll, a native of Massachusetts, brought a number of American settlers to the Ingersoll, Ontario, area of Oxford County following the American Revolution. He eventually settled near the mouth of the Credit River. The town of Ingersoll is named after his son Charles.

6. Following her husband's death, Laura Secord moved to a house in Niagara Falls in 1841, where she opened a private school to support herself. Now a designated heritage structure, it stands at 3800 Bridgewater Street, Niagara Falls.

7. W.H. Smith, *Smith's Canadian Gazetteer* (Toronto: H. & W. Rowsell, 1846), 155.

8. *Ibid.*

9. *Ibid.*

10. *Ibid.*

11. W.H. Smith, *Canada: Past, Present and Future*, Vol. 1 (Toronto: Thomas Maclear, 1852), 197.

12. H.R. Page and Co., *Illustrated Historical Atlas of the Counties of Lincoln and Welland Counties* (R. Cumming, Toronto, 1971), 14.

13. G. Heriot, *Travels Through the Canadas*, 156.

14. *Ibid.*, 180.

15. *Ibid.*

16. H.R. Page and Co., *Illustrated Historical Atlas of the Counties of Lincoln and Welland Counties* (R. Cumming, Toronto, 1971), 14.

17. W.H. Smith, *Canada: Past, Present and Future*, Vol. 1, 196.

18. *Ibid.*

19. Brown, Ron, *Behind Bars: Inside Ontario's Heritage Gaols* (Toronto: Natural Heritage Books, 2005).

20. Van Dougen, "Lovable Niagara Landmark, or a Highway Wreck," *Niagara Falls Blog — Travel and Tourism News*, January 2, 2007.

21. *Smith's Canadian Gazetteer*, 72.

Chapter 2: *The Head of the Lake*

1. W.H. Smith, *Canada: Past, Present and Future*, Vol. 1, 223.
2. *Ibid.*, 223.
3. The HMCS *Haida* was one of twenty-seven Tribal Class destroyers built in Britain during the Second World War, eight of which served in the Canadian Navy. Following the war, the *Haida* was converted to an anti-submarine vessel, serving with Canada's NATO fleet until 1965, when she was taken out of service and slated to be scrapped. Worried about losing such a piece of Canada's military history, a group of concerned Torontonians raised money to save her. After operating as a museum at Toronto's York Street, the ship was moved to Ontario Place and opened for tours. In 2002, Parks Canada bought the *Haida* and towed it to Hamilton Harbour, where it is now a National Historic Site.
4. The McQuesten family established Hamilton's first iron foundry in 1835. Calvin McQuesten, along with his cousin John Knox Fisher, built a foundry at James and Merrick streets, where they began to manufacture stoves. Following a fire in 1855, the foundry moved to the foot of Wellington Street and later became part of the Massey-Harris industrial empire.
5. W.H. Smith, *Canada: Past, Present and Future*, Vol. 1, 250.
6. Page and Smith, *Illustrated Historical Atlas of the County of Wentworth Ontario* (Dundas, ON: Dundas Valley School of Art, 1971), 21.
7. *Ibid.*

Chapter Three: *Lake Ontario's "West Coast"*

1. L.J. Chapman and D.F. Putnam, *The Physiography of Southern Ontario* (Toronto: University of Toronto Press, 1966), 37–51.
2. W.H. Smith, *Canada: Past, Present and Future*, Vol. 1, Wellington Square, 256.
3. *Ibid.*, 257.
4. Stonehooking is a long-lost occupation. With the growing demand for stones for construction, a great source of building stones lay in the bountiful flat shingles of shale that lay along the shoreline. Found nowhere else on Lake Ontario, the shale shingles were the product of wave erosion of the Queenston and Dundas shale that forms the shoreline in this area. To mine the stones, schooners would anchor near the shore while scows with long rakes would wrench the stones from the lake bottom, which they would then load onto the schooners. Most of the stones would then go to the wharves in Toronto, where they would be piled into rectangular containers known as "toises." Here they would be sorted by size: "builders," which were used for walls, "pavers," which would be used for pavement, and "cobblers" for smaller requirements.

Scattered among the shale were granite boulders picked up from the Canadian Shield by the glaciers. These were called "hardheads," as they were much harder than the shale, and were used mainly for roads and cribs. At the height of the industry, forty-three thousand tons of stone was offloaded onto the docks in Toronto. A few shingle beaches can still be found in the area.

5. The Charles Sovereign and Mazo de la Roche Heritage Centre, or the "Sovereign House," was built between 1824 and 1826 on the farm of Charles Sovereign. Sovereign was a major local figure, being a justice of the peace and a school inspector. For fifty years he maintained a personal journal and account book, both of which have survived and in which he depicts the lives of his family and neighbours. Mazo de la Roche lived in the house for about five years, prior to becoming a famous novelist. The house is maintained by the Bronte Historical Society.

6. Joseph Cawthra (1759–1842) had arrived from Yorkshire, England, in 1806 and set up an apothecary shop at the corner of today's Frederick and Front streets in Toronto. He became rich through profiteering during the War of 1812.

7. W.H. Smith, *Smith's Canadian Gazetteer* (Toronto: H. & W. Rowsell, 1846), 148.

8. The story of Joe Burk is cited in the *Royal Commission on Customs and Excise*, RG 35/88, on pages 15,575 and 75,591, Public Archives of Canada, 1936.

Chapter Four: Toronto By the Lake

1. Margaret Clyne's marriage certificate is housed at the Ontario Archives, and describes her as "formerly a prisoner of the Mohawk." She and Rousseau were married on October 15, 1795, at the home of Captain Joseph Brant on the Grand River.

2. Alan Rayburn, "The Story of How Toronto Got its Name," *Canadian Geographic*, Vol. 114, No. 5 (September/October 1994), 68–70.

3. William Berczy (1744–1813) was a German-born portrait artist, architect, and surveyor who helped Simcoe's colonization efforts by bringing a group of German settlers from New York State to establish a community north of York in what is now Thornhill. The men from the settlement helped clear Yonge Street northward. His much-praised portrait of Joseph Brant (*circa* 1805) hangs in the National Gallery in Ottawa.

4. G. Heriot, *Travels Through the Canadas*, 138–142.

5. William Lyon Somerville was a Toronto architect who received many contracts for monuments during the 1930s, including the memorial arch in Niagara Falls. Frances Loring was a Toronto-based sculptor with whom Somerville frequently collaborated. For more information on Frances Loring, see Rebecca Sisler, *The Girls: A Biography of Frances Loring and Florence Wyle* (Toronto: Clarke, Irwin & Company Limited, 1972).

6.   Born John Corby in Bengeo, England, in 1803, he moved to Canada with his wife in 1833, and soon after changed his name to John George Howard. A trained surveyor and architect, Howard began teaching geometrical drawing at Upper Canada College and was soon designing buildings. Among his more significant creations were Queen's College in Kingston and the Royal Mohawk Church at Tyendinaga, near Deseronto. In 1836 he purchased a forty-eight-hectare estate near Grenadier Pond on which to raise sheep, and it was here in the following year that he designed and built his Colborne Lodge, naming if after Sir John Colborne, Ontario's lieutenant governor. Source: Edith G. Firth, *Dictionary of Canadian Biography Online*, accessed July 8, 2009.

7.   According to the authoritative work on dance halls, *Let's Dance* by Peter Young, Bert Niosi began his musical career at the age of fourteen, playing with Guy Lombardo in London, Ontario. While Lombardo moved on to popularity in the United States, Niosi became an expert in many instruments, including the clarinet, flute, saxophone, and trumpet. His musical resumé included playing with the Dorsey Brothers, and on CBC's *The Happy Gang* and *The Tommy Hunter Show*. See Peter Young, *Let's Dance: A Celebration of Ontario's Dance Halls and Summer Dance Pavilions* (Natural Heritage Books, Toronto, 2002).

8.   For more on the Todmorden mills, see Eleanor Darke, *"A Mill Shall Be Built Thereon": An Early History of the Todmorden Mills* (Toronto: Natural Heritage Books, 1995).

9.   Carl Benn points out in *Historic Fort York, 1793–1993* (Toronto: Natural Heritage Books, 1993), that the term "Fort York" was not commonly used until restoration began in the 1930s. Instead, he tells us, it was more common in the early days to call it the "Garrison at York."

10. *Toronto Star*, various editions, October 6 to November 23, 1923.

11. Elizabeth Simcoe, *The Diary of Mrs. John Graves Simcoe: Wife of the First Lieutenant Governor of Upper Canada, With Notes By J. Ross Robertson* (Toronto: William Briggs, 1911), 180. Republished by Dundurn Press, Toronto, 2001.

12. The Toronto Maple Leaf baseball team would remain there until 1967 when the team folded and the stadium was demolished, despite vocal opposition by those who cherished the heritage of this handsome stadium. The building was considered to be the first purpose-built stadium for professional baseball in Toronto.

13. Arriving in Canada from Scotland in 1816, John Redpath recognized the need for sugar manufacturing in Canada. In 1854 he built the Canada Sugar Refinery in Montreal for the manufacture of loaf sugar. In 1911 Redpath perfected the making of packaged granulated sugar. The Toronto plant opened in June of 1959 on the occasion of the royal tour of Queen Elizabeth and the Duke of Edinburgh. For more information on John Redpath, see Richard Feltoe, *A Gentleman of Substance: The Life and Legacy of John Redpath (1796–1869)* (Toronto: Natural Heritage Books, 2004).

14. Elizabeth Simcoe, *The Diary of Mrs. John Graves Simcoe*, 180.

15. Charles P. Mulvaney, *History of Toronto and the County of York* (Toronto: C. Blackett Robinson, 1885), 103.

16. For more information on Sir William Mackenzie, see R.B. Fleming, *The Railway King of Canada: Sir William Mackenzie, 1849–1923* (Vancouver, BC: UBC Press, 1991).

Chapter 5: The Ghost Ports and the "Newports"

1. For more information on the Rouge River and the Rouge River Park, see James E. Garratt, *The Rouge River Valley: An Urban Wilderness* (Toronto: Natural Heritage Books, 2000).

2. Edward M. Hodder, *The Harbours and Ports of Lake Ontario* (Toronto: Maclear and Co., Toronto, 1857), 10.

3. W.H. Smith, *Smith's Canadian Gazetteer*, 23.

4. *Ibid.*

5. W.H. Smith, *Canada: Past, Present and Future*, Vol. 1, 202

6. *Ibid.*

7. W.H. Smith, *Smith's Canadian Gazetteer*, 17.

8. W.H. Smith, *Canada: Past, Present and Future*, Vol. 1, 202.

9. Edward M. Hodder, *The Harbours and Ports of Lake Ontario*, Bond Head, 10–14.

10. Port Britain, quote from *Prospectus of the Port Britain Harbour Company Situated in the Township of Hope and County of Durham*, by the Port Britain Harbour Company, signed by A. Degrassi, Secretary and Treasurer, 1856, and printed by Blackburn's City Steam Press, page 5, housed in the Metro Toronto Reference Library.

11. *Ibid.*

12. Hodder, *The Harbours and Ports of Lake Ontario*, 10–14.

13. *Ibid.*, 14.

14. *Ibid.*, 14.

15. W.H. Smith, *Canada: Past, Present and Future*, Vol. 1, 204.

16. Considered the "Hero of Batoche," Colonel Arthur Williams was a commander of the Midland Regiment during the Riel Rebellion. It was at Batoche, in 1885, that he led a daring charge that turned the tide against Louis Riel and his Métis rebels. Plans were made for a grand homecoming. Sadly, Williams died of pneumonia before he could bask in his glory.

17. W.H. Smith, *Canada: Past, Present and Future*, Vol. 1, 208.

18. Hodder, *The Harbours and Ports of Lake Ontario*, 14.

19. *Cobourg Daily Star*, November 14, 1832.

20. John "Jack" Wilson was born in Toronto in 1883. He graduated as a civil

engineer and worked several years in Moose Jaw, but returned to Toronto in 1914 to turn his talents to the federal government. After several visits to Presqu'ile Park, usually at the cottage of friends, the Wilsons decided to make the park their summer residence, and built "Stonehedge" in 1938.

Chapter 6: 'Round the Bay

1. W.H. Smith, *Smith's Canadian Gazetteer*, 198.
2. W.H. Smith, *Canada: Past, Present and Future*, Vol. 2, 213.
3. For more background on Belleville, see Gerry Boyce, *Belleville: A Popular History* (Toronto: Natural Heritage Books/Dundurn Press, 2008).
4. Smith, *Smith's Canadian Gazetteer*, 14.
5. *Ibid.*
6. *Ibid.*
7. Smith, *Canada: Past, Present and Future*, Vol. 2, 242.
8. Smith, *Smith's Canadian Gazetteer*, 168.
9. H. Belden, *Illustrated Historical Atlas of Hastings and Prince Edward Counties, Ontario* (Toronto: H. Belden and Co., 1878), xi.
10. While on a visit in 1860, the Prince of Wales invited Oronhyetakha to England to study at Oxford. After obtaining his medical degree, he returned to Deseronto where he practised medicine and became head of the Hastings County Medical Association. He is buried in the Christ Church cemetery.
11. Allan Macpherson was a prominent citizen who owned a gristmill, distillery, and a store in the community, and encouraged the building of churches and schools as well as road improvements. When he built his grand home on the north side of the river, growth of the town migrated to that location.
12. Smith, *Canada: Past, Present and Future*, Vol. 2, 271.

Chapter 7: The Bath Road: A Loyalist Trail

1. Linking the Loyalist heritage features is a route known as the Loyalist Parkway. This series of local roads and provincial Highway 33 runs between Carrying Place in Prince Edward County and Amherstview. Marked by a handsome stone-and-iron gate point of entry at Amherstview, the ninety-four-kilometre route was officially opened by Queen Elizabeth II in 1984, the two hundredth anniversary of the Loyalist landings. In 1988 a master plan for the parkway was adopted, which calls for local coordination in the designating and celebrating of the various Loyalist historic sites. More than thirty historic plaques describe the buildings, folk heroes, politicians, and significant sites along the route. Between Adolphustown and Millhaven, the route of the parkway frequently hugs the shoreline, making it one of Ontario's lesser-known scenic drives.

Views extend across the water to Amherst Island and the peninsulas of Prince Edward County. See "Loyalist Parkway," a booklet published by the Loyalist Parkway Group of Advisors, Picton, in 1997.

2. For more on La Salle's Seigneury, see Barbara La Roque, *Wolfe Island: A Legacy in Stone* (Toronto: Natural Heritage Books/Dundurn Press, 2009).

3. *Illustrated Historical Atlas of Frontenac and Lennox and Addington Counties, Ontario* (Toronto: J.H. Meacham and Co., 1878), ix.

4. This may have been Stephen Moore (1792–1883). The 3rd Earl of Mount Cashel, of Tipperary, Ireland, came to Canada with his family in 1833. He purchased a thousand-acre estate in Lobo Township, Middlesex County. For more information, see *The Heritage of Lobo, 1820–1990*, published by the Lobo Township Heritage Group; *www.brooksrealty.ca/kilworth/legends/castles. htm*, accessed January 25, 2010.

Chapter 8: Quinte's Isle: The Tranquility of Prince Edward County

1. H. Belden, *Illustrated Historical Atlas of Hastings and Prince Edward Counties, Ontario,* viii.

2. W.H. Smith, *Canada: Past, Present and Future*, Vol. 2, 259.

3. *Ibid.*, 259–60.

4. Ontario Department of Lands and Forests, unpublished correspondence, 1954, held at Presqu'ile Provincial Park headquarters.

5. *The Picton Gazette*, June 3, 1911.

6. Before refrigeration, cheese-making was strictly seasonal, occurring only when cows had open pasture on which to feed. Following the early morning milking, farmers within a five kilometre radius of a cheese factory would put out their milk cans for the seven o'clock pickup. At the factory, milk was kept cool through storage in deep wells until it was ready to become cheese.

7. William Canniff, *History of the Settlement of Upper Canada (Ontario) with Special Reference to the Bay of Quinte* (Toronto: Dudley and Burns, 1869), 384, 388.

8. *Ibid.*

9. *Ibid.*

10. Peter Van Alstine was a major in a Loyalist regiment during the American Revolution and led a group of Loyalists to Adolphustown in 1783. He subsequently operated a gristmill at Glenora.

11. Sir Thomas Picton had nothing to do with his namesake town. Born in 1758 at Poyston, Pembrokeshire, he joined the military and by the age of twenty-eight had achieved the rank of captain. After fighting in the West Indies in 1793, he became the governor of a territory that included St. Lucia, St. Vincent, and Trinidad. After fighting with the Duke of Wellington in Spain

and Portugal, he was knighted in 1813. Then, in 1815, although recovering from a previous wound, he led a charge against the army of Napoleon at the Battle of Waterloo, where he was shot and killed. He was often noted for his unusual apparel and when shot at Waterloo was wearing a top hat. See Ian S. Robertson in *County Magazine* and reproduced in *Prince Edward County: An Illustrated History* (Bloomfield, ON: County Printshop Magazine, 2009), 71.

12. W.H. Smith, *Canada: Past, Present and Future*, Vol. 2, 262.
13. *Ibid.*
14. *The Belleville Intelligencer*, May 28, 1879.

Chapter 9: The Old Stones of Kingston

1. For more on Alwington House and Charles Grant, see Barbara La Roque, *Wolfe Island: A Legacy in Stone* (Natural Heritage Books/Dundurn Press, 2009).
2. Originally a tailor, James Richardson entered the grain-shipping business in 1857, and bought the wharf in 1868. In 1880, along with his sons, he built Kingston's first grain elevator with a capacity of sixty thousand bushels. Richardson died in 1892.
3. City of Kingston, *The Official Plan for the City of Kingston* (City Hall Planning Department, 1981), sections 73–84.
4. One of the better critiques of Kingston's heritage preservation successes and failures is in the book *Kingston, Building on the Past* (note the double meaning) by Brian Osborne and Donald Swainson, published in 1988 by Butternut Press, Westport, Ontario.
5. Martello towers were first used by the British during the Napoleonic wars. These circular mini-forts stand roughly twelve metres high with two floors inside. The upper floor would contain artillery, while the lower level housed a garrison of usually a dozen troops. The world's first circular tower was designed by Giovan Fratino and built at Mortella in Corsica in 1565. It was copied around the world. The British built fourteen such forts in Canada, nine of which survive. The oldest among them is the Prince of Wales tower in Halifax, built in 1796. Those at Kingston were built in the 1840s in anticipation of hostilities emanating from the 1844 Oregon Crisis in which President James Polk of the United States claimed what is today British Columbia to be American territory. The crisis was resolved when negotiators agreed to the present boundary.
6. James A. Roy, *Kingston: The King's Town* (Toronto: McClelland & Stewart, 1952).
7. William Coverdale, a prominent architect in the Kingston area, also designed St. John's Anglican Church and the manse, and some private homes in Portsmouth. Along with Edward Horsey, he also designed the Kingston Penitentiary

8. Plans have been proposed to develop a new ambulatory hospital on the grounds of the Rockwood Asylum. Meanwhile, the asylum building remains vacant and fenced off.

9. One novel escape attempt occurred when inmates were assigned the job of repairing the commandant's yacht. On the pretext that they needed to take it on a test run, they headed toward Wolfe Island and didn't return. They were, however, recaptured soon after. See Stephen D. Mecredy, *Fort Henry: An Illustrated History* (Toronto: Lorimer and Co., 2000).

10. UNESCO's Site Description: The Rideau Canal, a monumental early nineteenth-century construction covering 202 kilometres of the Rideau and Cataraqui rivers from Ottawa south to Kingston Harbour on Lake Ontario, was built primarily for strategic military purposes at a time when Great Britain and the United States vied for control of the region. The site, one of the first canals to be designed specifically for steam-powered vessels, also features an ensemble of fortifications. It is the best-preserved example of a slack-water canal in North America, demonstrating the use of this European technology on a large scale. It is the only canal dating from the great North American canal-building era of the early nineteenth century to remain operational along its original line with most of its structures intact.

Bibliography

Books

A Decade of Sundays: Quinte Walking Tours, Vol. 1. Architectural Conservancy of Ontario, Quinte Region Branch, Belleville, 1994.

Alley, Lt-Col H.R. *Fort York, Toronto, Ontario: An Historical Sketch*. City of Toronto, 1936.

Ashenburg, Katherine. *Going to Town: Architectural Walking Tours in Southern Ontario*. Toronto: MacFarlane, Walter & Ross, 1996.

Bailey, T.M. *Hamilton: Chronicle of a City*. Northridge, CA: Windsor Publishing, 1983.

Benn, Carl. *Historic Fort York, 1793–1993*. Toronto: Natural Heritage Books, 1993.

Bonis, Robert R. *A History of Scarborough*. Scarborough Public Library, 1965.

Boyce, Gerald E. *Historic Hastings*. Hastings County Council, 1967.

Boyce, Gerry. *Belleville: A Popular History*. Toronto: Natural Heritage Books-Dundurn Press, 2008.

Boyer, Barbaranne. *The Boardwalk Album: Memories of the Beach*. Erin, ON: Boston Mills Press, 1985.

Brighton History Book Committee. *That's Just the Way We Were: Brighton Memories*, Municipality of Brighton. Altona, MB: Friesens Corporation, 2006.

Brimacombe, Philip. *The Story of Oakville Harbour*. Erin, ON: Boston Mills Press, 1975.

Brown, Ron. *Behind Bars: Inside Ontario's Heritage Gaols*. Toronto: Natural Heritage Books, 2004.

————. *Ghost Railways of Ontario*. Peterborough, ON: Broadview Press, Peterborough, 1994.

————. *Toronto's Lost Villages*. Toronto: Polar Bear Press, 1997.

Buildings of Architectural and Historical Significance. 3 Vols. Kingston, ON: Committee of Architectural Review, Kingston, 1974.

Byers, Mary, and Margaret McBurney. *The Governor's Road.* Toronto: University of Toronto Press, 1982.

Campbell, Mary, and Barbara Myrvold. *The Beach in Pictures, 1793–1932,* Toronto Public Library Board, 1988.

Campbell, Mary, and Barbara Myrvold. *Historical Walking Tour of Kew Beach.* Toronto Public Library Board, 1995.

Campbell, Steve, Janet Davies, and Ian Robertson. *Prince Edward County: An Illustrated History.* Bloomfield, ON: County Printshops Ltd., 2009.

Cane, Fred. *The Heritage Buildings of Darlington Township.* Town of Newcastle LACAC, 1986.

Caniff, William. *The Settlement of Upper Canada.* Toronto: Dudley and Burns, 1869 (reproduced by Mika Publishing, Belleville, 1983).

Chapman, L.J., and D.F. Putnam. *The Physiography of Southern Ontario.* Toronto: University of Toronto Press, 1966.

Chapple, Nina Perkins. *A Heritage of Stone.* Toronto: James Lorimer, 2006.

City of Hamilton Planning and Economic Development Department. *Hamilton's Heritage Vol. 1, 2nd Edition, List of Designated Properties and Heritage, Conservation Easements.* City of Hamilton, nd.

Clarkson, Betty. *At the Mouth of the Credit.* Erin, ON: Boston Mills Press, 1977.

Cooper, Charles. *Hamilton's Other Railway.* Ottawa: Bytown Railway Society, 2001.

Cruickshank, Tom. *The Settler's Dream: A Pictorial History of the Older Buildings of Prince Edward County.* Corporation of the County of Prince Edward, 1984.

Cruikshank, Tom, and John de Visser. *Port Hope: A Treasury of Early Houses.* Port Hope, ON: Bluestone House Inc., 1987.

Currell, Harvey. *The Mimico Story.* Town of Mimico, 1967.

Dale, Ronald, and Dwayne Coon. *Niagara-on-the-Lake: Its Heritage its Festival.* Toronto: James Lorimer and Co., 1999.

Emery, Claire, and Barbara Jean Ford. *From Pathway to Skyway: A History of Burlington.* Confederation Centennial Committee, of Burlington, 1967.

Filey, Mike. *Discover Toronto's Waterfront: A Walker's, Jogger's, Cyclist's, Boater's Guide to Toronto's Lakeside Sites and History.* Toronto: Dundurn Press, 1998.

Filey, Mike. *I Remember Sunnyside: The Rise and Fall of a Magical Era.* Toronto: Dundurn Press, 1996.

Footpaths to Freeways: The Story of Ontario's Roads, 1784–1984, Ontario Ministry of Transportation, 1984.

Freeman, Bill. *Hamilton, A People's History.* Toronto: James Lorimer and Co., 2001.

Gibson, Sally. *More Than an Island: A History of the Toronto Island.* Toronto: Irwin Publishing, 1984.

Givern, Robert A. *Etobicoke Remembered.* Toronto: Pro Familia Publishing, 2007.

Glazebrook, G.P. de T. *The Story of Toronto.* Toronto: University of Toronto Press, 1971.

Grantfield, Diana. *Bowmanville: Architectural and Social History, 1794–1999,* Municipality of Clarington, 1999.

Grieg, Roger, and Nick Mika. *The Splendour of Prince Edward County.* Belleville, ON: Mika Publishing, 1991.

Hayes, Derek. *Historic Atlas of Toronto.* Vancouver: Douglas & McIntyre, 2008.

Heriot, George. *Travels Through the Canadas.* 2 volumes, London, UK: Rich Phillips, 1807.

Heritage Buildings. Clarke Township, Municipality of Clarington, 1993.

Historic Prince Edward: An Historical Guide to Prince Edward County, Ontario, Prince Edward Historical Society, 2000.

Hodder, Edward M. *Harbours and Ports of Lake Ontario.* Toronto: Maclear and Co., 1857.

Hodgson, Lynn-Philip. *Inside – Camp X.* Oakville, ON: Blake Books, 1999.

Home Sweet Scarborough, Scarborough LACAC, 1996.

Houghton, Margaret. *First Here.* Burlington, ON: North Shore Publishing, 2008.

Hounsome, Eric. *Toronto in 1810 (The Town and Its Buildings).* Coles Publishing, 1975 (reproduction).

Hull, Harry and Blanche. *Humber Bay: The Way We Were, 1900–1950.* Self published, 1993.

Hunt, C.W. *Booze, Boats and Billions: Smuggling Liquid Gold.* Toronto: McClelland & Stewart, 1988.

_____. *Whisky and Ice: The Saga of Ben Kerr, Canada's Most Daring Rumrunner.* Toronto: Dundurn Press, 1995.

Interesting People and Places: A Guide to the Historical Architecture of Cobourg, Architectural Conservancy of Ontario, Cobourg Branch, nd.

Jackson, John N., and John Burtniak. *Railways in the Niagara Peninsula.* Belleville, ON: Mika Publishing, 1978.

James, Doug, and the Port Hope LACAC. *Historical Port Hope Buildings,* 2 volumes. Port Hope, ON: Legend Publishing, nd.

Kelly, Orval E. *In the Beginning: Presqu'ile Point and Brighton.* Brighton, ON: Enslow Printing Office, 1942.

Kyte, E.C., ed. *Old Toronto: A Selection from John Ross Robertson's Landmarks of Toronto.* Toronto: Macmillan Company of Canada, 1954.

Lincoln County, 1856–1956. Lincoln County Council, St. Catharines, 1956.

Lorne Park Estates Historical Committee. *A Village Within the City.* Erin, ON: Boston Mills Press, 1980.

McCullough, A.B. *The Commercial Fishery of the Canadian Great Lakes.* Ottawa: Parks Canada, 1989.

McHugh, Patricia. *Toronto Architecture: A City Guide*. Toronto: McClelland & Stewart, Toronto, 1985.

McKendry, Jennifer. *Chronology of Kingston Architecture*. Accessed at *www. mckendry.net*.

————. *Portsmouth Village, Kingston: An Illustrated History*. Kingston, ON: Jennifer McKendry, 2005.

McShane, Myron. *The Presqu'ile Lighthouse: Its History and Its Keepers*. Friends of Presqu'ile Park and the Ministry of Natural Resources, nd.

Memories of Haldimand. Erin, ON: Boston Mills Press for Haldimand's History Committee, 1997.

Mika, Nick. *Prince Edward County Heritage*. Belleville, ON: Mika Publishing, 1980.

Mika, Nick and Helma. *Community Spotlight: Leeds, Frontenac, Lennox and Addington, and Prince Edward Counties*. Belleville, ON: Mika Publishing, Belleville, 1974.

————. *A Mosaic of Belleville: An Illustrated History*. Belleville, ON: Mika Publishing, 1965.

————. *Places in Ontario*. 3 volumes. Belleville, ON: Mika Publishing, 1983.

Montagues, Ian. *Port Hope: A History*. Port Hope, ON: Ganaraska Press, 2007.

Mulvaney, Charles P. *History of Toronto and the County of York, 1888*. Toronto: C. Blackett Robinson, 1885.

Peacock, David and Suzanne. *Old Oakville: A Character Study*. Oakville, ON: John White and Anthony Hawke, 1979.

Rennie, Wm. F. *Lincoln: Story of an Ontario Town*, Lincoln, ON: W.F. Rennie Publishing, 1974.

Reynolds, John L. *Burlington's History: Who We Are, Where We've Been, and Where We're Going*. Burlington Committee for the Ontario Bi-Centennial, 1984.

Riddell, John. *The Railways of Toronto: The First 100 Years*. Calgary, AB: BRMNA, 1991.

Riendeau, R.E. *Mississauga: An Illustrated History*. Windsor, ON: Windsor Publishing, 1965.

Rosenbaum, Linda, and Peter Dean. *The Essential Guide to Toronto Island*. Toronto: Island Ad/Ventures, Toronto, 2004.

St. Lawrence Hall. Don Mills, ON: Thomas Nelson and Sons, 1969.

Scenic and Sporting Tours of Lake Ontario, the Bay of Quinte, and the Kawartha Lakes. The Lake Ontario and Bay of Quinte Steamship Co., Season 1901.

Schmid, Helen, and Sid Rutherford. *Out of the Mists: A History of Clarke Township*. Orono, ON: *Orono Weekly Times*, 1976. (Republished by Helen Schmid, 2005.)

Schofield, Richard, Meredyth Schofield and Karen Whynot. *Scarborourgh, Then and Now*. Scarborough Board of Education and Scarborough Historical Society, 1996.

Smith, W.H. *Smith's Canadian Gazetteer*. Toronto: H. and W. Russell, 1846.

_____. *Canada: Past, Present and Future.* Toronto: Thomas Maclear, 1852.

Squair, John. *The Townships of Darlington and Clarke: Including Bowmanville and Newcastle, Province of Ontario, Canada.* Toronto: University of Toronto Press, 1927.

Stamp, Robert. *Riding the Radials: Toronto's Suburban Electric Streetcar Lines.* Erin, ON: Boston Mills Press, 1989.

Symbols of Our Past: Hope Township Architectural and Historic Inventory. The Architectural Conservancy of Ontario, Port Hope Branch, 1982.

Toronto Harbour Commission. *Toronto Harbour: The Passing Years,* Toronto Harbour Commission, Toronto, 1985.

Track, Norman S. *Canada's Royal Garden: Portraits and Reflections.* New York: Viking Press, 1994.

Trent Canal Reference and Guide Book. Department of Railways and Canals of Canada, 1911.

Turcotte, Dorothy. *Greetings from Grimsby Park: The Chautauqua of Canada* Grimsby, ON: Grimsby Historical Society, 1985.

_____. *The Sand Strip: Hamilton and Burlington Beaches,* St. Catharines, ON: Stonehouse Publishing, 1987.

The Villages of Etobicoke. Etobicoke Historical Board, 1983.

Walker, Susan. *Exploring Niagara-on-the-Lake and the Niagara Peninsula.* Toronto: Grey de Pencier Books, 1977.

Waterfront Regeneration Trust. *The Waterfront Trail.* Toronto, May 1995.

Weaver, John. *Hamilton: An Illustrated History.* Toronto: James Lorimer, 1982.

Wickson, Ted. *Reflections of Toronto Harbour.* Toronto Port Authority, 2002.

Wilson, Donald M. *Lost Horizons: The Story of the Rathbun Company and the Bay of Quinte Railway.* Belleville, ON: Mika Publishing, 1983.

Withrow, William Henry. *Our Own Country: Canada, Scenic and Descriptive.* Toronto: W. Briggs, 1889.

Wright, Larry. *Great Lakes Lighthouses Encyclopaedia.* Erin Mills, ON: Boston Mills Press, 2006.

Wright, Ruth M. *The Front of South Fredericksburg.* South Fredericksberg Historical Committee, Brockville, 1999.

Young, Peter. *Let's Dance: A Celebration of Ontario's Dance Halls and Summer Dance Pavilions.* Toronto: Natural Heritage Books, 2002.

Papers/Pamphlets/Booklets

Benn, Carl. *Fort York: A Short History and Guide.* City of Toronto Culture, 2007.

Cobourg: A Guide to the Historic and Architectural Heritage of the Town of Cobourg. Cobourg LACAC, nd.

Cobourg Illustrated: Canada's Most Beautiful Summer Resort. Town of Cobourg, 1905.

Ellis, John Jr. "Windermere." Swansea Historical Society, Booklet No. 2, 1992.

"Heritage Walking Tours of Picton." Prince Edward County Heritage Advisory Committee, 1999.

Made in Hamilton: 20th Century Industrial Trial. Sponsored by DOFASCO, nd.

Napanee Ontario Walking Tour. Pamphlet, Heritage Napanee, nd.

Oshawa Community Museum and Archives, heritage plaque information. "Entertainment in the Park," "The Oshawa Harbour," "Lakeview Park."

Redner, D.K. *It Happened in Port Credit: A Heritage Tour.* Pamphlet, City of Mississauga Recreation and Parks, Heritage Section, nd.

"Stonehedge": Its Family and Neighbours, Memories of John Melville, "Jack" and Luta Alberta Welch Wilson. Files of Presqu'ile Point Provincial Park.

Tate, Marsha Ann. "The American Connection." Paper presented to the Cobourg Historical Society in conjunction with the Cobourg District Collegiate Institute, nd.

Trenton Heritage Walking Tour. Pamphlet, Trent Port Historical Society, nd.

The Walker's Guide to Old Oakville. Oakville Historical Society, 1994.

Wellington Walking Tour. Pamphlet, Wellington and District Business Association, nd.

Journals/Magazines

Eberspaecher, Alex and Judy. "Desjardins Canal Railway Disaster," *Goodlife Magazine*, Vol. 10, Issue 8, November 8, 2008.

"Public Notice to Designate 171 Midland Ave, Under the Ontario Heritage Act (Scarborough Bluffs Refreshment Room)," City Clerk, City of Toronto, October 17, 2007.

Rayburn, Alan. "The Real Story of How Toronto Got Its Name," *Canadian Geographic*, Vol. 114, No. 5 (September/October, 1994), 68–70.

Newspapers

Blackburn, Angela. "Bronte Remembered as Fishing Village." *Oakville Beaver*, July 18, 2007.

Faulkner, Robert. "Feelings Heated Over Dynes." *Hamilton Spectator*, August 4, 2007.

Hume Christopher. "Motels Check Out, Condos Check In." *Toronto Star*, March 24, 2008.

Sprague, Terry. "The Ghosts of Main Duck Island." *The Kingston Whig Standard*, June 20, 2009.

Versace, Vince. "On the Waterfront: A Look Back at the History of Cobourg's Waterfront." *Northumberland News*, August 2, 2003.

Websites

"About Our Great Lakes: Lake by Lake Profiles." National Oceanic and Atmospheric Advisory Administration, Great Lakes Environmental Research Laboratory: *www.glerl.noaa.gov/pr/ourlakes/lakes.html.*

"About Paletta Lakefront and Park." City of Burlington: *www.burlington.ca.*

"Ashbridge Estate, Toronto." Ontario Heritage Trust: *www.heritagefnd.on.ca.*

"Asylum by the Lake." *www.asylumbythelake.com.*

"Barley Days." The Archives and Collection Society, Picton: *www.aandc.org.*

"Biography of Doris McCarthy." *www.dorismccarthy.com.*

Bell, Bruce. "TO History Revisited and the Gooderham and Worts Factory Complex." Accessed November 10, 2005: *www.travelandtransitions.com.*

Bell, Bruce. "TO History Revisited, Toronto Islands, Travel and Transitions." Accessed November 10, 2005: *www.travelandtransitions.com.*

Brookes, Ivan S. *Hamilton Harbour, 1826–1900,* a transcription of Walter Lewis, *Maritime History of the Great Lakes.* 2001. Accessed at *www.halinet.on.ca/ GreatLakes/documents/Brookes.*

"Campbell House, The History and the Move." *www.campbellhousemuseum.ca.*

"City Designates Lorne Park Estates Cottage." City of Mississauga Heritage Planning: *www.mississauga.ca.*

"Closed Canadian Parks." The Coaster Enthusiasts of Canada: *cec.chebucto.org.*

"Distillery District Heritage." *www.distillerydistrictheritage.com.*

"Early Shipping in Prince Edward County." The Archives and Collection Society, Picton: *www.aandc.org.*

"Fort Henry History." *www.forthenry.com.*

"Gairloch Gardens History." *www.gairlochgardesn.com.*

"Glenora Ferries." The Archives and Collection Society, Picton: *www.aandc.org.*

"History in Gibbard Furniture." *www.gibbardfurniture.ca.*

"History of Agriculture." The County: *www.pec.on.ca.*

"History of the Barracks." Cobourg History: *www.cobourghistory.ca.*

"History of Burlington." Burlington Public Library: *www.bpl.on.ca/localhistory.*

"History of the Humber River." *www.finchavehomes.com.*

"History of Industry in Hamilton." *Industrial Hamilton: Trail to the Future.* Library and Archives Canada Electronic Collection. Accessed at *epe.lac-bac. gc.ca/100/205/301/ic/cdc/industrial/history.htm.*

"History of Massassauga Point." Friends of Massassauga Point: *www.fom. quinteconservation.ca.*

History of Mississauga. Mississauga Historical Society: *www.heritagemississauga.ca.*

"History of the St. Lawrence Market." *www.stlawrencemarket.com.*

"The History of Sugar." Redpath Sugar Museum: *www.redpathsugars.com.*

HMCS *Haida,* History: *hmcshaida.ca.*

Maloney, Sean M. "Avro Arrow: The Obsession and the Myth." *www.seanmmaloney.com/articles/i0068.html*.

McCowan, Bea. "Scarborough Heights." HomeLife Best-Seller Realty Inc., Scarborough: *www.beamccowan.com/historic*.

"Mimico Asylum." *www.newtorontohistorical.com /Mimico%20Asylum.htm*.

"Palace Street School" and "Cherry Street Hotel," on Lost River Walks in Points of Interest along Lost Streams: *www.lostrivers.ca*.

"The Parish of Tyendinaga." The Dioces of Ontario: *www.ontario.anglican.ca*.

"Point Anne," Ontario Ghost Towns: *www.ghosttownpix.com*.

"Rideau Canal World Heritage Site." Rideau Canal Waterway: *www.rideau-info.com*.

"Southern Ontario Railway, Overview."CN website: *cnplus.cn.ca*.

"Stelco Inc., Company History." FundingUniverse: *www.fundinguniverse.com*.

"Toronto City Centre Airport: A History." Toronto Port Authority: *www.torontoport.com*.

Toronto Hunt Club, History: *www.torontohunt.com*.

Toronto Island Park, City of Toronto Parks, Forestry and Recreation: *www.toronto.ca*.

Town of Deseronto, Archives and History: *deseronto.ca*.

Note: all websites accessed between May and August 2009.

Index

About the Author

Ron Brown is a freelance travel writer and photographer. He has published twenty books on the visual heritage of Ontario, including *The Lake Erie Shore: Ontario's Forgotten South Coast*; *Behind Bars: Inside Ontario's Heritage Gaols*; *The Train Doesn't Stop Here Any More: An Illustrated History of Railway Stations in Canada*; *Ontario's Ghost Town Heritage*; and *Top 100 Unusual Things To See In Ontario*. He is past chair of the Writers Union of Canada, and is active with the Travel Media Association of Canada, Access Copyright, where he sits on the board of directors, and the Book and Periodical Council. He lectures and directs bus tours based on his book topics. He lives in East York with his wife, June.

Also by Ron Brown

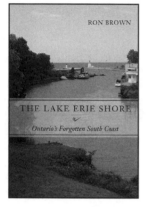

The Lake Erie Shore
Ontario's Forgotten South Coast
978-1-55488-388-2
$24.99

The Lake Erie shoreline has witnessed some of Ontario's earliest history, yet remains largely unspoiled. Ron Brown has traversed this most southern coastline in Ontario, fleshing out forgotten stories of the past, from War of 1812 skirmishes and links with the Underground Railroad, to forgotten outposts and canals, the introduction of wineries, and the legacy of the many towns and villages that hug the shore.

The Train Doesn't Stop Here Anymore
An Illustrated History of Railway Stations in Canada,
3rd Edition
978-1-55002-794-5
$29.99

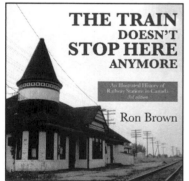

At one time, railways were the country's lifeline, and the railway station our social centre. Across Canada, many stations have been bulldozed and rails ripped up; once the heart of communities, this practice has left little more than gaping holes in the landscape. This book celebrates the survival of our railway heritage in the stations that have been preserved or remain in use today.

Available at your favourite bookseller.

 **DUNDURN PRESS**
www.dundurn.com

What did you think of this book?
Visit www.dundurn.com for reviews, videos, updates, and more!